Practice*Planners*®

Arthur E. Jongsma, Jr., Series Editor

Helping therapists help their clients . . .

P9-AGT-043

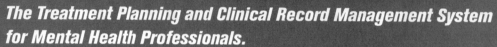

TheraScribe®

The Treatment Planning and Clinical Record Management System for Mental Health Professionals.

Spend More Time on Patients— Not Paperwork

Thera*Scribe*®—the latest version of our popular treatment planning, patient record-keeping software. Facilitates intake/assessment reporting, progress monitoring, and outcomes analysis. Supports group treatment and multiprovider treatment teams. Compatible with our full array of **Practice*Planners*®** libraries, including our *Treatment Planner* software versions.

- This bestselling, easy-to-use Windows®-based software allows you to generate fully customized psychotherapy treatment plans that meet the requirements of all major accrediting agencies and most third-party payers.

- In just minutes, this user-friendly program's on-screen help enables you to create customized treatment plans.

- Praised in the *National Psychologist* and *Medical Software Reviews,* this innovative software simplifies and streamlines record-keeping.

- Available for a single user, or in a network version, this comprehensive software package suits the needs of all practices—both large and small.

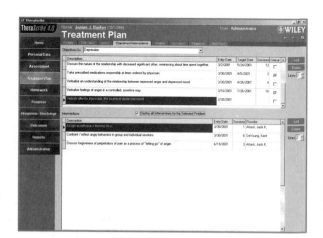

Treatment Planner Upgrade to Thera*Scribe*®

The behavioral definitions, goals, objectives, and interventions from this *Treatment Planner* can be imported into Thera*Scribe*®. For purchase and pricing information, please send in the coupon below or call 1-866-888-5158 or e-mail us at planners@wiley.com.

For more information about **Thera*Scribe*®** or the Upgrade to this *Treatment Planner,* fill in this coupon and mail it to: R. Crucitt, John Wiley & Sons, Inc., 7222 Commerce Center Dr., Ste. 240, Colorado Springs, CO 80919 or e-mail us at planners@wiley.com.

❏ Please send me information on **Thera*Scribe*®**

❏ Please send me information on the *Treatment Planner* Upgrade to **Thera*Scribe*®**
Name of *Treatment Planner* _____

❏ Please send me information on the network version of **Thera*Scribe*®**

Name _____

Affiliation _____

Address _____

City/State/Zip _____

Phone _____ E-mail _____

For a free demo, visit us on the web at: therascribe.wiley.com ⊛WILEY

Practice*Planners*®   Order Form

Treatment Planners cover all the necessary elements for developing formal treatment plans, including detailed problem definitions, long-term goals, short-term objectives, therapeutic interventions, and DSM-IV™ diagnoses.

❏ **The Complete Adult Psychotherapy Treatment Planner,** Second Edition
0-471-31924-4 / $44.95

❏ **The Child Psychotherapy Treatment Planner,** Second Edition
0-471-34764-7 / $44.95

❏ **The Adolescent Psychotherapy Treatment Planner,** Second Edition
0-471-34766-3 / $44.95

❏ **The Addiction Treatment Planner,** Second Edition
0-471-41814-5 / $44.95

❏ **The Couples Psychotherapy Treatment Planner**
0-471-24711-1 / $44.95

❏ **The Group Therapy Treatment Planner**
0-471-37449-0 / $44.95

❏ **The Family Therapy Treatment Planner**
0-471-34768-X / $44.95

❏ **The Older Adult Psychotherapy Treatment Planner**
0-471-29574-4 / $44.95

❏ **The Employee Assistance (EAP) Treatment Planner**
0-471-24709-X / $44.95

❏ **The Gay and Lesbian Psychotherapy Treatment Planner**
0-471-35080-X / $44.95

❏ **The Crisis Counseling and Traumatic Events Treatment Planner**
0-471-39587-0 / $44.95

❏ **The Social Work and Human Services Treatment Planner**
0-471-37741-4 / $44.95

❏ **The Continuum of Care Treatment Planner**
0-471-19568-5 / $44.95

❏ **The Behavioral Medicine Treatment Planner**
0-471-31923-6 / $44.95

❏ **The Mental Retardation and Developmental Disability Treatment Planner**
0-471-38253-1 / $44.95

❏ **The Special Education Treatment Planner**
0-471-38872-6 / $44.95

❏ **The Severe and Persistent Mental Illness Treatment Planner**
0-471-35945-9 / $44.95

❏ **The Personality Disorders Treatment Planner**
0-471-39403-3 / $44.95

❏ **The Rehabilitation Psychology Treatment Planner**
0-471-35178-4 / $44.95

❏ **The Pastoral Counseling Treatment Planner**
0-471-25416-9 / $44.95

❏ **The Juvenile Justice Treatment Planner**
0-471-43320-9 / $44.95

❏ **The Psychiatric Evaluation & Psychopharmacology Treatment Planner**
0-471-43322-5 / $44.95 (available 2/02)

❏ **The Adult Corrections Treatment Planner**
0-471-20244-4 / $44.95 (available 6/02)

❏ **The School Counseling and School Social Work Treatment Planner**
0-471-08496-4 / $44.95 (available 8/02)

Progress Notes Planners contain complete prewritten progress notes for each presenting problem in the companion Treatment Planners.

❏ **The Adult Psychotherapy Progress Notes Planner**
0-471-34763-9 / $44.95

❏ **The Adolescent Psychotherapy Progress Notes Planner**
0-471-38104-7 / $44.95

❏ **The Child Psychotherapy Progress Notes Planner**
0-471-38102-0 / $44.95

❏ **The Addiction Progress Notes Planner**
0-471-09158-8/ $44.95

Name_____

Affiliation_____

Address_____

City/State/Zip_____

Phone/Fax_____

E-mail_____

To order, call 1-800-225-5945
(Please refer to promo #1-4019 when ordering.)
Or send this page with payment* to:
John Wiley & Sons, Inc., Attn: J. Knott
605 Third Avenue, New York, NY 10158-0012

❏ Check enclosed   ❏ Visa   ❏ MasterCard   ❏ American Express
Card #_____

Expiration Date_____

Signature_____

On the web: practiceplanners.wiley.com   *Please add your local sales tax to all orders.

The Addiction
Treatment Planner

PRACTICE*PLANNERS*® SERIES

Treatment Planners

The Complete Adult Psychotherapy Treatment Planner, Second Edition
The Child Psychotherapy Treatment Planner, Second Edition
The Adolescent Psychotherapy Treatment Planner, Second Edition
The Continuum of Care Treatment Planner
The Couples Psychotherapy Treatment Planner
The Employee Assistance Treatment Planner
The Pastoral Counseling Treatment Planner
The Older Adult Psychotherapy Treatment Planner
The Behavioral Medicine Treatment Planner
The Group Therapy Treatment Planner
The Gay and Lesbian Psychotherapy Treatment Planner
The Family Therapy Treatment Planner
The Severe and Persistent Mental Illness Treatment Planner
The Mental Retardation and Developmental Disability Treatment Planner
The Social Work and Human Services Treatment Planner
The Crisis Counseling and Traumatic Events Treatment Planner
The Personality Disorders Treatment Planner
The Rehabilitation Psychology Treatment Planner
The Addiction Treatment Planner, Second Edition
The Special Education Treatment Planner
The Juvenile Justice Treatment Planner

Progress Notes Planners

The Child Psychotherapy Progress Notes Planner
The Adolescent Psychotherapy Progress Notes Planner
The Adult Psychotherapy Progress Notes Planner
The Addiction Progress Notes Planner

Homework Planners

Brief Therapy Homework Planner
Brief Couples Therapy Homework Planner
Chemical Dependence Treatment Homework Planner
Brief Child Therapy Homework Planner
Brief Adolescent Therapy Homework Planner
Brief Employee Assistance Homework Planner
Brief Family Therapy Homework Planner
Grief Counseling Homework Planner
Group Therapy Homework Planner
Divorce Counseling Homework Planner

Documentation Sourcebooks

The Clinical Documentation Sourcebook
The Forensic Documentation Sourcebook
The Psychotherapy Documentation Primer
The Chemical Dependence Treatment Documentation Sourcebook
The Clinical Child Documentation Sourcebook
The Couple and Family Clinical Documentation Sourcebook
The Clinical Documentation Sourcebook, Second Edition
The Continuum of Care Clinical Documentation Sourcebook

PracticePlanners®

Arthur E. Jongsma, Jr., Series Editor

The Addiction Treatment Planner

Second Edition

Robert R. Perkinson

Arthur E. Jongsma, Jr.

JOHN WILEY & SONS, INC.

New York • Chichester • Weinheim • Brisbane • Singapore • Toronto

Library of Congress Cataloging-in-Publication Data:

Perkinson, Robert R.
    The addiction treatment planner / Robert R. Perkinson, Arthur E. Jongsma, Jr.—2nd ed.
      p. ; cm. — (Practice planners series)
    Rev. ed. of: The chemical dependence treatment planner. c1998.
    Includes bibliographical references and index.
   ISBN 0-471-41814-5 (pbk. : alk. paper)
    1. Substance abuse—Treatment—Handbooks, manuals, etc. 2. Substance abuse—
Treatment—Planning. I. Jongsma, Arthur E., 1943– II. Perkinson, Robert R. Chemical dependence treatment planner. III. Title. IV. Practice planners.
   [DNLM: 1. Substance-Related Disorders—therapy. 2. Patient Care Planning. WM 270 P4505a 2001]
   RC564.15 .P47 2001
   616.86'06—dc21

2001026217

Printed in the United States of America.

10 9 8 7 6 5 4 3

To the dedicated and humble staff at The Salvation Army who for so many years and so few dollars have given so much acceptance, love, and quality treatment to those addicted to mood-altering chemicals around the world. God's love is reflected in their work and attitude.

—*Art Jongsma*

CONTENTS

SERIES PREFACE

The practice of psychotherapy has a dimension that did not exist 30, 20, or even 15 years ago—accountability. Treatment programs, public agencies, clinics, and even group and solo practitioners must now justify the treatment of patients to outside review entities that control the payment of fees. This development has resulted in an explosion of paperwork.

Clinicians must now document what has been done in treatment, what is planned for the future, and what the anticipated outcomes of the interventions are. The books and software in this Practice Planners series are designed to help practitioners fulfill these documentation requirements efficiently and professionally.

The Practice Planners series is growing rapidly. It now includes not only the *Complete Adult Psychotherapy Treatment Planner,* the *Child Psychotherapy Treatment Planner,* and the *Adolescent Psychotherapy Treatment Planner,* but also Treatment Planners targeted to specialty areas of practice, including: chemical dependence, the continuum of care, couples therapy, employee assistance, behavioral medicine, therapy with older adults, pastoral counseling, family therapy, group therapy, neuropsychology, therapy with gays and lesbians, and more.

In addition to the Treatment Planners, the series also includes *TheraScribe®,* the latest version of the popular treatment-planning, patient record–keeping software, as well as adjunctive books, such as the *Brief, Chemical Dependence, Couple, Child,* and *Adolescent Therapy Homework Planners, The Psychotherapy Documentation Primer,* and *Clinical, Forensic, Child, Couples and Family, Continuum of Care,* and *Chemical Dependence Documentation Sourcebooks*—containing forms and resources to aid in mental health practice management. The goal of the series is to provide practitioners with the resources they need in order to provide high-quality care in the era of accountability—or, to put it simply, we seek to help you spend more time on patients, and less time on paperwork.

ARTHUR E. JONGSMA, JR.
Grand Rapids, Michigan

xiii

ACKNOWLEDGMENTS

We are grateful to the substance abuse treatment community for their overwhelming acceptance of the first edition of this book, *The Chemical Dependence Treatment Planner*. Only the success of that book has created the momentum for us to attempt to refine our original work and add new material to broaden the scope. We have tried to incorporate the suggestions that readers have given to us from their use of the first edition. We eagerly await your review and feedback on the latest efforts.

We are indebted to our supportive friends, colleagues, and family members who recharged our batteries when we were running low on energy and motivation to see this project to its completion. We all need a support network and we are grateful for ours. Thanks to Jen Byrne for her persistent efforts to produce a transcribed manuscript that contains all the various pieces sent over the Internet from South Dakota and Michigan. Her organizational and word-processing skills were invaluable. Thanks also to the many staff at John Wiley & Sons who support the Practice Planner project: Peggy Alexander, Cris Wojdylo, Judi Knott, Lynne Marsala, and Kelly Franklin. Finally, thanks to our gracious wives who have encouraged us and excused us when we have been preoccupied with this revision.

—Robert R. Perkinson
Art Jongsma

The Addiction
Treatment Planner

INTRODUCTION

PLANNER FOCUS

The Addiction Treatment Planner has been written for individual, group, and family counselors and psychotherapists who are working with adults who are struggling with addictions to mood-altering chemicals, gambling, abusive eating, nicotine, or sexual promiscuity. The problem list or chapter titles reflect those addictive behaviors and the emotional, behavioral, interpersonal, social, personality, legal, medical, and vocational issues associated with those addictions. Whereas the focus of the original *Chemical Dependence Treatment Planner* was limited exclusively to substance abuse and its associated problems, the focus of this second edition has been expanded to include the other common addictive behaviors. The original problem chapters have been altered slightly from the first edition to be more generic in their language so as to include these other addictions. Beyond adding chapters for eating disorders, gambling, sexual promiscuity, and nicotine dependence, additional entirely new chapters have been created for dependent traits, oppositional defiant behavior, parent/child relational problems, and social anxiety/withdrawal.

Interventions can be found in each chapter that reflect a 12-step recovery program approach, but you will also find interventions based on a broader psychological and pharmacological model. Because addictions treatment is often done in a residential setting through a team approach, interventions have been created that can be assigned to staff members of various disciplines and modalities: nursing, medical, group counseling, family therapy, or individual therapy. We hope that we have provided a broad, eclectic menu of objectives and interventions from which you can select to meet your client's unique needs. Hopefully, we have also provided a stimulus for you to create new objectives and interventions from your own clinical experience that have proven to be helpful to addictive clients.

HISTORY AND BACKGROUND

Since the early 1960s, formalized treatment planning has gradually become a vital aspect of the entire health care delivery system, whether it is treatment related to physical health, mental health, child welfare, or substance abuse. What started in the medical sector in the 1960s, spread into the mental health sector in the 1970s as clinics, psychiatric hospitals, agencies, and so on began to seek accreditation from bodies such as the Joint Commission on Accreditation of Healthcare Organizations (JCAHO) to qualify for third-party reimbursements. For most treatment providers to achieve accreditation, they had to begin developing and strengthening their documentation skills in the area of treatment planning. Previously, most mental health and substance abuse treatment providers had, at best, a "bare-bones" plan that looked similar for most of the individuals they treated. As a result, clients were uncertain as to what they were trying to attain in mental health treatment. Goals were vague, objectives were nonexistent, and interventions were applied equally to all clients. Outcome data were not measurable, and neither the treatment provider nor the client knew exactly when treatment was complete. The initial development of rudimentary treatment plans made inroads toward addressing some of these issues.

With the advent of managed care in the 1980s, treatment planning has taken on even more importance. Managed care systems *insist* that clinicians move rapidly from assessment of the problem to the formulation and implementation of the treatment plan. The goal of most managed care companies is to expedite the treatment process by prompting the client and treatment provider to focus on identifying and changing behavioral problems as quickly as possible. Treatment plans must be specific as to the problems and interventions, individualized to meet the client's needs and goals, and measurable in terms of setting milestones that can be used to chart his/her progress. Pressure from third-party payers, accrediting agencies, and other outside parties has therefore increased the need for clinicians to produce effective, high-quality treatment plans in a short time frame. However, many mental health providers have little experience in treatment plan development. Our purpose in writing this book is to clarify, simplify, and accelerate the treatment planning process.

TREATMENT PLAN UTILITY

Detailed written treatment plans can benefit not only the client, therapist, treatment team, insurance community, and treatment agency, but also the overall psychotherapy profession. The client is served by a written plan because it stipulates the issues that are the focus of the treatment process. It is very easy for both the provider and the client to lose sight of what the issues were that brought the client into therapy. The treatment plan is a guide that structures the focus of the therapeutic contract. Because issues can change as therapy progresses, the treatment plan must be viewed as a dynamic document that can and must be updated to reflect any major change of problem, definition, goal, objective, or intervention.

Clients and therapists benefit from the treatment plan, which forces both to think about therapy outcomes. Behaviorally stated, measurable objectives clearly focus the treatment endeavor. Clients no longer have to wonder what therapy is trying to accomplish. Clear objectives also allow the client to channel effort into specific changes that will lead to the long-term goal of problem resolution. Therapy is no longer a vague contract to just talk honestly and openly about emotions and cognitions until the client feels better. Both the client and the therapist are concentrating on specifically stated objectives using specific interventions.

Providers are aided by treatment plans because they are forced to think analytically and critically about therapeutic interventions that are best suited for objective attainment for the client. Therapists were traditionally trained to "follow the patient," but now a formalized plan is the guide to the treatment process. The therapist must give advance attention to the technique, approach, assignment, or cathartic target that will form the basis for interventions.

Clinicians benefit from clear documentation of treatment because it provides a measure of added protection from possible patient litigation. Malpractice suits are increasing in frequency and insurance premiums are soaring. The first line of defense against allegations is a complete clinical record detailing the treatment process. A written, individualized formal treatment plan that is the guideline for the therapeutic process, that has been reviewed and signed by the client, and that is coupled with problem-oriented progress notes is a powerful defense against exaggerated or false claims.

A well-crafted treatment plan that clearly stipulates presenting problems and intervention strategies facilitates the treatment process carried out by team members in inpatient, residential, or intensive outpatient settings. Good communication between team members about what approach is being implemented and who is responsible for which intervention is critical. Team meetings to discuss client treatment used to be the only source of interaction between providers; often, therapeutic conclusions or assignments were not recorded. Now, a thorough treatment plan stipulates in writing the details of the objectives and the varied interventions (e.g., pharmacological, milieu, group therapy, didactic, recreational, individual therapy, etc.) and who will implement them.

Every treatment agency or institution is constantly looking for ways to increase the quality and uniformity of the documentation in the clinical record. A standardized, written treatment plan with problem definitions, goals, objectives, and interventions in every client's file enhances that uniformity of documentation. This uniformity eases the task of record reviewers inside and outside the agency. Outside reviewers, such as JCAHO, insist on documentation that clearly outlines assessment, treatment, progress, and discharge status.

The demand for accountability from third-party payers and health maintenance organizations (HMOs) is partially satisfied by a written treatment plan and complete progress notes. More and more managed care systems are demanding a structured therapeutic contract that has measurable objectives and explicit interventions. Clinicians cannot avoid this move toward being accountable to those outside the treatment process.

The psychotherapy profession stands to benefit from the use of more precise, measurable objectives to evaluate success in mental health treatment. With the advent of detailed treatment plans, outcome data can be more easily collected for interventions that are effective in achieving specific goals.

HOW TO DEVELOP A TREATMENT PLAN

The process of developing a treatment plan involves a logical series of steps that build on each other much like constructing a house. The foundation of any effective treatment plan is the data that are gathered in a thorough biopsychosocial assessment. As the client presents himself or herself for treatment, the clinician must sensitively listen to and understand what the client struggles with in terms of family-of-origin issues, current stressors, emotional status, social network, physical health, coping skills, interpersonal conflicts, self-esteem, and so on. Assessment data may be gathered from a social history, physical exam, clinical interview, psychological testing, or contact with a client's significant others. The integration of the data by the clinician or the multidisciplinary treatment team members is critical for understanding the client, as is an awareness of the basis of the client's struggle. We have identified six specific steps for developing an effective treatment plan based on the assessment data.

Step One: Problem Selection

Although the client may discuss a variety of issues during the assessment, the clinician must ferret out the most significant problems on which to focus the treatment process. Usually, a *primary* problem will surface, and *secondary* problems may also be evident. Some *other* problems may have to be set aside as not urgent enough to require treatment at this time. An effective treatment plan can only deal with a few selected problems or treatment will lose its direction. *The Addiction Treatment Planner* offers 37 problems from which to select those that most accurately represent your client's presenting issues.

As the problems to be selected become clear to the clinician or the treatment team, it is important to include opinions from the client as to his or her prioritization of issues for which help is being sought. A client's motivation to participate in and cooperate with the treatment process depends, to some extent, on the degree to which treatment addresses his or her greatest needs.

Step Two: Problem Definition

Each individual client presents with unique nuances as to how a problem behaviorally reveals itself in his or her life. Therefore, each problem that is selected for treatment focus requires a specific definition about how it is evidenced in the particular client. The symptom pattern should be associated with diagnostic criteria and codes such as those found in the *Diagnostic and Statistical Manual* or the *International Classification of Diseases*. The Planner, following the pattern established by *DSM-IV,* offers such behaviorally specific definition statements to choose from or to serve as a model for your own personally crafted statements. You will find several behavior symptoms or syndromes listed that may characterize one of the 37 presenting problems.

Step Three: Goal Development

The next step in treatment plan development is that of setting broad goals for the resolution of the target problem. These statements need not be crafted in measurable terms but can be global, long-term goals that indicate a desired positive outcome to the treatment procedures. The Planner suggests several possible goal statements for each problem, but one statement is all that is required in a treatment plan.

Step Four: Objective Construction

In contrast to long-term goals, objectives must be stated in behaviorally measurable language. It must be clear when the client has achieved the established objectives; therefore, vague, subjective objectives are not acceptable. Review agencies (e.g., JCAHO), HMOs, and managed care organizations insist that psychological treatment outcome be measurable. The objectives presented in this Planner are designed to meet this demand for accountability. Numerous alternatives are presented to allow construction of a variety of treatment plan possibilities for the same presenting problem. The clinician must exercise professional judgment as to which objectives are most appropriate for a given client.

Each objective should be developed as a step toward attaining the broad treatment goal. In essence, objectives can be thought of as a series of steps that, when completed, will result in the achievement of the long-term goal. There should be at least two objectives for each problem, but the clinician may construct as many as are necessary for goal achievement. Target attainment dates should be listed for each objective. New objectives should be added to the plan as the individual's treatment progresses. When all of the necessary objectives have been achieved, the client should have resolved the target problem successfully.

Step Five: Intervention Creation

Interventions are the actions of the clinician designed to help the client complete the objectives. There should be at least one intervention for every objective. If the client does not accomplish the objective after the initial intervention, new interventions should be added to the plan.

Interventions should be selected on the basis of the client's needs and the treatment provider's full therapeutic repertoire. *The Addiction Treatment Planner* contains interventions from a broad range of therapeutic approaches, including cognitive, motivational enhancement, dynamic, behavioral, pharmacological, family-oriented, client-centered therapy and 12-step-oriented (the exercises used in the Planner are available in one volume in *Chemical Dependency Counseling: A Practical Guide,* by Robert R. Perkinson, published by Sage Publications, Thousand Oaks, California, or one at a time from the Hazelden Foundation, located in Center City, Minnesota). Other interventions may be written by the provider to reflect his or her own training and experience. The addition of new problems, definitions, goals, objectives, and interventions to those found in the Planner is encouraged because doing so adds to the database for future reference and use.

Some suggested interventions listed in the Planner refer to specific books that can be assigned to the client for adjunctive bibliotherapy. Appendix A contains a full bibliographic reference list of these materials. The books are arranged under each problem for which they are appropriate as assigned reading for clients. When a book is used as part of an intervention plan, it should be reviewed with the client after it is read, enhancing the application of the content of the book to the specific client's circumstances. For further information about self-help books, mental health professionals may wish to consult *The Authoritative Guide to Self-Help Books* (1994) by Santrock, Minnett, and Campbell (available from The Guilford Press, New York, NY).

Assigning an intervention to a specific provider is most relevant if the patient is being treated by a team in an inpatient, residential, or intensive outpatient setting. Within these settings, personnel other than the primary clinician may be responsible for implementing a specific intervention. Review agencies require that the responsible provider's name be stipulated for every intervention.

Step Six: Diagnosis Determination

The determination of an appropriate diagnosis is based on an evaluation of the client's complete clinical presentation. The clinician must compare the behavioral, cognitive, emotional, and interpersonal symptoms that the client presents with the criteria for diagnosis of a mental illness condition as described in *DSM-IV*. The issue of differential diagnosis is admittedly a difficult one that research has shown to have rather low interrater reliability. Psychologists have also been trained to think more in terms of maladaptive behavior than disease labels. In spite of these factors, diagnosis is a reality that exists in the world of mental health care, and it is a necessity for third-party reimbursement. (However, recently, managed care agencies are more interested in behavioral indices that are exhibited by the client than the actual diagnosis.) It is the clinician's thorough knowledge of *DSM-IV* criteria and a complete understanding of the client assessment data that contribute to the most reliable, valid diagnosis. An accurate assessment of behavioral indicators will also contribute to more effective treatment planning.

HOW TO USE THIS PLANNER

Our experience has taught us that learning the skills of effective treatment plan writing can be a tedious and difficult process for many clinicians. It is more stressful to try to develop this expertise when under the pressure of increased patient load and short time frames placed on clinicians today by managed care systems. The documentation de-

mands can be overwhelming when we must move quickly from assessment to treatment plan to progress notes. In the process, we must be
very specific about how and when objectives can be achieved, and how
progress is exhibited in each client. *The Addiction Treatment Planner*
was developed as a tool to aid clinicians in writing a treatment plan in
a rapid manner that is clear, specific, and highly individualized accord-
ing to the following progression:

1. Choose one presenting problem (Step One) that you have identified through your assessment process. Locate the corresponding
   page number for that problem in the Planner's table of contents.
2. Select two or three of the listed behavioral definitions (Step Two)
   and record them in the appropriate section on your treatment
   plan form. Feel free to add your own defining statement if you
   determine that your client's behavioral manifestation of the
   identified problem is not listed. (Note that while our design for
   treatment planning is vertical, it will work equally well on plan
   forms formatted horizontally.)
3. Select a single long-term goal (Step Three) and again write the
   selection, exactly as it is written in the Planner or in some appropriately modified form, in the corresponding area of your own
   form.
4. Review the listed objectives for this problem and select the ones
   that you judge to be clinically indicated for your client (Step
   Four). Remember, it is recommended that you select at least two
   objectives for each problem. Add a target date or the number of
   sessions allocated for the attainment of each objective.
5. Choose relevant interventions (Step Five). The Planner offers
   suggested interventions related to each objective in the parentheses following the objective statement. But do not limit yourself to those interventions. The entire list is eclectic and may
   offer options that are more tailored to your theoretical approach
   or preferred way of working with clients. Also, just as with definitions, goals, and objectives, there is space allowed for you to
   enter your own interventions into the Planner. This allows you
   to refer to these entries when you create a plan around this problem in the future. You will have to assign responsibility to a specific person for implementation of each intervention if the
   treatment is being carried out by a multidisciplinary team.
6. Several *DSM-IV* diagnoses are listed at the end of each chapter
   that are commonly associated with a client who has this problem. These diagnoses are meant to be suggestions for clinical
   consideration. Select a diagnosis listed or assign a more appropriate choice from the *DSM-IV* (Step Six).

Note: To accommodate those practitioners that tend to plan treatment in terms of diagnostic labels rather than presenting problems, Appendix B lists all of the *DSM-IV* diagnoses that have been presented in the various presenting problem chapters as suggestions for consideration. Each diagnosis is followed by the presenting problem that has been associated with that diagnosis. The provider may look up the presenting problems for a selected diagnosis to review definitions, goals, objectives, and interventions that may be appropriate for their clients with that diagnosis.

Congratulations! You should now have a complete, individualized treatment plan that is ready for immediate implementation and presentation to the client. It should resemble the format of the sample plan presented on the next page.

A FINAL NOTE

One important aspect of effective treatment planning is that each plan should be tailored to the individual client's problems and needs. Treatment plans should not be mass produced, even if clients have similar problems. The individual's strengths and weaknesses, unique stressors, social network, family circumstances, and symptom patterns *must* be considered in developing a treatment strategy. Drawing upon our own years of clinical experience, we have put together a variety of treatment choices. These statements can be combined in thousands of permutations to develop detailed treatment plans. Relying on their own good judgment, clinicians can easily select the statements that are appropriate for the individuals they are treating. In addition, we encourage readers to add their own definitions, goals, objectives, and interventions to the existing samples. It is our hope that *The Addiction Treatment Planner* will promote effective, creative treatment planning—a process that will ultimately benefit the client, the clinician, and the mental health community.

SAMPLE TREATMENT PLAN

PROBLEM: SUBSTANCE ABUSE/DEPENDENCE

Definitions: Inability to stop or cut down the use of the mood-altering drug once started, despite the verbalized desire to do so and the negative consequences that continued use brings.

Denial that chemical dependence is a problem despite feedback from significant others that the use of the substance is negatively affecting him/her and others.

Frequent blackouts when using.

Continued substance use despite the knowledge of experiencing persistent physical, legal, financial, vocational, social, or relationship problems that are directly caused by the use of the substance.

Increased tolerance for the drug demonstrated by the need to use more to become intoxicated or to recall the desired effect.

Suspension of important social, recreational, or occupational activities because they interfere with use.

Goals: Accept the powerlessness and unmanageability over mood-altering substances and participate in a recovery-based program.

Withdraw from mood-altering substance, stabilize physically and emotionally, and then establish a supportive recovery plan.

Short-Term Objectives

1. Cooperate with a medical assessment and an evaluation of the necessity for pharmacological intervention.

Therapeutic Interventions

1. Physician perform a physical exam and write treatment orders, including, if necessary, prescription of medications.

   *RP: Dwight Kessler, M.D. Psychiatrist

2. Physician monitor the side effects and effectiveness of medication, titrating as necessary.

   RP: Dwight Kessler, M.D. Psychiatrist

---

*RP = responsible professional.   *(Continued)*

2. Take prescribed medications as directed by the physician, and report as to compliance, side effects, and effectiveness.

1. Staff administer the client's prescribed medications.
   RP: Jane Doe, R.N.
        Nurse

2. Monitor the client's prescribed psychotropic medications for compliance, side effects, and effectiveness.
   RP: Jane Doe, R.N.
        Nurse

3. Report acute withdrawal symptoms.

1. Assess and monitor the client's condition during withdrawal using a standardized procedure (e.g., Clinical Institute of Withdrawal scale) as needed.
   RP: Jane Doe, R.N.
        Nurse

4. Provide honest and complete information for a chemical dependence biopsychosocial history.

1. Complete a thorough family and personal biopsychosocial history that has a focus on addiction.
   RP: Molly Evans, M.A.
        Substance Abuse
        Counselor

5. Verbally admit to powerlessness over the mood-altering substances.

1. Assign the client to complete an Alcoholics Anonymous (AA) first-step paper admitting to powerlessness over mood-altering chemicals, and present it in group therapy for feedback.
   RP: John Smith, Psy.D.
        Psychologist, Group
        Therapist

(Continued)

6. List 10 negative consequences resulting from or exacerbated by substance dependence.

1. Ask the client to make a list of the ways in which chemical use has negatively impacted his/her life, and process the list with the therapist or group.
RP: Molly Evans, M.A.
Substance Abuse
Counselor

7. Verbalize an understanding of the problems caused by the use of mood-altering substances and, therefore, the need to stay in treatment.

1. Assist the client in listing reasons why he/she should stay in chemical dependence treatment.
RP: Molly Evans, M.A.
Substance Abuse
Counselor

8. Make a written plan to cope with each high-risk or trigger situation.

1. Using a 12-step recovery program's relapse prevention exercise, help the client to uncover his/her triggers for relapse.
RP: Molly Evans, M.A.
Substance Abuse
Counselor

2. Teach the client about high-risk situations (e.g., negative emotions, social pressure, interpersonal conflict, positive emotions, and test personal control); assist him/her in making a written plan to cope with each high-risk situation.
RP: Molly Evans, M.A.
Substance Abuse
Counselor

DIAGNOSIS

Axis I: 303.90 Alcohol Dependence

Note: The numbers in parentheses accompanying the short-term objectives in each chapter correspond to the list of suggested therapeutic interventions in that chapter. Each objective has specific interventions that have been designed to assist the client in attaining that objective. Clinical judgment should determine the exact intervention to be used, including any outside of those suggested.

ADULT-CHILD-OF-AN-ALCOHOLIC TRAITS

BEHAVIORAL DEFINITIONS

1. A history of being raised in an alcoholic home that resulted in having experienced emotional abandonment, role confusion, abuse, and a chaotic, unpredictable environment.
2. Inability to trust others, share feelings, or talk openly about self.
3. Overly concerned with the welfare of other people.
4. Passively submissive to the wishes, wants, and needs of others; too eager to please others.
5. Chronically fearful of interpersonal abandonment and desperately clings to destructive relationships.
6. Tells other people what they want to hear rather than the truth.
7. Persistent feelings of worthlessness and a belief that being treated with disdain is normal and expected.
8. Strong feelings of panic and helplessness when faced with being alone as a close relationship ends.
9. Chooses partners and friends who are chemically dependent or have other serious problems.
10. Distrusts authority figures—only trusts peers.
11. Takes on the parental role in a relationship.
12. Feels less worthy than those who had a more normal family life.
13. Chronic feelings of alienation from others.

__. _____
   _____
__. _____
   _____
__. _____
   _____

LONG-TERM GOALS

1. Recovery from addiction that reduces the impact of adult-child-of-an-alcoholic (ACOA) traits on sobriety.
2. Decrease dependence on relationships while beginning to meet own needs, build confidence, and practice assertiveness.
3. Reduce the frequency of behaviors exclusively designed to please others.
4. Demonstrate healthy communication that is honest, open, and self-disclosing.
5. Recognize ACOA traits and their detrimental effects on abstinence.
6. Replace negative, self-defeating thinking with self-enhancing messages to self.
7. Begin to choose partners and friends that are responsible, respectful, and reliable.
8. Overcome fears of abandonment, loss, and neglect.

—. _____

_____

—. _____

_____

_____

—. _____

_____

SHORT-TERM OBJECTIVES	THERAPEUTIC INTERVENTIONS
1. Acknowledge the feelings of powerlessness that result from ACOA traits and addiction. (1, 6, 8)	1. Probe the feelings of powerlessness that the client experienced as a child in the alcoholic home, and explore similarities to his/her feelings when abusing chemicals. *RP: _____ _____
2. Verbalize the relationship between being raised in an addictive family and now repeating the pattern of addiction. (2, 3)	
3. Verbalize the rules of "don't talk, don't trust, don't feel,"	2. Teach the client the relationship between his/her

_____

*RP = responsible professional.

which were learned as a child, and how these rules have made interpersonal relationships more difficult. (3, 4)

4. Verbalize an understanding of how three ACOA traits contributed to addiction. (5, 6)

5. Identify how the tendency to take on the parental role in interpersonal relationships is related to maintaining a feeling of security and control. (7, 8)

6. Identify the causes for the fear of abandonment that were experienced in the alcoholic home. (9, 10)

7. Share the feeling of worthlessness that was learned in the alcoholic home, and directly relate this feeling to abuse of substances as a coping mechanism. (3, 11, 12)

8. Identify the pattern in the alcoholic family of being ignored or punished when honest feelings were shared. (3, 4, 13)

9. List five qualities and behaviors that should be evident in others before interpersonal trust can be built. (14)

10. Increase the frequency of telling the truth rather than saying only what the patient thinks the other person wants to hear. Record the incidents and

childhood experience in an addictive family and how this increased the likelihood of repeating addictive behavior pattern as an adult.
RP: _____

_____

3. Explore how the dysfunctional family rules lead to uncomfortable feelings and escape into addiction.
RP: _____

_____

4. Educate the client about the ACOA rules of "don't talk, don't trust, don't feel," and explain how these rules make healthy relationships impossible.
RP: _____

_____

5. Teach the client the effects that modeling, fear, and shame have on choosing a lifestyle of addiction.
RP: _____

_____

6. Assist the client in identifying his/her ACOA traits and the relationship between ACOA traits and addiction.
RP: _____

_____

7. Assist the client in understanding how his/her early childhood experiences led to fears of abandonment, rejection, neglect, and to assumption of the caretaker

feelings in a journal.
(15, 16)

11. List the steps to effectively and independently solving problems. (17)

12. Acknowledge the resistance to sharing personal problems. Share at least one problem in each therapy session. (13, 18, 19)

13. Verbalize an understanding of how ACOA traits contribute to choosing partners and friends that have problems and need help.
(6, 7, 20)

14. Initiate the encouragement of others in recovery to help reestablish a feeling of self-worth. (21, 22)

15. List 10 reasons why regular attendance at recovery group meetings is necessary to arrest ACOA traits and addiction. (21, 23)

16. Discuss three fears that are related to attending recovery group meetings, and develop specific, written plans to deal with each fear.
(7, 24)

17. Verbalize how a recovery group can become the healthy family that one never had. (21, 23, 25, 26)

18. List five ways in which belief in and interaction with a higher power can reduce fear and aid in recovery.
(27, 28)

19. Verbalize a feeling of serenity that results from turn-

role, which is detrimental to intimate relationships.
RP: _____
_____

8. Assist the client in identifying the many ways in which he/she takes on the parental role of caretaker.
RP: _____
_____

9. Probe the client's fear of violence, abandonment, unpredictability, and embarrassment when the parent was abusing chemicals.
RP: _____
_____

10. Explore specific situations when the client experienced fear of abandonment or feelings of rejection during childhood.
RP: _____
_____

11. Explore the client's feelings of worthlessness; assess their depth and origins.
RP: _____
_____

12. Teach the client how low self-esteem results from being raised in an alcoholic home due to experiencing emotional rejection, broken promises, abuse, neglect, poverty, and lost social status.
RP: _____
_____

ing out-of-control problems over to a higher power. (27, 28, 29)

20. Practice assertiveness skills, and keep a daily journal of the times these skills were used in interpersonal conflict. (30, 31)

21. Three times each day, begin a sentence with the words "I feel . . ." when talking to a trustworthy friend. (30, 31)

22. To practice intimacy skills, share the personal experiences of each day (feelings, thoughts, behaviors) with one person that day. (32, 33)

23. Cooperate with a physician's evaluation regarding whether psychopharmacological intervention is warranted. (34)

24. Take medications as prescribed, and report on their effectiveness and side effects. (35, 36)

__. _____
   _____

__. _____
   _____

__. _____
   _____

13. Probe how the client's family responded to expressions of feelings, wishes, and wants and why it became dangerous for the client to share feelings with others.
RP: _____
_____

14. Assist the client in developing a set of character traits in others (e.g., honesty, sensitivity, kindness, etc.) that qualify them as trustworthy.
RP: _____
_____

15. Teach the client that the behavior of telling other people what we think they want to hear rather than speaking the truth is based on fear of rejection, which was learned in the alcoholic home. Use modeling, role playing, and behavior rehearsal to teach the client more honest communication skills.
RP: _____
_____

16. Assign the client to keep a journal of incidents in which he/she told the truth rather than saying only what others want to hear.
RP: _____
_____

17. Teach the client problem-solving skills (i.e., identify the problem, brainstorm alternate solutions, examine the advantages and disad-

vantages of each option, select an option, implement a
course of action, and evaluate the result), and role-
play solving a current
problem in his/her life.

RP: _____

_____

18. Educate the client about
healthy interpersonal relationships based on open-
ness, respect, and honesty,
and explain the necessity of
sharing feelings to build
trust and mutual under-
standing.

RP: _____

_____

19. Explore the client's pattern
of resisting to share personal problems and prefer-
ring, instead, to focus on
helping others with their
problems.

RP: _____

_____

20. Help the client to understand that the strong need
to help others is based on
low self-esteem and the
need for acceptance, which
were learned in the alco-
holic family of origin. Relate
this caretaking behavior to
choosing friends and partners who are chemically dependent or psychologically
disturbed.

RP: _____

_____

21. Teach the client that active involvement in a recovery group can aid in building trust in others and confidence in himself/herself.
RP: _____

_____

22. Assist the client in developing an aftercare plan that is centered around regular attendance at Alcoholics Anonymous/Narcotics Anonymous (AA/NA) meetings.
RP: _____

_____

23. Assist the client in listing 10 reasons why 12-step recovery group attendance is helpful to overcome ACOA traits.
RP: _____

_____

24. Probe the relationship between ACOA traits and the fear of attending recovery group meetings. Develop plans to cope with the fear.
RP: _____

_____

25. Discuss how the home group of AA/NA can function as the healthy family the client never had. Help the client to realize why he/she needs such a family to recover.
RP: _____

_____

26. Educate the client about the family atmosphere in a home AA/NA recovery group and how helping others can aid in recovery and reestablishing a feeling of worth.

    RP: _____

    _____

27. Teach the client how faith in a higher power can aid in recovery and arrest ACOA traits and addiction.

    RP: _____

    _____

28. Assign the client to read the Alcoholics Anonymous *Big Book* on the topic of spirituality and the role of a higher power. Process the material in an individual or group therapy session.

    RP: _____

    _____

29. Review problematic circumstances in the client's life which could be turned over to a higher power to increase serenity.

    RP: _____

    _____

30. Use modeling, behavior rehearsal, and role playing to teach the client healthy assertive skills. Apply these skills to several current problem situations, and then ask the client to journal his/her assertiveness experiences.

    RP: _____

    _____

31. Teach the client the assertive formula of "I feel . . . When you . . . I would prefer it if. . . ." Role-play several applications in his/her life.
    RP: _____

    _____

32. Teach the client the *share-check method* of building trust, in which the degree of shared information is related to a proven level of trustworthiness. Use behavior rehearsal of several situations in which the client shares feelings.
    RP: _____

    _____

33. Review and reinforce instances when the client has shared honestly and openly with a trusted person.
    RP: _____

    _____

34. Refer the client to a physician to evaluate if psychopharmacological interventions are warranted.
    RP: _____

    _____

35. Medical staff administer medications as prescribed.
    RP: _____

    _____

36. Monitor medications for effectiveness and side effects.
    RP: _____

    _____

—. _____

_____

RP: _____

_____

—. _____

_____

RP: _____

_____

—. _____

_____

RP: _____

_____

DIAGNOSTIC SUGGESTIONS

Axis I: 311   Depressive Disorder NOS
             300.00   Anxiety Disorder NOS
             309.81   Posttraumatic Stress Disorder
             V61.20   Parent-Child Relational Problem

             _____   _____

             _____   _____

Axis II: 301.82   Avoidant Personality Disorder
             301.6   Dependent Personality Disorder
             301.9   Personality Disorder NOS

             _____   _____

             _____   _____

ANGER

BEHAVIORAL DEFINITIONS

1. History of explosive, aggressive outbursts, particularly when intoxicated, that lead to assaultive acts or destruction of property.
2. Tendency to blame others rather than accept the responsibility for own problems.
3. Angry overreaction to perceived disapproval, rejection, or criticism.
4. Passively withholds feelings, then explodes in a violent rage.
5. Abuses substances to cope with angry feelings and relinquish responsibility for aggression.
6. Persistent pattern of challenging or disrespecting authority figures.
7. Body language of tense muscles (e.g., clenched fists or jaw, glaring looks, or refusal to make eye contact).
8. Views aggression as a means to achieve needed power and control.
9. Use of verbally abusive language.

__. _____
   _____
__. _____
   _____
__. _____
   _____

LONG-TERM GOALS

1. Maintain a program of recovery that is free of addiction and violent behavior.
2. Decrease the frequency of occurrence of angry thoughts, feelings, and behaviors.

3. Implement the assertive skills that are necessary to solve problems in a less aggressive and more constructive manner.
4. Think positively in anger-producing situations.
5. Stop blaming others for problems, and begin to accept responsibility for own feelings, thoughts, and behaviors.
6. Learn and implement stress management skills to reduce the level of stress and the irritability that accompanies it.
7. Understand the relationship between angry feelings and the feelings of hurt and worthlessness that are experienced in the family of origin.
8. Learn the assertive skills that are necessary to reduce angry feelings and solve problems in a less aggressive and more constructive manner.

—. _____
   _____
   _____

—. _____
   _____
   _____

—. _____
   _____
   _____

SHORT-TERM OBJECTIVES

1. Keep a daily anger log, writing down each situation that produced angry feelings and the thoughts that were associated with the situation. Rate the level of anger on a scale from 1 to 100. (1)

2. Verbalize an understanding of the relationship between the feelings of worthlessness and hurt that were experienced in the family of origin and the current feelings of anger. (2, 3)

THERAPEUTIC INTERVENTIONS

1. Assign the client to keep a log of situations that precipitate angry feelings; ask him/her to record the thoughts, feelings, and depth of anger, rating these on a scale from 1 to 100.
   *RP:_____
   _____

2. Assign the client to list experiences of his/her life that have hurt and have lead to anger and resentment.
   RP: _____
   _____

*RP = responsible professional.

3. Verbalize an understanding of how anger has been reinforced as a coping mechanism for stress. (4)

4. Implement the impulse control technique of "stop, look, listen, think, and plan." (5)

5. Verbalize regret and remorse for the harmful consequences of anger. (6)

6. Decrease the frequency of negative, self-defeating thinking, and increase the frequency of positive, self-enhancing self-talk. (1, 7, 10)

7. Increase the frequency of assertive behaviors while reducing the frequency of aggressive behaviors. (8)

8. Verbalize an understanding of the need for and process of forgiving others to reduce anger. (9, 17)

9. Ask others what they think and how they feel rather than assuming that they have malicious intent. (10)

10. Verbalize an understanding of how angry thoughts and feelings can lead to increased risk of addiction. List instances when anger has resulted in addiction. (11, 12)

11. List five reasons why angry thoughts, feelings, and behaviors increase the risk of relapse. (11, 12)

12. Make a list of the thoughts that trigger angry feelings, and replace each thought

3. Probe the client's experience with his/her family of origin and help him/her to see how these experiences led to a tendency to see people and situations as dangerous and threatening.
   RP: _____
   _____

4. Teach the client how anger blocks the awareness of pain, discharges uncomfortable feelings, erases guilt, and places the blame for problems on others.
   RP: _____
   _____

5. Teach the client the impulse control skill of "stop, look, listen, think, and plan" before acting.
   RP: _____
   _____

6. Use modeling and role reversal to make the client more aware of how his/her aggressive behavior has had negative consequences on others (e.g., spouse, children) who have been the target of or witness to violence.
   RP: _____
   _____

7. Help the client to develop a list of positive, self-enhancing statements to use daily in building a positive and accurate self-image. Use role playing and modeling to demonstrate

with a more positive and accurate thought that is supportive to self and recovery. (13, 14)

13. Practice relaxation skills twice a day for 10 to 20 minutes. (15, 16)

14. Verbalize an understanding of the concept of a higher power and the benefits of acceptance of such a concept. (17)

15. Implement regular physical exercise to reduce tension. (18)

16. Attend 12-step recovery group meetings regularly, and share feelings with others there. (19)

17. Engage in at least one or two pleasurable activities per week. (20)

18. Implement proactive steps to meet the needs of self without expecting other people to meet those needs and angrily blaming them when they fail to. (8, 21)

19. Implement cognitive and behavioral techniques designed to stop the impulsive angry reaction when feeling angry. (22)

20. Practice the time-out technique to reduce impulsive anger expression. Keep a record of utilization of the technique in daily interactions. (22, 23)

21. Develop an aftercare program that details

implementation of positive self-talk.
RP: _____
_____

8. Teach assertiveness and its benefits through the use of role playing and modeling, assigning appropriate reading material (e.g., *Your Perfect Right* by Alberti and Emmons), or participating in an assertiveness training group.
RP: _____
_____

9. Assist the client in identifying who he/she needs to forgive, and educate him/her as to the long-term process that is involved in forgiveness versus a magical single event. Recommend reading *Forgive and Forget* by Smedes.
RP: _____
_____

10. Explore the client's tendency to read malicious intent into the words and actions of others. Use modeling, role playing, and behavior rehearsal to show him/her to ask other people what they think and feel.
RP: _____
_____

11. Educate the client about the tendency to engage in addictive behavior as a means of relieving uncomfortable feelings. Develop a

healthy, constructive alternatives to impulsive, destructive anger expression. (14, 15, 17, 18, 19, 24)

22. Cooperate with a physician's evaluation regarding whether psychopharmacological intervention is warranted. (25)

23. Take medications as prescribed, and report as to the effectiveness and side effects. (26, 27)

—. _____
     _____
     _____

—. _____
     _____

—. _____
     _____

list of several instances of occurrence.
RP: _____
     _____

12. Teach the client about the high-risk situations of negative emotions, social pressure, interpersonal conflict, strong positive emotions, and testing personal control. Discuss how anger, as a strong negative emotion, places them at high risk for addiction.
RP: _____
     _____

13. Educate the client about how the thoughts of abandonment and rejection trigger feelings of worthlessness, hurt, and then anger.
RP: _____
     _____

14. Assist the client in identifying a list of distorted thoughts that trigger feelings of anger; teach him/her to replace such thoughts with positive, realistic thoughts.
RP: _____
     _____

15. Teach the client progressive relaxation skills, and encourage their utilization twice a day for 10 to 20 minutes.
RP: _____
     _____

16. Review the client's application of relaxation skills; reinforce success and redirect for failure.
RP: _____

_____

17. Teach the client about the 12-step recovery program concept of a higher power and how to turn over perpetrators of pain to his/her higher power for judgment and punishment.
RP: _____

_____

18. Teach the client the benefits of regular physical exercise. Assign a program of implementation.
RP: _____

_____

19. Teach the client the importance of actively attending 12-step recovery meetings, getting a sponsor, reinforcing people around him/her, and sharing feelings.
RP: _____

_____

20. Assist the client in identifying a list of pleasurable leisure activities that he/she could engage in to reduce stress and increase enjoyment of life. Solicit a contract to engage in one or two such activities per week.
RP: _____

_____

21. Assist the client in developing a list of his/her own needs and wishes and then the personal actions necessary to attain these rather than being angry with others for not meeting his/her needs and wishes.
    RP: _____

    _____

22. Using modeling, role playing, and behavior rehearsal, show the client how to stop the impulse to react with anger (e.g., relax muscles; use positive, comforting self-talk; implement a time-out procedure; and speak softly in frustrating, threatening, or hurtful situations).
    RP: _____

    _____

23. Develop a time-out contract between the client and his/her significant other. Role-play applying the time-out procedure in five different anger-producing situations.
    RP: _____

    _____

24. Help the client to develop a list of what adaptive actions he/she is going to take to cope with angry feelings during aftercare (e.g., calling a sponsor, being assertive but not aggressive, taking a time-out, implementing relaxation, practic-

ing positive self-talk, praying to a higher power, etc.)
to avoid relapse.

RP: _____

_____

25. Refer the client to a
physician to evaluate if psychopharmacological inter-
ventions are warranted.

RP: _____

_____

26. Medical staff administer
medications as prescribed.

RP: _____

_____

27. Monitor medications for effectiveness and side effects.

RP: _____

_____

__. _____

_____

RP: _____

_____

__. _____

_____

RP: _____

_____

__. _____

_____

RP: _____

_____

DIAGNOSTIC SUGGESTIONS

Axis I:	312.8	Conduct Disorder
	313.81	Oppositional Defiant Disorder
	296.xx	Bipolar I Disorder
	296.89	Bipolar II Disorder
	312.34	Intermittent Explosive Disorder
	312.30	Impulse-Control Disorder NOS
	309.4	Adjustment Disorder With Mixed Disturbance of Emotions and Conduct
	V71.01	Adult Antisocial Behavior
	V71.02	Child or Adolescent Antisocial Behavior
	_____	_____
	_____	_____
Axis II:	301.0	Paranoid Personality Disorder
	301.70	Antisocial Personality Disorder
	301.83	Borderline Personality Disorder
	301.9	Personality Disorder NOS
	301.81	Narcissistic Personality Disorder
	_____	_____
	_____	_____

ANTISOCIAL BEHAVIOR

BEHAVIORAL DEFINITIONS

1. A history of breaking the rules or the law (often under the influence of drugs or alcohol).
2. A pervasive pattern of disregard for and violation of the rights of others.
3. Consistently blames other people for own problems and behaviors.
4. Uses aggressive behavior to manipulate, intimidate, or control others.
5. Chronic pattern of dishonesty.
6. Hedonistic, self-centered lifestyle with little regard for the needs and welfare of others.
7. Lack of empathy for the feelings of others, even if they are friends or family.
8. A pattern of criminal activity and addiction going back into the adolescent years.
9. Engages in dangerous, thrill-seeking behavior without regard for the safety of self or others.
10. Impulsively makes decisions without giving thought to the consequences for others.
11. Failure to keep commitments, promises, or obligations toward others, including own children, family, or significant others.
12. A history of many broken relationships with a lack of loyalty shown in intimate, as well as superficial, relationships.

__. _____
   _____

__. _____
   _____

__. _____
   _____

LONG-TERM GOALS

1. Develop a program of recovery that is free from addiction and the negative influences of antisocial behavior.
2. Stop committing crimes and understand why illegal activity is harmful to self and others.
3. Implement a program of recovery that demands rigorous honesty.
4. Learn and practice behaviors that are prosocial.
5. Respect the rights and feelings of others.
6. Take responsibility for own behavior.
7. Demonstrate honesty, reliability, empathy, and commitment in relationships.
8. Become abstinent from addictive behavior as a necessary part of controlling and changing antisocial impulses and behavior.

—. _____

_____

—. _____

_____

—. _____

_____

SHORT-TERM OBJECTIVES

1. Verbalize an acceptance of powerlessness and unmanageability over antisocial behavior and addiction. (1, 2)

2. Verbalize how addiction fosters antisocial behavior and how antisocial behavior encourages addiction. (3)

3. State how antisocial behavior and addiction are associated with irrational thinking [Alcoholics Anony-

THERAPEUTIC INTERVENTIONS

1. Assist the client in recognizing and acknowledging without projection or denial his/her pattern of antisocial behavior; list the behaviors that fit this pattern.
   *RP:_____

   _____

2. Help the client to understand the self-defeating nature of antisocial behavior and addiction.
   RP: _____

   _____

_____

*RP = responsible professional.

mous's (AA's) concept of *insanity*]. (4)

4. Consistently follow all rules. (5)

5. Identify and verbalize the consequences that failure to comply with the rules/limits has had on self and others. (6, 7)

6. List five occasions when antisocial behaviors led to negative consequences, and list the many decisions that were made along the way. (7, 8)

7. List the ways in which dishonesty is self-defeating. (9)

8. List the reasons why criminal activity leads to a negative self-image. (10)

9. Verbalize how criminal thinking leads to antisocial behavior and addiction. (11)

10. Verbalize an understanding of why blaming others prevents learning from mistakes of the past. (12)

11. Decrease the frequency of statements of blaming others or blaming circumstances, and increase the frequency of statements of accepting responsibility for own behavior, thoughts, and feelings. (12, 13, 14)

12. Identify historic and current sources for the pattern of blaming others. (14)

13. Develop a list of prosocial behaviors, and practice one of these behaviors each day. (15)

3. Help the client to see the reciprocal relationship between antisocial behavior and addiction.
   RP: _____
   _____

4. Help the client to understand how doing the same things over and over but expecting different results is irrational and what 12-step recovery programs call insane.
   RP: _____
   _____

5. Review with the client all rules that must be kept, and assign appropriate consequences when he/she fails to follow the rules.
   RP: _____
   _____

6. Review with the client several examples of his/her rule/limit breaking leading to negative consequences to himself/herself and others.
   RP: _____
   _____

7. Teach the client that many negative consequences are preceded by decisions based on criminal thinking.
   RP: _____
   _____

8. Attempt to sensitize the client to his/her lack of empathy for others by revisiting consequences of his/her

14. Write a list of typical criminal thoughts, and then list an alternative thought that is respectful to self and others. (16, 17)

15. List five ways that 12-step recovery group meetings and a higher power can assist in overcoming antisocial behavior and addiction. (18)

16. Receive feedback/redirection from the staff/therapist without making negative gestures or remarks. (5, 19)

17. Develop a written plan to address all pending legal problems in a constructive manner. (20)

18. Verbalize why it is essential in recovery from antisocial traits and addiction to give assistance to others. (21)

19. Give examples of a daily supportive behavior that has been demonstrated toward others. (22, 23)

20. State the reasons why having the trust of others is important. (24)

21. Articulate antisocial and addictive behaviors that have resulted in others' pain and disappointment and, therefore, a loss of their trust. (13, 25, 26)

22. Verbalize a desire to keep commitments to others, and list ways to prove self to be responsible, reliable, loyal, and faithful. (27)

behavior on others. Use role reversal techniques.

RP: _____

_____

9. Assist the client in understanding why dishonesty results in more lies, loss of trust from others, and ultimate rejection from others.

RP: _____

_____

10. Help the client to understand why criminal activity leads to feelings of low self-esteem. (e.g., others are hurt by his/her behavior, others lose respect for him/her, society does not give recognition or praise for his/her accomplishments, negative legal and moral judgments result from his/her behavior, etc.).

RP: _____

_____

11. Teach the client how criminal thinking (e.g., superoptimism, little empathy for others, power orientation, a sense of entitlement, self-centeredness, etc.) leads to antisocial behavior and addiction.

RP: _____

_____

12. Help the client to understand how blaming others results in a failure to learn from mistakes and, there-

23. Verbalize several ways that a sponsor can be helpful in recovery, and then make contact with a temporary sponsor. (28)

24. List the recovery groups and continuing therapy that will be a part of aftercare. (29)

25. Family members verbalize an understanding of the client's antisocial thought processes and the need to confront distorted thinking. (30)

26. Family members develop an aftercare plan that focuses on what they are expected to do to help the client recover. (31, 32, 33)

27. Family members verbalize a plan for reaction to the client's lapses into antisocial or addictive behavior. (33)

28. In a family session, each family member lists three things that he/she can do to help the client recover. (31, 33, 34)

—. _____
   _____

—. _____
   _____

—. _____
   _____

fore, a recurrence of making the same mistakes.
RP: _____
    _____

13. Confront the client's projection of blame for his/her behavior, feelings, and thoughts; reinforce acceptance of personal responsibility.
RP: _____
    _____

14. Explore with the client his/her reasons for blaming others for his/her own problems and behaviors and how he/she may have learned this behavior in a punishing family environment.
RP: _____
    _____

15. Teach the client the difference between antisocial and prosocial behaviors. Help him/her to develop a list of prosocial behaviors (e.g., helping others) to practice each day.
RP: _____
    _____

16. Confront the client's antisocial beliefs about the lack of respect for the rights and feelings of others, and model thoughtful attitudes and beliefs about the welfare of others.
RP: _____
    _____

17. Assist the client in identifying his/her typical antisocial thoughts; list an alternate, respectful, trusting empathic thought.
RP: _____

_____

18. Discuss with the client the various ways that recovery groups and a higher power can assist him/her in recovery.
RP: _____

_____

19. Confront the client when he/she breaks the rules, blames others, or makes excuses.
RP: _____

_____

20. Assist the client in addressing each legal problem honestly, taking responsibility for his/her behavior.
RP: _____

_____

21. Teach the client why it is essential to attend recovery groups and help others.
RP: _____

_____

22. Using modeling, role playing, and behavior rehearsal, practice with the client how he/she can encourage others in recovery.
RP: _____

_____

23. Assign the client to engage in at least one helpful be-

havior per day and to record these acts in a journal.

RP: _____

_____

24. Assist the client in developing a list of reasons why the trust in others is important as a basis for any human relationship.

RP: _____

_____

25. Encourage the client to be honest in acknowledging how he/she has hurt others.

RP: _____

_____

26. Confront any denial of responsibility for irresponsible, self-centered, and impulsive behaviors. Relate these behaviors to others' lack of trust in him/her.

RP: _____

_____

27. Discuss the importance of the client keeping commitments and promises to others and ways to prove himself/herself as trustworthy in relationships.

RP: _____

_____

28. Introduce the client to his/her 12-step recovery group sponsor or encourage him/her to ask a stable recovery person to be a sponsor; teach the client the

many ways that a sponsor
can be helpful in recovery.
RP: _____

_____

29. Help the client to develop
an aftercare program that
specifically outlines which
12-step recovery group
meetings will be attended
and with which psychother-
apist he/she will be working.
RP: _____

_____

30. Teach family members
about criminal thinking,
and show them how to help
the client correct his/her in-
accurate thoughts.
RP: _____

_____

31. Encourage family members
to work their own program
of recovery. Teach them the
need to overcome the denial
of making excuses for reinforcing or being intimidated
by the client's antisocial
behavior.
RP: _____

_____

32. Use behavior rehearsal,
modeling, and role playing
to teach family members
conflict resolution skills.
RP: _____

_____

33. Educate the family members about the client's aftercare program, and develop a
plan for reaction to his/her

lapses into antisocial or addictive behavior.

RP: _____

_____

34. Assist each family member
in identifying and listing
these things that he/she can
do to encourage the client to
recover from antisocial behavior and addiction.

RP: _____

_____

__. _____

_____

RP: _____

_____

__. _____

_____

RP: _____

_____

__. _____

_____

RP: _____

_____

DIAGNOSTIC SUGGESTIONS

Axis I: 312.80   Conduct Disorder
313.81   Oppositional Defiant Disorder
309.3   Adjustment Disorder With Disturbance of
Conduct
312.34   Intermittent Explosive Disorder
V71.01   Adult Antisocial Behavior
V71.02   Child or Adolescent Antisocial Behavior

_____   _____

_____   _____

Axis II: 301.70   Antisocial Personality Disorder
301.83   Borderline Personality Disorder
301.81   Narcissistic Personality Disorder

_____   _____

_____   _____

ANXIETY

BEHAVIORAL DEFINITIONS

1. Excessive fear and worry about several life circumstances that have no factual or logical basis.
2. Constant worry about family, job, social interactions, or health.
3. Tendency to blame self for the slightest imperfection or mistake.
4. Fear of saying or doing something foolish in a social situation due to lack of confidence in social skills.
5. Symptoms of autonomic hyperactivity, such as cardiac palpitations, shortness of breath, sweaty palms, dry mouth, trouble swallowing, nausea, or diarrhea.
6. Symptoms of motor tension, such as restlessness, tiredness, shakiness, or muscle tension.
7. Abuse of substances in an attempt to control anxiety symptoms.
8. Symptoms of hypervigilance, such as feeling constantly on edge, difficulty concentrating, sleep problems, irritability.

—. _____

_____

—. _____

_____

—. _____

_____

LONG-TERM GOALS

1. Maintain a program of recovery that is free from addiction and excessive anxiety.
2. End addictive behavior as a means of escaping anxiety, and practice constructive coping behaviors.

3. Decrease anxious thoughts, and increase positive self-enhancing self-talk.
4. Reduce overall stress levels, reducing excessive worry and muscle tension.
5. Learn the relationship between anxiety and addiction.
6. Develop the social skills necessary to reduce excessive anxiety in social situations, and terminate reliance on addiction as a coping mechanism.

—. _____
   _____
   _____
—. _____
   _____
   _____
—. _____
   _____

SHORT-TERM OBJECTIVES

1. Keep a daily journal of anxiety, including the situation that caused anxious feelings, the negative thoughts that fueled anxiety, and a ranking of each anxiety-producing situation on a scale from 1 to 100. (1)

2. Acknowledge the powerlessness and unmanageability caused by excessive anxiety and addiction. (2, 3)

3. List reasons why anxiety led to more addiction and addiction led to more anxiety. (3)

4. Verbalize the irrationality (12-step program's "insanity") of excessive anxiety and addiction. (3, 4)

THERAPEUTIC INTERVENTIONS

1. Assign the client to keep a daily record of anxiety, including each situation that caused anxious feelings, the negative thoughts precipitating anxiety, and a ranking of the severity of the anxiety from 1 to 100.
   *RP: _____
   _____

2. Help the client to see how anxiety and powerlessness over addiction has made his/her life unmanageable.
   RP: _____
   _____

3. Teach the client about the relationship between anxiety and addiction (i.e., how

_____

*RP = responsible professional.

5. Verbalize an understanding of the principal of how irrational thoughts form the basis for anxiety. (5)

6. List specific worries, and use logic and reasoning to replace irrational thoughts with reasonable thoughts. (6, 7)

7. Implement positive self-talk to reduce or eliminate the anxiety. (7, 8)

8. List 10 positive self-enhancing statements that will be read several times a day, particularly when feeling anxious. (9, 10, 11)

9. Comply with a physician's evaluation to determine if psychopharmacological intervention is warranted. Take any medications as directed. (12, 13, 14)

10. List several ways that a higher power can assist in a program of recovery from anxiety and addiction. (15)

11. Report on the instances that worries and anxieties have been turned over to the higher power. (16, 17)

12. Identify the fears that were learned in the family of origin, and relate these fears to current anxiety levels. (18, 19, 20)

13. Write a specific plan to follow when anxious and craving substance use. (9, 16, 21)

14. Develop a leisure program that will increase the fre-

the substance was used to treat the anxious symptoms and why more substance use became necessary).
RP: _____

_____

4. Teach the client about the 12-step program concept of *insanity,* and help him/her to see how anxiety and addictive behavior are insane.
RP: _____

_____

5. Assist the client in understanding the irrational nature of his/her thoughts that underlie the fears.
RP: _____

_____

6. Process the client's anxiety journal material to help him/her to identify the distorted thoughts that fueled the anxiety.
RP: _____

_____

7. Help the client to identify his/her specific worries. Facilitate his/her use of logic and reasoning to challenge the irrational thoughts associated with the worries and to replace those thoughts with reasonable ones.
RP: _____

_____

8. Help the client develop reality-based cognitive messages that will increase

quency of engaging in pleasurable activities and will
affirm self. (22)

15. Practice relaxation techniques twice a day for 10 to
20 minutes. (23)

16. Exercise at least three
times a week at a training
heart rate for at least 20
minutes. (24)

17. Write an autobiography detailing those behaviors in
the past that are related to
current anxiety or guilt and
the use of addiction as
means of escape.
(18, 19, 25)

18. Increase assertive behaviors to deal more effectively
and directly with stress,
conflict, and responsibilities. (26, 27)

19. Increase the frequency of
speaking up with confi-
dence in social situations.
(26, 27, 28)

20. Develop a program of recovery that includes regularly
helping others at recovery
group meetings. (28, 29)

21. Each family member list
three ways that he/she can
assist the client in recovery.
(30, 33)

22. Family members verbalize
an understanding of anxi-
ety, addiction, and the tools
that the client has learned
to use in recovery. (31, 32)

23. Family members state
what each can do in contin-

his/her self-confidence in
coping with fears and anxieties.
RP: _____

_____

9. Assist the client in developing a list of 10 positive
statements to read to him-
self/herself several times a
day, particularly when feeling anxious.
RP: _____

_____

10. Assign the client to read
*What to Say When You Talk
to Yourself* (Helmstetter)
and to process key ideas
with the therapist.
RP: _____

_____

11. Reinforce the client's use of
more realistic, positive messages to himself/herself in
interpreting life events.
RP: _____

_____

12. Physician will determine if
psychopharmacological in-
tervention is warranted,
order medication, titrate
medication, and monitor for
side effects.
RP: _____

_____

13. Staff will administer medication as directed by the
physician.
RP: _____

_____

uing care to become involved in a 12-step program of recovery. (33)

—. _____
_____
—. _____
_____
—. _____
_____

14. Monitor the client's use of medication for side effects and effectiveness.
    RP: _____
    _____

15. Teach the client the benefits of turning his/her will and life over to the care of a higher power of his/her own understanding.
    RP: _____
    _____

16. Using a 12-step program's step-three exercise, show the client how to turn over problems, worries, and anxieties to a higher power and to trust that the higher power is going to help him/her resolve the situation.
    RP: _____
    _____

17. Review the client's implementation of turning anxieties over to a higher power; reinforce success and redirect failure.
    RP: _____
    _____

18. Probe the client's family-of-origin experiences for fear-producing situations, and help him/her to relate these past events to current anxious thoughts, feelings, and behaviors.
    RP: _____
    _____

19. Encourage and support the client in verbally expressing

and clarifying his/her feelings that are associated with past rejection experiences, harsh criticism, abandonment, or trauma.
RP: _____

_____

20. Assign the client to read the books *Healing the Shame That Binds You* (Bradshaw) and *Facing Shame* (Fossum and Mason). Process key concepts.
RP: _____

_____

21. Help the client to develop an alternative constructive plan of action (e.g., relaxation exercises, physical exercise, calling a sponsor, going to a meeting, calling the counselor, talking to someone, etc.) when feeling anxious and craving substance use.
RP: _____

_____

22. Help the client to develop a plan of engaging in pleasurable leisure activities (i.e., clubs, hobbies, church, sporting activities, social activities, games, etc.) that will increase enjoyment of life and affirm himself/herself.
RP: _____

_____

23. Using relaxation techniques, such as progressive relaxation, guided imagery,

and biofeedback, teach the client how to relax completely. Assign him/her to relax twice a day for 10 to 20 minutes.

RP: _____

_____

24. Using the client's current physical fitness levels, increase his/her exercise by 10 percent a week, until he/she is exercising three times a week, at a training heart rate for at least 20 minutes.

RP: _____

_____

25. Using a 12-step program's step-four exercise, have the client write an autobiography detailing the exact nature of his/her wrongs, then teach the client how to begin to forgive himself/herself and others.

RP: _____

_____

26. Teach assertiveness skills to help the client communicate thoughts, feelings, and needs more openly and directly.

RP: _____

_____

27. Use role playing, modeling, and behavior rehearsal to help the client apply assertiveness to his/her daily life situations.

RP: _____

_____

28. Teach social skills to the client (see *Intimate Connections* by Burns and *Shyness* by Zimbardo).
    RP: _____

    _____

29. Help the client to develop a structured program of recovery that includes regularly helping others at 12-step program recovery groups.
    RP: _____

    _____

30. Assist each family member in developing a list of three things that he/she can do to assist the client in recovery; hold a family session to facilitate communication of the actions on the list.
    RP: _____

    _____

31. Provide the family members with information about anxiety disorders and the tools that are used to assist the client in recovery.
    RP: _____

    _____

32. Discuss with the family the connection between anxiety and addiction.
    RP: _____

    _____

33. In a family session, discuss
with the family members
what each one must do in
aftercare to maximize the
client's recovery and to become involved themselves
in a 12-step recovery
program.

RP: _____

_____

__. _____

_____

RP: _____

_____

__. _____

_____

RP: _____

_____

__. _____

_____

RP: _____

_____

DIAGNOSTIC SUGGESTIONS

Axis I:	309.21	Separation Anxiety Disorder
	291.89	Alcohol-Induced Anxiety Disorder
	292.89	Other (or Unknown) Substance–Induced Anxiety Disorder
	296.90	Mood Disorder NOS
	300.01	Panic Disorder Without Agoraphobia
	300.21	Panic Disorder With Agoraphobia
	300.29	Specific Phobia
	300.23	Social Phobia
	300.3	Obsessive-Compulsive Disorder
	309.81	Posttraumatic Stress Disorder
	308.3	Acute Stress Disorder
	300.02	Generalized Anxiety Disorder

	309.24	Adjustment Disorder With Anxiety
	309.28	Adjustment Disorder With Mixed Anxiety and Depressed Mood
	———	————————————
	———	————————————
Axis II:	301.0	Paranoid Personality Disorder
	301.83	Borderline Personality Disorder
	301.50	Histrionic Personality Disorder
	301.82	Avoidant Personality Disorder
	301.6	Dependent Personality Disorder
	301.4	Obsessive-Compulsive Personality Disorder
	301.9	Personality Disorder NOS
	———	————————————
	———	————————————

ATTENTION-DEFICIT/HYPERACTIVITY DISORDER (ADHD)

BEHAVIORAL DEFINITIONS

1. A pattern of restlessness and hyperactivity leading to attention deficit or learning disability.
2. Unable to focus attention long enough to learn appropriately.
3. Often fidgets with hands or squirms in seat.
4. Often leaves seat in situations where sitting is required.
5. Moves about excessively in situations in which it is inappropriate to do so.
6. Unable to exclude extraneous stimulation.
7. Blurts out answers before the questions have been completed.
8. Has difficulty waiting in line or awaiting a turn.
9. Often intrudes or talks excessively.
10. Acts too quickly on feelings without thought or deliberation.
11. Low self-esteem and poor social skills that lead to alienation from peers.

__. _____
   _____

__. _____
   _____

__. _____
   _____

LONG-TERM GOALS

1. Maintain a program of recovery from addiction, and reduce the negative effects of attention-deficit/hyperactivity disorder (ADHD) on learning, social interaction, and self-esteem.
2. Develop the skills that are necessary to bring ADHD symptoms under control.
3. Develop the coping skills that are necessary to improve ADHD symptoms and addiction.
4. Understand the relationship between ADHD symptoms and addiction.

—. _____
   _____
—. _____
   _____
—. _____
   _____

SHORT-TERM OBJECTIVES

1. Complete psychological testing to confirm the diagnosis of ADHD. (1, 3)
2. Complete psychological testing to rule out emotional factors or learning disabilities as the basis for maladaptive behavior. (2, 3)
3. Identify and monitor symptoms of ADHD on a daily basis, and rate the severity of symptoms each day on a scale from 1 to 100. (4, 5)
4. Verbalize the powerlessness and unmanageability that resulted from treating

THERAPEUTIC INTERVENTIONS

1. Arrange for thorough psychological testing to confirm the presence of ADHD in the client.
   *RP: _____
   _____

2. Arrange for psychological testing to rule out emotional factors or learning disabilities as the basis for the client's maladaptive behavior.
   RP: _____
   _____

3. Give feedback to the client and his/her family regard-

_____
*RP = responsible professional.

ADHD symptoms with addictive behavior. (6)

5. Verbalize the relationship between ADHD and addictive behavior. (7)

6. Implement a program of recovery that is structured enough to bring ADHD and addiction under control. (8)

7. List five ways in which a higher power can be used to assist in recovery from ADHD and addiction. (9)

8. Comply with a physician evaluation to determine if a psychotropic intervention is warranted. Take any medications as directed. (10, 11)

9. Report as to the effectiveness and side effects of psychotropic medications prescribed for ADHD. (10, 12)

10. Implement remedial procedures for any learning disabilities that add to frustration. (13)

11. Reduce environmental stimulation to the point that concentration can improve and new learning can take place. (14)

12. Keep lists and use a calendar as reminders of daily appointment and obligations. (15)

13. Practice taking time-outs and breaks when feeling restless or irritable. (18)

14. Practice extending concentration in gradual incre-

ing the psychological testing results.

RP: _____

_____

4. Explore the client's pattern of ADHD symptoms and their impact on his/her daily living.

RP: _____

_____

5. Teach the client how to monitor ADHD symptoms, and rate the severity of symptoms on a scale from 1 to 100 each day.

RP: _____

_____

6. Using a 12-step recovery program's step-one exercise, help the client accept his/her powerlessness and unmanageability over ADHD symptoms and addiction.

RP: _____

_____

7. Using a biopsychosocial approach, teach the client about the relationship between ADHD symptoms and the use of substances to control symptoms.

RP: _____

_____

8. Help the client to develop a program of recovery that includes the elements necessary to bring ADHD and addictive behavior under control (e.g., medication, behavior modification, envi-

ments, and self-reinforce each extension. (16, 17)

15. Verbalize an understanding of the importance of learning in small increments of time and taking enough breaks to keep ADHD symptoms under control. (16, 18)

16. Reduce impulsive behavior, and demonstrate the ability to stop, think, and plan before acting. (19, 20)

17. Verbalize the feelings of shame and frustration that accompany failure to learn because of ADHD. (21)

18. List the negative messages given to self in a learning situation, and replace each with an encouraging, affirming message. (22, 23)

19. Identify specific instances when the negative emotions associated with failure to learn were a trigger for addictive behavior, and verbalize constructive coping mechanisms to use in future learning situations. (21, 24, 25)

20. Increase the frequency of positive interaction with peers. (26, 27)

21. Verbalize satisfaction with self and others regarding fitting in socially. (26, 27, 28)

22. Practice relaxation techniques two times a day for 10 to 20 minutes. (29, 30)

ronmental controls, aftercare meetings, further therapy, etc.).
RP: _____
_____

9. Teach the client about the 12-step recovery program concept of a higher power and how this power can assist him/her in recovery.
RP: _____
_____

10. A physician orders psychotropic medications as warranted, titrates medications, and monitors for side effects.
RP: _____
_____

11. Staff will administer medications as ordered by the physician.
RP: _____
_____

12. Monitor the client's psychotropic medication for effectiveness and side effects.
RP: _____
_____

13. Refer the client to an educational specialist to design remedial procedures for any learning disabilities that may be present in addition to ADHD.
RP: _____
_____

14. Help the client to create an environment that is free

23. Report instances when relaxation techniques reduced
tension and frustration
while increasing focus in a
learning situation.
(29, 30, 31)

24. Develop and implement an
exercise program that in-
cludes exercise at a training
heart rate for at least 20
minutes at least three times
per week. (32)

25. Develop an aftercare program that includes regular
attendance at recovery
group meetings, getting a
sponsor, and continuing the
therapy necessary to bring
ADHD and addiction under
control. (8, 33, 34)

26. Family members verbalize
an understanding of the
connection between ADHD
and addiction. (35)

27. Family members verbalize
what each person can do to
assist the client in recovery.
(36, 37)

___. _____
    _____

___. _____
    _____

___. _____
    _____

enough of extraneous stimulation so that learning can
take place.
RP: _____
    _____

15. Teach the client how to
make lists and use a calendar to remind himself/her-
self about appointments
and daily obligations.
RP: _____
    _____

16. Using modeling, role playing, and behavior re-
hearsal, show the client
how to take time-outs and
breaks when feeling rest-
less or irritable.
RP: _____
    _____

17. Show the client how to ex-
tend periods of concentration in small increments.
Teach him/her how to reinforce himself/herself each
time.
RP: _____
    _____

18. Assist the client in setting
up learning periods in small
increments of time, taking
enough breaks to keep
ADHD symptoms under
control.
RP: _____
    _____

19. Review the client's impulsive behavior pattern and

the negative consequences
that have resulted from it.
RP: _____

_____

20. Using modeling, role playing, and behavior rehearsal,
show the client how to stop,
think, and plan before acting. Practice this technique
several times.
RP: _____

_____

21. Explore the client's negative
emotions associated with
his/her failure to learn.
RP: _____

_____

22. Assist the client in identifying the distorted, negative
self-talk that he/she engages
in any learning situation.
RP: _____

_____

23. Train the client to replace
negative expectations and
disparaging self-talk with
positive self-talk in a learning situation.
RP: _____

_____

24. Review specific instances of
failure to learn and the negative emotions that were associated with the experience.
Focus on how addictive behavior was used to escape
from negative emotions.
RP: _____

_____

25. Role-play and model constructive alternative coping behaviors to cope with negative emotions (e.g., focus cognitively, breathe deeply, make lists, reduce distractions, shorten learning sessions, repeat instructions verbally, etc.).
RP: _____

_____

26. Using role playing, modeling, and behavior rehearsal, teach social skills (e.g., use calm tones, respectfully time verbal contribution, consider the impact of comments, use appropriate humility, etc.) that control impulsivity, reduce alienation, and build self-esteem.
RP: _____

_____

27. Direct group therapy sessions that focus on social skill enhancement, getting feedback from peers for the client's socialization behavior.
RP: _____

_____

28. Reinforce the client's positive social interaction with peers, and explore the positive self-esteem that results from his/her successful interactions.
RP: _____

_____

29. Using techniques (e.g., progressive relaxation, guided

imagery, and/or biofeed-
back), teach the client how
to completely relax, then assign him/her to relax twice
a day for 10 to 20 minutes.
RP: _____

_____

30. Encourage the client to implement relaxation skills as
a coping and focusing mechanism when feeling tense
and frustrated by a learning
situation.
RP: _____

_____

31. Review the client's implementation of relaxation
techniques; reinforce success and redirect on failure.
RP: _____

_____

32. Using current fitness levels,
help the client develop an
exercise program. Increase
the exercise by 10 percent
each week until he/she is
exercising at a training
heart rate for at least 20
minutes at least three times
per week.
RP: _____

_____

33. Encourage the client to use
adaptive techniques in aftercare (e.g., relaxation, exercise, talking to someone,
taking a time-out, etc.)
when feeling restless or irritable.
RP: _____

_____

34. Help the client to develop an aftercare program that includes regular attendance at recovery group meetings, getting a sponsor, and continuing the therapy necessary to bring ADHD and addictive behavior under control.
    RP: _____

    _____

35. Discuss with the family members the connection between ADHD and addictive behavior.
    RP: _____

    _____

36. In a family session, go over what each family member can do to assist the client in recovery (e.g., attend recovery group meetings, reinforce the client's positive coping skills, be patient, keep expectations realistic, go to ADHD support group, etc.).
    RP: _____

    _____

37. Provide the family members with information about ADHD and the tools that are used to assist the client in recovery.
    RP: _____

    _____

___. _____
        _____

RP: _____
        _____

___. _____
        _____

RP: _____
        _____

___. _____
        _____

RP: _____
        _____

DIAGNOSTIC SUGGESTIONS

Axis I:	315.9	Learning Disorder NOS
	314.01	Attention-Deficit/Hyperactivity Disorder, Combined Type
	314.01	Attention-Deficit/Hyperactivity Disorder, Predominantly Hyperactive-Impulsive Type
	314.9	Attention-Deficit/Hyperactivity Disorder NOS
	312.8	Conduct Disorder
	313.81	Oppositional Defiant Disorder
	312.9	Disruptive Behavior Disorder NOS
	291.89	Alcohol-Induced Mood Disorder
	292.84	Other (or Unknown) Substance–Induced Mood Disorder
	309.4	Adjustment Disorder With Mixed Disturbance of Emotions and Conduct
	312.30	Impulse-Control Disorder NOS
	_____	_____
	_____	_____
Axis II:	301.70	Antisocial Personality Disorder
	301.83	Borderline Personality Disorder
	_____	_____
	_____	_____

ATTENTION-DEFICIT/INATTENTIVE DISORDER

BEHAVIORAL DEFINITIONS

1. Inability to sustain attention long enough to learn normally at work or school.
2. Fails to give sufficient attention to details and tends to make careless mistakes.
3. Has difficulty sustaining attention at work, school, or play.
4. Often does not seem to listen when spoken to directly.
5. Often does not follow through on instructions and fails to finish tasks.
6. Has difficulty organizing events, material, or time.
7. Avoids tasks and activities that require concentration.
8. Too easily distracted by extraneous stimulation.
9. Often forgets daily obligations.

__. _____

_____

__. _____

_____

__. _____

_____

LONG-TERM GOALS

1. Maintain a program of recovery that is free from addiction and the negative effects of attention-deficit disorder (ADD).
2. Demonstrate sustained attention and concentration for consistently longer periods of time.

3. Understand the negative influence of ADD on addictive behavior.
4. Structure a recovery program that is sufficient to maintain abstinence and reduce the negative effects of ADD on learning and self-esteem.

—. _____

_____

—. _____

_____

—. _____

_____

SHORT-TERM OBJECTIVES

1. Complete psychological testing to confirm the diagnosis of ADD. (1, 3)
2. Complete psychological testing to rule out emotional factors or learning disabilities as the basis for maladaptive behavior. (2, 3)
3. Verbalize several reasons why attention-deficit symptoms can lead to addictive behavior. (4)
4. List the ways that using addictive behavior to cope with symptoms of ADD and the feelings that result from it leads to powerlessness and unmanageability. (5)
5. Verbalize the interpersonal difficulties that are caused by or exacerbated by symptoms of ADD and addictive behavior. (6, 7)

THERAPEUTIC INTERVENTIONS

1. Arrange for thorough psychological testing to confirm the presence of ADD in the client.
   *RP: _____

   _____

2. Arrange for psychological testing to rule out emotional factors or learning disabilities as the basis for the client's maladaptive behavior.
   RP: _____

   _____

3. Give feedback to the client and his/her family regarding the psychological testing results.
   RP: _____

   _____

4. Explain how the ADD symptoms (e.g., learning

_____

*RP = responsible professional.

6. Verbalize an understanding of the etiology of ADD and addiction. (4, 8)

7. Identify the feelings of shame and frustration that are experienced when dealing with a failure to learn due to ADD, and state how addictive behavior was used to control uncomfortable feelings. (9)

8. List the negative messages given to self in a learning situation, and replace each with an encouraging, affirming message. (10, 11)

9. Identify specific instances when the negative emotions that are associated with a failure to learn were a trigger for addictive behavior; verbalize constructive coping mechanisms to use in future learning situations. (12)

10. List ways in which a program of recovery can eliminate the negative effects of ADD and addictive behavior. (13, 18, 20)

11. Comply with a physician's evaluation to determine if psychopharmacological intervention is warranted. Take any medications as directed. (14, 15)

12. Report as to the effectiveness and side effects of psychotropic medications that have been prescribed for ADD. (14, 16)

difficulties, impulsivity, and social alienation) can make the client vulnerable to addictive behavior.
RP: _____
_____

5. Using a 12-step recovery program's step-one exercise, help the client to correlate ADD and addiction with powerlessness and unmanageability.
RP: _____
_____

6. Probe the relationship problems that are caused by or exacerbated by ADD and addictive behavior.
RP: _____
_____

7. Confront statements in which the client blames others for his/her impulsive behaviors and fails to accept responsibility for the consequences of his/her actions.
RP: _____
_____

8. Teach the client about the biopsychosocial events that cause ADD and addictive behavior.
RP: _____
_____

9. Probe the feelings the client had when trying to deal with the failure to learn due to symptoms of ADD, and discuss how addictive be-

13. Implement remedial procedures for learning disabilities that add to frustration. (17)

14. List five ways in which a higher power can assist in dealing with the symptoms of ADD and addiction. (13, 18)

15. Keep lists of all scheduled activities and obligations, and mark off each item as it is completed. (19)

16. List techniques that can be used to reduce the negative effects of ADD. (20, 21, 22, 23)

17. Create and utilize a learning environment that is relatively free of extraneous stimulation so that productive learning can take place. (21)

18. Develop and demonstrate the relapse prevention skills to use when experiencing ADD symptoms or craving for addictive behavior. (22, 23)

19. Practice relaxation techniques twice a day for at least 10 to 20 minutes. (23)

20. Report instances when a relaxation technique reduced tension and frustration while increasing focus in a learning situation. (24)

21. Exercise at a training heart rate for at least 20 minutes per day, at least three times per week. Utilize exercise

havior was used to avoid uncomfortable feelings.
RP: _____

10. Assist the client in identifying distorted, negative self-talk that he/she engages in during a learning situation.
RP: _____

11. Train the client to replace negative expectations and disparaging self-talk with positive self-talk in a learning situation.
RP: _____

12. Review specific instances of failure to learn and the negative emotions that were associated with the experience. Role-play and model constructive alternative coping behaviors (e.g., focus cognitively, breathe deeply, make lists, reduce distractions, shorten learning sessions, repeat instructions verbally, etc.)
RP: _____

13. Help the client to see how working on a program of recovery can aid in reducing the negative influence of ADD and addictive behavior.
RP: _____

14. Physician examine the client to determine if psy-

as a coping mechanism when tense. (25)

22. Family members verbalize an understanding of the connection between ADD and addiction. (26)

23. Family members verbalize what each person can do to assist the client in recovery. (27, 28)

__. _____

_____

__. _____

_____

__. _____

_____

chopharmacological intervention is warranted, order medications as indicated, titrate the medications, and observe for side effects.
RP: _____

_____

15. Staff administer medications as ordered by the physician.
RP: _____

_____

16. Monitor the client's psychotropic medication use for side effects and effectiveness.
RP: _____

_____

17. Design remedial procedures for any learning disabilities that may be present in addition to ADD.
RP: _____

_____

18. Help the client to understand the 12-step recovery program concept of a higher power, and teach him/her the ways that a higher power can assist them in recovery.
RP: _____

_____

19. Assist the client in developing calendars and lists detailing activities and obligations.
RP: _____

_____

20. Help the client to develop a list of the things that he/she can do to reduce the negative effects of ADD (i.e., reduce extraneous stimulation, make lists and reminders, take medication, utilize relaxation techniques, talk to someone, go to recovery group meetings, engage in physical exercise).
RP: _____

_____

21. Help the client to develop a quiet place that is free of extraneous stimulation where he/she can concentrate and learn.
RP: _____

_____

22. Teach the client about the relapse prevention skills (e.g., going to meetings, talking to someone, calling a sponsor, utilizing relaxation techniques, engaging in physical exercise, and turning worries over to a higher power).
RP: _____

_____

23. Using relaxation techniques (e.g., progressive relaxation, guided imagery, and biofeedback), teach the client how to relax. Assign him/her to relax twice a day for 10 to 20 minutes.
RP: _____

_____

24. Encourage the client to implement relaxation skills as a coping and focusing mechanism when feeling tense and frustrated by a learning situation.
RP: _____

_____

25. Using current physical fitness levels, help the client develop an exercise program. Increase the exercise until he/she is exercising at a training heart rate at least three times a week for at least 20 minutes. Encourage exercise as a means of reducing the level of stress and frustration.
RP: _____

_____

26. Discuss with the family members the connection between ADD and addictive behavior.
RP: _____

_____

27. In a family session, go over what each family member can do to assist the client in recovery (e.g., attend recovery group meetings, reinforce the client's positive coping skills, be patient, keep expectations realistic, go to an ADD support group, etc.).
RP: _____

_____

28. Provide the family members with information about

ADD and the tools that are used to assist the client in recovery.

RP: _____

_____

—. _____

_____

RP: _____

_____

—. _____

_____

RP: _____

_____

—. _____

_____

RP: _____

_____

DIAGNOSTIC SUGGESTIONS

Axis I:	315.9	Learning Disorder NOS
	314.01	Attention-Deficit/Hyperactivity Disorder, Combined Type
	314.00	Attention-Deficit/Hyperactivity Disorder, Predominantly Inattentive Type
	314.9	Attention-Deficit/Hyperactivity Disorder NOS
	312.8	Conduct Disorder
	313.81	Oppositional Defiant Disorder
	312.9	Disruptive Behavior Disorder NOS
	291.89	Alcohol–Induced Mood Disorder
	292.xx	Other (or Unknown) Substance–Induced Mood Disorder
	309.4	Adjustment Disorder With Mixed Disturbance of Emotions and Conduct
	312.30	Impulse-Control Disorder NOS
	_____	_____
	_____	_____

Axis II: 301.70   Antisocial Personality Disorder
                301.83   Borderline Personality Disorder
                _____   _____
                _____   _____

BORDERLINE TRAITS

BEHAVIORAL DEFINITIONS

1. Extreme emotional reactivity (anger, anxiety, or depression) under minor stress that usually does not last beyond a few hours to a few days.
2. A pattern of intense, chaotic interpersonal relationships.
3. Marked identity disturbance.
4. Impulsive behaviors that are potentially self-damaging.
5. Recurrent suicidal gestures, threats, or self-mutilating behavior.
6. Chronic feelings of emptiness, boredom, or dissatisfaction with life or other people.
7. Frequent eruptions of intense, inappropriate anger.
8. Easily feels unfairly treated or that others can't be trusted.
9. Analyzes most issues in simple terms of right and wrong (black and white, trustworthy or deceitful) without regard for extenuating circumstances or complex situations.
10. Becomes very anxious or angry with any hint of perceived abandonment in a relationship.

__. _____
   _____
__. _____
   _____
__. _____
   _____

LONG-TERM GOALS

1. Develop a program of recovery from addiction that reduces the impact of borderline traits on abstinence.
2. Develop and demonstrate coping skills to deal with mood swings.
3. Develop the ability to control impulses.
4. Understand how borderline traits can foster a pattern of continued addictive behavior.
5. Modify dichotomous thinking.
6. Develop and demonstrate anger management skills.
7. Learn and practice interpersonal relationship skills.
8. Learn stress management skills.
9. Reduce the frequency of self-damaging behaviors (e.g., substance abuse, reckless driving, sexual acting out, binge eating, or suicidal behaviors).

__. _____
   _____

__. _____
   _____

__. _____
   _____

SHORT-TERM OBJECTIVES	THERAPEUTIC INTERVENTIONS
1. Keep a daily feelings journal. (1)	1. Assign the client to write a daily journal of emotions that he/she experienced, why the feelings developed, and what actions resulted from those feelings.
2. Keep a daily record of negative self-defeating thinking that leads to failure. (2, 3)	*RP: _____
3. Make a list of positive, accurate self-statements to use in daily positive self-talk. (4)	
4. Practice replacing self-defeating thoughts with	2. Help the client to differentiate between and list his/her self-defeating and self-

*RP = responsible professional.

self-enhancing, realistic thoughts. (2, 3, 4, 5)

5. List five occasions when borderline traits have led to addictive behavior. (6)

6. Describe situations in which self-damaging behaviors led to negative consequences, and list alternative adaptive behaviors. (7)

7. Verbalize five reasons why borderline traits make recovery from addictive behavior more difficult. (8)

8. Verbalize a plan to decrease the frequency of sudden mood swings. (9)

9. Verbalize how impulsivity has led to negative consequences. (10)

10. Practice the impulse control skills of stopping, looking, listening, thinking, and planning before acting. (11, 12, 13)

11. Verbalize an understanding of how anger toward others or fear of abandonment is expressed in suicidal gestures or self-mutilating behavior. (14, 15)

12. Identify interpersonal situations that easily trigger feelings of anger or fear of abandonment. (15, 16)

13. Verbalize the negative social consequences of frequent expressions of untamed anger or extreme dependency. (17)

enhancing thoughts. Assign the client to keep a daily record of his/her self-defeating thoughts.
RP: _____

_____

3. Using cognitive therapy techniques, help the client to see how negative, self-defeating thinking leads to negative consequences, both emotionally and behaviorally.
RP: _____

_____

4. Assist the client in building a list of positive reinforcing statements to use daily for self-enhancement.
RP: _____

_____

5. Using cognitive therapy techniques, help the client replace self-derogatory, distorted thinking with positive, self-enhancing statements.
RP: _____

_____

6. Help the client to see how poor impulse control, poor anger management, fear of abandonment, and intense mood swings increase the probability of addictive behavior. Explore instances when these borderline traits led to addictive behavior.
RP: _____

_____

14. Verbalize alternative, constructive ways to cope with feelings of anger or fear. (18, 19)

15. Role-play expressing anger in a calm, assertive manner. (19, 20)

16. Five times this week, talk calmly to someone when feeling upset. (20, 21)

17. Meet with the physician to be evaluated for the need for psychopharmacological treatment. (22, 23)

18. Take psychotropic medications as prescribed, and report as to their effectiveness and side effects. (23, 24, 25)

19. Practice the health communication skills of listening to others, using "I" statements, and sharing feelings. (26)

20. Verbalize what will help in developing a feeling of interpersonal safety. (27, 28)

21. Verbalize five ways in which a higher power can assist in resolving dependency needs. (29)

22. Verbalize an understanding of how dichotomous thinking leads to interpersonal difficulties. (30, 31)

23. List the good and bad points of five friends or family members. (31, 32)

24. Practice relaxation techniques two times a day for 10 to 20 minutes. (18, 33)

7. Review several self-damaging behaviors (e.g., gambling, substance abuse, binge eating, explosive anger, sexual acting out, self-mutilation, or suicidal gestures) and their negative consequences; help the client to discover what he/she could have done adaptively in each situation.
RP: _____

_____

8. Assist the client in defining the criteria for borderline traits, identifying each in himself/herself, and how each trait makes recovery from addictive behavior more difficult.
RP: _____

_____

9. Help the client to develop a list of coping skills to be used in dealing with sudden dysphoric mood swings (e.g., delaying the reaction to his/her moodiness, writing down his/her feelings in their causes, checking with others as to the rationality of his/her feelings, etc.).
RP: _____

_____

10. Teach the client how impulsivity leads to negative consequences and how self-control leads to positive consequences.
RP: _____

_____

25. Exercise at least three times a week for at least 20 minutes. (18, 34)

26. Write an aftercare program that lists resources that will be used when feeling angry, abandoned, or depressed, rather than reverting to addictive behavior. (35)

27. Family members verbalize a connection between borderline traits and addictive behavior. (36)

28. Family members verbalize what each can do to assist the client in recovery. (37, 38)

__. _____

_____

__. _____

_____

__. _____

_____

11. Teach the client self-control strategies (e.g., "stop, look, listen, think, and plan") to control impulses.

RP: _____

_____

12. Using role playing, behavior rehearsal, and modeling, apply the "stop, look, listen, think, and plan" strategy to the client's daily life situations.

RP: _____

_____

13. Review the client's impulse control progress; reinforce success and redirect for failure.

RP: _____

_____

14. Probe the relationship between the client's feelings of anger and/or fear and the behavior of suicide gestures or self-mutilation.

RP: _____

_____

15. Explore childhood and more recent experiences that have shaped the client's psyche such that he/she is so reactive to any hint of abandonment.

RP: _____

_____

16. Assist the client in identifying current triggers for his/her feelings of anger or fear of abandonment, and

relate these to historical causes for these feelings.

RP: _____

   _____

17. Help the client to understand the self-defeating, alienating consequences of frequently expressing anger and/or desperately clinging to others.

RP: _____

   _____

18. Develop with the client a list of constructive reactions to feelings of anger or fear (e.g., writing about his/her feelings, talking to a counselor, delaying expression for 24 hours, tracing feelings to his/her own background, substituting a physical exercise for outlet, practicing a relaxation exercise, etc.) that reduce impulsive acting out of feelings.

RP: _____

   _____

19. Model verbalization of anger in a controlled, respectful manner, delaying the response, if necessary, to gain more control. Ask the client to role-play calm anger expression.

RP: _____

   _____

20. Help the client to make a list of the people to call or visit when he/she becomes upset, and then role-play

several situations in which he/she discusses a problem calmly.

RP: _____

_____

21. Assign the client the task of talking to someone calmly when feeling angry, fearful, or depressed.

RP: _____

_____

22. Physician to evaluate if psychopharmacological intervention is warranted.

RP: _____

_____

23. Physician prescribe and adjust medication to maximize its effectiveness and reduce the side effects.

RP: _____

_____

24. Staff administer medications as ordered by physician.

RP: _____

_____

25. Monitor the client's psychotropic medication for compliance, effectiveness, and side effects.

RP: _____

_____

26. Teach the client how to listen, use "I" statements, and share feelings.

RP: _____

_____

27. Assist the client in developing healthy self-talk and good communication skills as a means of increasing his/her feelings of interpersonal safety.
    RP: _____
    _____

28. Assist the client in resolving feelings of rejection from childhood to decrease his/her current feelings of vulnerability.
    RP: _____
    _____

29. Teach the client about the higher-power concept in 12-step recovery programs, and give examples of how he/she can turn problems over to the higher power in recovery.
    RP: _____
    _____

30. Assist the client in understanding how dichotomous thinking leads to feelings of interpersonal mistrust.
    RP: _____
    _____

31. Challenge the extremes of the client's thinking as it relates to decisions about good or bad, trustworthy or deceitful people.
    RP: _____
    _____

32. Assist the client in reviewing the strengths and weak-

nesses of his/her friends
and family members.

RP: _____

_____

33. Using techniques (e.g., progressive relaxation, biofeedback, or guided imagery),
teach the client how to
relax; encourage application
of this skill to reduce feelings of tension and anger.

RP: _____

_____

34. Help the client to develop
an exercise program that
will help in reducing his/her
stress level.

RP: _____

_____

35. Assist the client in developing a structured aftercare
program that lists resources
he/she can use when feeling
angry, anxious, abandoned,
or depressed.

RP: _____

_____

36. Discuss with family members the connection between
borderline traits and addictive behavior.

RP: _____

_____

37. In a family session, review
what each member can do to
assist the client in recovery.

RP: _____

_____

38. Provide the family members with information about borderline syndrome and the steps that the client must take to recover successfully.

RP: _____

_____

___. _____

_____

RP: _____

_____

___. _____

_____

RP: _____

_____

___. _____

_____

RP: _____

_____

DIAGNOSTIC SUGGESTIONS

Axis I: 296.xx   Major Depressive Disorder
              300.4   Dysthymic Disorder
              296.xx   Bipolar Disorder I
              296.89   Bipolar Disorder II
              309.81   Posttraumatic Stress Disorder
              313.82   Identity Problem

              _____   _____

              _____   _____

Axis II: 301.83   Borderline Personality Disorder
              301.50   Histrionic Personality Disorder
              301.22   Schizotypal Personality Disorder
              301.70   Antisocial Personality Disorder
              301.0   Paranoid Personality Disorder
              301.81   Narcissistic Personality Disorder
              301.6   Dependent Personality Disorder

              _____   _____

              _____   _____

CHILDHOOD TRAUMA

BEHAVIORAL DEFINITIONS

1. History of childhood physical, sexual, or emotional abuse.
2. Unresolved psychological conflicts caused by childhood abuse or neglect.
3. Irrational fears, suppressed rage, low self-esteem, identity conflicts, depression, or anxious insecurity related to painful early life experiences.
4. Use of addiction to escape emotional pain tied to childhood trauma.
5. Intrusive memories, guilt, or emotional numbing from early childhood trauma.
6. Unresolved emotions and maladaptive behavior that is the result of childhood trauma.
7. Inability to trust others, bond in relationships, communicate effectively, and maintain healthy interpersonal relationships because of early childhood neglect or abuse.

—. _____
   _____
—. _____
   _____
—. _____
   _____

LONG-TERM GOALS

1. Resolve conflictual feelings that are associated with painful childhood traumas, and terminate addiction that has been used as a means of coping with those unresolved feelings.

2. Develop an awareness of how childhood issues have contributed to addictive behavior.
3. Maintain a program of recovery that is free of addiction and the negative effects of childhood trauma.
4. Forgive perpetrators of childhood trauma, and turn them over to a higher power.
5. Resolve childhood/family issues leading to less fear, anger, depression, greater self-esteem, and confidence.
6. Attend a continuing care program to resolve past childhood trauma and addiction.

—. _____
_____
_____

—. _____
_____

—. _____
_____

SHORT-TERM OBJECTIVES

THERAPEUTIC INTERVENTIONS

1. Verbalize powerlessness and unmanageability experienced as a child, and relate these feelings directly to addiction. (1, 2)

2. Describe the traumatic experiences that were endured and the feelings of helplessness, rage, hurt, and sadness that resulted from those experiences. (2, 3)

3. Identify the unhealthy rules and roles that were learned in the family of origin. (2, 4)

4. Verbalize an understanding of how childhood abandon-

1. Using a 12-step recovery program's step-one exercise, help the client to see the powerlessness and unmanageability that resulted from using addiction to deal with the negative feelings associated with the childhood trauma.
   *RP: _____
   _____

2. Explore the painful experiences endured in the client's family of origin, and help him/her to identify the unhealthy emotional and behavioral patterns that

*RP = responsible professional.

ment, neglect, or abuse led to current interpersonal distrust, anger, low self-esteem, or depression. (5, 6)

5. Identify a pattern of using drugs or alcohol abuse as a means of escape from psychological pain associated with childhood trauma, and verbalize more constructive means of coping. (1, 7)

6. Verbalize the unresolved grief that is tied to unmet needs, wishes, and wants of the childhood years. (8, 9)

7. Verbalize a plan as to how to fulfill the unmet needs of childhood now that adulthood has been reached. (10)

8. List the dysfunctional thoughts learned during the childhood trauma/neglect. (11)

9. Replace each self-defeating thought with a new thought that is positive and self-enhancing. (12)

10. Attend group therapy sessions to share thoughts and feelings that are related to childhood trauma and how addictive behavior has been used to avoid negative feelings. (7, 13)

11. Verbalize how the family of origin handled conflict, and then practice healthy rules of conflict resolution. (14)

12. List current maladaptive interpersonal relationship/ communication skills, and then develop and demon-

evolved from those experiences.

RP: _____

_____

3. Use the empty-chair technique to facilitate the client's expression of feelings toward the perpetrator of the abuse that he/she experienced in childhood.

RP: _____

_____

4. Teach the client about the unhealthy rules and roles that develop in dysfunctional families, and help him/her to identify what role he/she played in the family dynamics.

RP: _____

_____

5. Explore the client's current pattern of distrust of others and feelings of low self-esteem, anger, and/or depression.

RP: _____

_____

6. Help the client to understand the relationship between his/her childhood trauma experiences and his/her current problems with trust, anger, self-esteem, or depression.

RP: _____

_____

7. Confront the client's addictive behavior as a means of coping with emotional pain,

strate new skills that are adaptive and healthy. (14, 15)

13. List five ways in which a higher power can assist in recovery from childhood trauma and addictive behavior. (16)

14. Verbalize an understanding of the power of forgiving perpetrators and turning them over to the higher power. (16, 17)

15. Write a letter to the perpetrator detailing the childhood abuse and its effect on thoughts, feelings, and behavior. (18)

16. Write a letter to each primary caregiver, describing the childhood abuse and current feelings, wishes, and wants. (19)

17. Learn and demonstrate honesty, openness, and assertiveness in communicating with others. Practice these skills daily in recovery. (20, 21, 22)

18. Identify any patterns of repeating the abandonment, neglect, or abuse experienced as a child. (23)

19. Verbalize an understanding of how the home group in a 12-step recovery program can provide a substitute for the healthy home that was never experienced. (24)

20. Develop and agree to participate in an aftercare program to continue to recover

and assist him/her in identifying the self-defeating, negative consequences of this behavior. Process healthier, constructive means of coping (e.g., sharing pain with others, attending 12-step recovery program meetings, confronting and then forgiving perpetrator, turning the issue over to a higher power, etc.)

RP: _____

_____

8. Assist the client in identifying, understanding, and verbalizing unresolved needs, wishes, and wants from the childhood years.

RP: _____

_____

9. Have the client read *Healing the Shame That Binds You* (Bradshaw) and *Outgrowing the Pain* (Gil). Help him/her to identify unresolved feelings, wishes, and wants.

RP: _____

_____

10. Develop a written plan to meet each of the client's unmet needs, wishes, or wants.

RP: _____

_____

11. Assist the client in identifying distorted, dysfunctional thoughts that were learned during experiences of child-

from childhood abuse and addiction. (25)

21. Share with family members the pain of childhood trauma, and commit to working with the family in continuing care. (26)

22. Family members verbalize a connection between childhood trauma and addictive behavior. (27, 28)

23. Family members verbalize what each can do to assist the client in recovery. (29)

—. _____
   _____

—. _____
   _____

—. _____
   _____

hood trauma/neglect. Relate these thoughts and behaviors to current feelings.

RP: _____
    _____

12. Teach the client realistic, positive self-talk to replace distorted messages that were learned from childhood experiences.

RP: _____
    _____

13. Direct or refer the client to group therapy sessions in which he/she is encouraged to share his/her story of childhood trauma, allowing for feedback of empathy, acceptance, and affirmation from group members.

RP: _____
    _____

14. Explore the client's family of origin reaction to conflict, teaching him/her the healthy conflict resolution skills of active listening, using "I" messages, cooperation, compromise, and mutual respect.

RP: _____
    _____

15. Help the client to identify the maladaptive relationship/communication skills learned as a child. Use modeling, role playing, and behavior rehearsal to teach him/her the healthy

problem-solving and communication skills to use in recovery.

RP: _____

_____

16. Teach the client about the 12-step recovery program's concept of a higher power and how the higher power can assist them in forgiving others and reestablishing self-esteem.

RP: _____

_____

17. Help the client to understand that, often, perpetrators were wounded children, too, and that they need to be forgiven and turned over to the higher power in order to escape from harboring rage at them.

RP: _____

_____

18. Assign the client to write a letter to his/her perpetrator detailing the emotional trauma that resulted from the abuse.

RP: _____

_____

19. Assist the client in writing a letter to each parent, or primary caregiver, detailing the childhood abuse, and sharing what he/she wants from each person in recovery.

RP: _____

_____

20. Assign the client to read *Taking Charge of Your Social Life* (Gumbrill and Richey) to enhance social communication skills. Process these concepts in session.

    RP: _____

    _____

21. Teach the client the healthy communication skills of being honest, asking for wants, and sharing feelings.

    RP: _____

    _____

22. Using modeling, role playing, and behavior rehearsal, teach the client healthy assertive skills, then practice these skills in several current problem situations.

    RP: _____

    _____

23. Explore whether the client has a tendency to repeat a pattern of abuse and neglect toward his/her own children when he/she has experienced it on a regular basis in childhood.

    RP: _____

    _____

24. Help the client to see that the new home 12-step recovery program group can help to substitute for a healthy home that he/she never had.

    RP: _____

    _____

25. Help the client to develop an aftercare program that includes regular attendance at recovery group meetings and the continued therapy that is necessary to recover from childhood trauma and addiction.

    RP: _____

    _____

26. Hold a family therapy session in which the client is supported in sharing the pain associated with his/her childhood trauma/abuse.

    RP: _____

    _____

27. Discuss with family members the connection between childhood trauma and addictive behavior.

    RP: _____

    _____

28. In a family session, review what each member can do to assist the client in recovery.

    RP: _____

    _____

29. Provide the family members with information about childhood trauma and the steps that the client must take to recover successfully.

    RP: _____

    _____

—. _____

_____

RP: _____

_____

—. _____

_____

RP: _____

_____

—. _____

_____

RP: _____

_____

DIAGNOSTIC SUGGESTIONS

Axis I:	300.4	Dysthymic Disorder
	296.xx	Major Depressive Disorder
	300.02	Generalized Anxiety Disorder
	309.81	Posttraumatic Stress Disorder
	300.14	Dissociative Identity Disorder
	V61.21	Sexual Abuse of Child (995.53, Victim)
	V61.21	Physical Abuse of Child (995.54, Victim)
	V61.21	Neglect of Child (995.52, Victim)
	_____	_____
	_____	_____
Axis II:	301.70	Antisocial Personality Disorder
	301.83	Borderline Personality Disorder
	301.60	Dependent Personality Disorder
	_____	_____
	_____	_____

DEPENDENT TRAITS

BEHAVIORAL DEFINITIONS

1. Passively submissive to the wishes, wants, and needs of others; too eager to please others.
2. Chronically fearful of interpersonal abandonment and desperately clings to destructive relationships.
3. Goes to excessive lengths to gain acceptance from others to the point of volunteering to do unpleasant things.
4. A history of being anxious about making decisions without an excessive amount of advice and support from others.
5. Inability to trust own judgment about everyday life decisions.
6. Overly concerned with the opinions of others for fear of the loss of social support.
7. Persistent feelings of worthlessness and a belief that being rejected is inevitable.
8. Needs others to assume the responsibility and make decisions for most major areas of life.
9. Fears group situations unless certain of being accepted.
10. Chronic feelings of alienation from others.

__. _____
   _____

__. _____
   _____

__. _____
   _____

LONG-TERM GOALS

1. Recovery from substance abuse that reduces the impact of dependent traits on addiction-free living.
2. Demonstrate increased independence and self-confidence through autonomous decision making, honest expression of feelings and ideas, and reduced fear of rejection.
3. Decrease dependence on relationships while beginning to meet own needs, build confidence, and practice assertiveness.
4. Demonstrate healthy communication that is honest, open, and self-disclosing.
5. Reduce the frequency of behaviors that are exclusively designed to please others.
6. Reduce feelings of alienation by learning similarity to others who were raised in a more normal home.
7. Improve feelings of self-worth by helping others in recovery.

—. _____
   _____
   _____
—. _____
   _____
   _____
—. _____
   _____

SHORT-TERM OBJECTIVES

1. Acknowledge the feelings of powerlessness and unmanageableness that result from dependent traits and addictive behavior. (1, 3, 7)

2. Identify at least two dynamics of early family life that contributed to developing dependent traits. (2, 3, 4, 8)

3. Identify at least five incidents in which dependent

THERAPEUTIC INTERVENTIONS

1. Probe the feelings of powerlessness that the client experienced as a child and how these feelings are similar to how the client feels when engaging in addictive behavior.
   *RP: _____
   _____

2. Educate the client about the childhood etiology of

*RP = responsible professional.

traits were used to avoid the anxiety of making decisions that could have resulted in failure. (5, 6, 7, 8)

4. Verbalize an understanding of how dependent traits contributed to addictive behavior. (1, 5, 9)

5. Identify how the tendency to take on the child role in interpersonal relationships is related to maintaining a feeling of security. (2, 4, 10)

6. Identify abandonment experiences in the family of origin and how this influenced current relationships. (4, 5, 11)

7. Share the feeling of worthlessness that was learned in the family, and relate this feeling to addictive behavior as a coping mechanism. (3, 8, 11, 12)

8. Identify the pattern in the family of being ignored or punished when honest feelings or thoughts were shared. (8, 13)

9. Practice relaxation techniques twice a day for at least 10 minutes as a means of coping with anxiety. (12, 14)

10. Report three incidents per week in which relaxation skills were implemented to counteract anxiety in interpersonal situations. (14, 15)

11. Acknowledge the resistance to sharing personal prob-

his/her fear of making decisions and how this is not appropriate as an adult.
RP: _____

_____

3. Explore how the dysfunctional family's inconsistent rules led to the client's fear of failure.
RP: _____

_____

4. Assist the client in understanding how his/her early childhood experiences led to fear of abandonment, rejection, and neglect, and the assumption of a childlike role that is detrimental to intimate relationships.
RP: _____

_____

5. Explore the influence that the client's fear and shame had on choosing a lifestyle of dependent traits and addictive behavior.
RP: _____

_____

6. Ask the client to identify at least five instances when he/she avoided making decisions out of fear of failure or rejection.
RP: _____

_____

7. Probe the client's inability to trust his/her own judgment; raise his/her aware-

lems. Share at least one problem in each therapy session. (13, 16)

12. Report two incidents per week of telling the truth rather than only saying what the other person wanted to hear. Record the incidents and feelings in a journal. (16, 17, 18)

13. Verbalize an understanding of how dependent traits contributed to choosing partners and friends that were controlling. (4, 8, 19)

14. Identify the six steps that are necessary for effective problem solving and decision making. (20)

15. Implement decision-making skills in at least three situations per week. Document and report on the process and feelings that are associated with the experience. (21, 22)

16. Encourage others in recovery to help reestablish a feeling of self-worth. (23, 24)

17. Discuss fears that are related to attending recovery group meetings, and verbalize specific plans to deal with each fear. (24)

18. Make a list of 10 reasons why regular attendance at recovery group meetings is necessary in arresting dependent traits and addictions. (25, 26)

ness of this tendency and explore its origins.

RP: _____

_____

8. Teach the client about how low self-esteem and fear of making the wrong choice resulted from being raised in a home in which people were overly controlling and critical.

RP: _____

_____

9. Discuss the relationship between dependent traits and addictive behavior.

RP: _____

_____

10. Raise the client's awareness of his/her tendency to take over the child role in relationships; explore causes for this pattern.

RP: _____

_____

11. Explore the client's childhood experiences of abandonment and neglect; relate these to his/her dependent traits and addictive behavior.

RP: _____

_____

12. Assist the client in identifying a pattern of using addictive behavior as an escape from feelings of anxiety and worthlessness.

RP: _____

_____

19. Report on successfully contacting a sponsor within the 12-step community. (27)

20. List five ways in which belief in an interaction with a higher power can reduce fears and aid in recovery. (28)

21. Verbalize a feeling of serenity that results from turning own out-of-control problems over to the higher power. (28, 29)

22. Read portions of recovery literature six days per week, and share insights obtained with others. (30)

23. Practice assertiveness skills and keep a daily journal of the times when these skills were used in interpersonal conflict. (18, 31)

__. _____

   _____

__. _____

   _____

__. _____

   _____

13. Explore how the client's family responded to expressions of feelings, wishes, and wants, and why the client became anxious when he/she expressed a choice, feeling, or decision.
RP: _____

   _____

14. Teach the client relaxation techniques (e.g., deep muscle release, rhythm, deep breathing, positive imagery, etc.) as a coping technique for anxiety.
RP: _____

   _____

15. Role-play instances when the client could implement relaxation techniques as a healthy escape from anxiety. Monitor and reinforce the implementation of this skill in daily life.
RP: _____

   _____

16. Educate the client about healthy interpersonal relationships based on openness, respect, and honesty, and explain the necessity of sharing feelings to build trust and mutual understanding.
RP: _____

   _____

17. Teach the client about how the behavior of telling other people what we think they want to hear, rather than telling them the truth, is

based on the fear of rejection that is learned in the family. Using behavioral rehearsal, teach the client more honest communication skills.

RP: _____

_____

18. Teach the client the assertive formula of "I feel . . . When you . . . I would prefer it if . . .," roleplaying several applications to his/her life. Have the client journal one assertive situation each day.

RP: _____

_____

19. Review the client's choice of friends and intimate partners; relate his/her dependency traits to the selection of controlling people.

RP: _____

_____

20. Teach problem-solving skills (e.g., identify the problem, brainstorm alternate solutions, examine the advantages and disadvantages of each option, select an option, implement a course of action, and evaluate the result), and roleplay solving a problem from the client's life experience.

RP: _____

_____

21. Educate the client about how the fear of making decisions is based on low

self-esteem and need for acceptance.

RP: _____

_____

22. Assign the client to implement decision-making skills at least three times per week, and record the process and feelings. Review, reinforce, and redirect when necessary.

RP: _____

_____

23. Teach the client how becoming actively involved in a 12-step recovery group can aid in building trust in others and confidence in himself/herself.

RP: _____

_____

24. Probe the relationship between the client's dependent traits and his/her fear of attending recovery group meetings. Assist him/her in identifying coping skills (e.g., relaxation techniques, positive self-talk, assertiveness skills, etc.) to overcome fears.

RP: _____

_____

25. Assist the client in developing an aftercare plan that is centered around regular attendance at a 12-step recovery group meeting.

RP: _____

_____

26. Discuss how the 12-step home group can be like the healthy family that the client never had. Help the client realize why he/she needs such a group to recover.
    RP: _____

    _____

27. Educate the client about the importance of sponsorship within the 12-step community, and facilitate his/her establishment of a relationship with a temporary sponsor.
    RP: _____

    _____

28. Teach the client about the positive ways that faith in a higher power can aid in recovery, and arrest the fear that is associated with dependent traits and addiction.
    RP: _____

    _____

29. Review and reinforce the client's enactment of faith in a higher power in his/her daily life.
    RP: _____

    _____

30. Assign the client to read recovery literature (e.g., Alcoholics Anonymous *Big Book*), and process the material in an individual or group therapy session.
    RP: _____

    _____

31. Use modeling, behavior rehearsal, and role playing to teach the client healthy assertiveness skills, and then assign application of these skills to several current problem situations.

RP: _____

_____

__. _____

_____

RP: _____

_____

__. _____

_____

RP: _____

_____

__. _____

_____

RP: _____

_____

DIAGNOSTIC SUGGESTIONS

Axis I:

311	Depressive Disorder NOS
300.00	Anxiety Disorder NOS
300.02	Generalized Anxiety Disorder
300.23	Social Phobia
300.21	Panic Disorder With Agoraphobia
309.81	Posttraumatic Stress Disorder
V61.20	Parent-Child Relational Problem
_____	_____
_____	_____

Axis II:

301.82	Avoidant Personality Disorder
301.60	Dependent Personality Disorder
301.50	Histrionic Personality Disorder
301.90	Personality Disorder NOS
_____	_____
_____	_____

DEPRESSION

BEHAVIORAL DEFINITIONS

1. Feels sad or down most days of the week.
2. Vegetative symptoms, including sleep disturbance, appetite disturbance, anhedonia, fatigue, and weight change.
3. Persistent feelings of helplessness, hopelessness, worthlessness, or guilt.
4. Loss of energy, excessive fatigue.
5. Poor concentration, indecisiveness.
6. Low self-esteem.
7. Mood-congruent hallucinations or delusions.
8. Engages in addictive behavior as a means of escaping from feelings of sadness, worthlessness, and hopelessness.
9. Suicidal thoughts
10. Expresses a wish to die without a suicidal thought or plan.

__. _____
_____

__. _____
_____

__. _____
_____

LONG-TERM GOALS

1. Elevate mood and develop a program of recovery that is free from addiction.
2. Alleviate depressed mood and return to previous level of effective functioning.

100

3. Decrease dysfunctional thinking and increase positive self-enhancing self-talk.
4. Understand affective disorder and how these symptoms increase vulnerability to addiction.
5. Develop a program of recovery that includes healthy and regular exercise, relaxation, and eating and sleeping habits.
6. Improve social skills and attend recovery groups regularly.
7. Resolve interpersonal conflicts and grief issues.
8. Increase feelings of self-worth and self-esteem.

—. _____
_____
—. _____
_____
—. _____
_____

SHORT-TERM OBJECTIVES

1. Verbalize the powerlessness and unmanageability that result from using addictive behavior to cope with depression. (1, 5)

2. Describe the signs and symptoms of depression that are experienced. (2, 4)

3. Verbally identify, if possible, the source of depressed mood. (3, 4)

4. Verbalize an understanding of how depression leads to addictive behavior and how addictive behavior leads to depression. (5)

5. Identify a pattern of using drug or alcohol abuse as a

THERAPEUTIC INTERVENTIONS

1. Using a 12-step recovery program's step-one exercise, help the client to admit powerlessness and unmanageability over addictive behavior and depression.
   *RP: _____
   _____

2. Explore how depression is experienced in the client's day-to-day living.
   RP: _____
   _____

3. Ask the client to make a list of what he/she is depressed

---

*RP = responsible professional.

means of escape from depression, and verbalize more constructive means of coping. (6, 7)

6. Report no longer feeling the desire to take own life. (6, 8, 9)

7. State a desire to live and an end to wishes for death. (8, 9)

8. Verbalize an understanding of how depression and addictive behavior lead to a condition that a 12-step recovery program calls *insane*. (5, 10)

9. List five ways in which a higher power can be useful in recovery from addiction and depression. (11)

10. Keep a daily record of dysfunctional thinking that includes each situation that was associated with the depressed feelings and the thoughts that triggered those feelings. (12)

11. Replace negative, self-defeating thinking with positive, accurate, self-enhancing self-talk. (13)

12. Learn and demonstrate the ability to use positive conflict resolution skills to resolve interpersonal discord. (14, 15)

13. Visit with the physician to determine if psychopharmacological intervention is warranted, and take all medication as prescribed. (16, 17)

about, and process the list with the therapist.
RP: _____
_____

4. Encourage sharing feelings of depression in order to clarify them and gain insight as to causes.
RP: _____
_____

5. Teach the client that addictive behavior results in negative psychological effects and that addictive behavior is often used to control psychological symptoms in a vicious cycle.
RP: _____
_____

6. Confront the addictive behavior as a means of coping with depression; assist the client in identifying the self-defeating, negative consequences of this behavior.
RP: _____
_____

7. Process healthier, more constructive means of coping with depression (sharing pain with others, attending 12-step recovery program meetings, developing positive cognitions, taking medication, turning conflicts over to a higher power, etc.).
RP: _____
_____

8. Assess and monitor the client's suicide potential, ar-

14. Report as to the effectiveness and side effects of psychotropic medication that have been prescribed. (18)

15. Participate in a psychological assessment to determine the extent of depression and addictive behavior. (19)

16. Verbalize unresolved grief and make a written plan to recover from grief issues. (20)

17. Identify the positive and negative aspects of the relationship with the deceased person. (21)

18. Write a plan to develop new relationships. (22)

19. Report an awareness of anger toward the deceased spouse or significant other for leaving. (23)

20. Write a good-bye letter to the person who has died, sharing unresolved feelings. (24)

21. Write an autobiography detailing the exact nature of wrongs, and turn past misbehavior over to a higher power. (25)

22. Read aloud 10 positive self-enhancing statements each morning. (26)

23. Encourage someone in recovery each day. Write each incident down and discuss it with the primary therapist. (27)

24. Verbalize an understanding of own importance to others in the recovery group. (28)

ranging for suicide precautions, if necessary.
RP: _____
_____

9. Reinforce the client's positive statements regarding his/her life and the future.
RP: _____
_____

10. Teach the client about the 12-step recovery program's concept of *insanity,* and relate this concept to his/her addiction and depression.
RP: _____
_____

11. Teach the client about the 12-step recovery program's concept of a higher power and the ways in which a higher power can assist in recovery.
RP: _____
_____

12. Assign the client to keep a daily record of dysfunctional thinking that includes listing each situation that associated with the depressed feelings, and the dysfunctional thinking about that situation that triggered depression.
RP: _____
_____

13. Using logic and reality, challenge each of the client's dysfunctional thoughts for accuracy, re-

25. Develop written plans and express hope for the future. (29)

26. Develop and implement an exercise program that includes training at a training heart rate for at least 20 minutes at least three times a week. (30)

27. Write down five things each night for which gratitude is felt. (31)

28. Attend group therapy sessions to share thoughts and feelings that are related to depression and how addictive behavior has been used to avoid these negative feelings. (32)

29. Develop an aftercare program that includes regular attendance at recovery groups and any therapy that the primary therapist deems appropriate. (33)

30. Family members verbalize a connection between depression and addictive behavior. (34)

31. Family members verbalize what each can do to assist the client in recovery. (35, 36)

__. _____

   _____

__. _____

   _____

__. _____

   _____

placing any dysfunctional thinking with positive, accurate thoughts.
RP: _____

   _____

14. Teach the client conflict resolution skills (e.g., empathy, active listening, "I" messages, respectful communication, assertiveness without aggression, compromise, etc.), and then use modeling, role playing and behavior rehearsal to work through several of his/her current conflicts.
RP: _____

   _____

15. In conjoint sessions, help the client apply conflict resolution skills to resolve interpersonal conflicts and problems.
RP: _____

   _____

16. Physician will examine the client and order medications as appropriate, titrate them, and monitor them for side effects.
RP: _____

   _____

17. Medical staff will administer medications as prescribed by the physician.
RP: _____

   _____

18. Monitor the client's psychotropic medications for

side effects and effectiveness.

RP: _____

_____

19. Psychologist will complete
     a psychological assessment
     to determine the extent of
     depression and addictive
     behavior and make recom-
     mendations for treatment.

     RP: _____

     _____

20. Help the client to identify
     grief issues and develop a
     written plan for resolving
     grief (e.g., visit the grave,
     write a good-bye letter, at-
     tend a support group, begin
     social activities, volunteer
     to help others, etc.).

     RP: _____

     _____

21. Probe the positive and neg-
     ative elements of the rela-
     tionship with the deceased
     individual.

     RP: _____

     _____

22. Help the client to develop a
     plan for making new rela-
     tionships (e.g., through 12-
     step recovery program
     meetings, work relation-
     ships, church acquain-
     tances, school, or special
     group contacts, etc.).

     RP: _____

     _____

23. Encourage the client to
     share his/her feelings of

anger and resentment felt toward the significant other for leaving.

RP: _____

_____

24. Probe the client's grief and help him/her to say good-bye in a letter to the person who has died.

RP: _____

_____

25. Using a 12-step recovery program's step-four inventory, assign the client to write an autobiography that details the exact nature of his/her wrongs; then, help the client to turn over past misbehavior to a higher power.

RP: _____

_____

26. Help the client to develop a list of 10 accurate, self-enhancing statements to read each morning.

RP: _____

_____

27. Teach the client the importance of helping others to build their own sense of self-worth and self-esteem. Assign the client to encourage someone in the 12-step recovery program each day.

RP: _____

_____

28. Help the client to understand that he/she is needed in a 12-step recovery program to help others. Dis-

cuss specific ways to help others and how this builds the client's self-esteem and self-worth.

RP: _____

_____

29. Assist the client in developing future plans, and show that these plans create new hope for tomorrow.

RP: _____

_____

30. Using current physical fitness levels, increase the client's exercise by 10 percent each week until the client is exercising at a training heart rate for at least 20 minutes three times a week.

RP: _____

_____

31. Teach the client about the 12-step recovery program's concept of *an attitude of gratitude*. Assign him/her to write down five things for which he/she is grateful each day.

RP: _____

_____

32. Direct group therapy sessions in which the client is encouraged to share his/her feelings of depression, allowing for feedback of empathy, acceptance, and affirmation from group members.

RP: _____

_____

33. Help the client to develop
    an aftercare program that
    includes regular attendance
    at 12-step recovery groups
    and any other therapy that
    the client needs to improve
    his/her health.
    RP: _____

    _____

34. Discuss with the family
    members the connection be-
    tween depression and addic-
    tive behavior.
    RP: _____

    _____

35. In a family session, review
    what each member can do to
    assist the client in recovery.
    RP: _____

    _____

36. Provide the family members
    with information about de-
    pression and the steps that
    the client must take to re-
    cover successfully.
    RP: _____

    _____

__. _____

    _____

    RP: _____

    _____

__. _____

    _____

    RP: _____

    _____

__. _____

    _____

    RP: _____

    _____

DIAGNOSTIC SUGGESTIONS

Axis I:

309.0	Adjustment Disorder With Depressed Mood
309.28	Adjustment Disorder With Mixed Anxiety and Depressed Mood
311	Depressive Disorder NOS
296.xx	Bipolar I Disorder
296.89	Bipolar II Disorder
300.4	Dysthymic Disorder
301.13	Cyclothymic Disorder
296.2x	Major Depressive Disorder, Single Episode
296.3x	Major Depressive Disorder, Recurrent
295.70	Schizoaffective Disorder
310.1	Personality Change Due to (*Axis III Disorder*)
V62.82	Bereavement
_____	_____
_____	_____

Axis II:

301.83	Borderline Personality Disorder
301.9	Personality Disorder NOS
_____	_____
_____	_____

EATING DISORDERS

BEHAVIORAL DEFINITIONS

1. A sense of loss of control over eating, feeling that one cannot stop eating or control how much food is consumed.
2. Intense fear of gaining weight or becoming fat.
3. Marked body image disturbance: perceives self as overweight even when thin.
4. Intermittent starving, gorging, purging, use of laxatives, enemas, excessive exercise, or other dysfunctional behaviors aimed at weight control.
5. Chronic feelings of depression revolving around the belief that one is fat.
6. Frequent unsuccessful attempts to bring the abnormal eating behavior under control.
7. Uses food consumption as a means of relaxation or escape from stress.
8. Self-evaluation is unduly influenced by body shape and weight.
9. Becomes very anxious when thinking of body weight, food, or eating.

__. _____
   _____
   _____
__. _____
   _____
   _____
__. _____
   _____

LONG-TERM GOALS

1. Eat nutritionally and develop healthy, realistic attitudes about body image and weight.
2. Terminate overeating, purging, use of laxatives, enemas, and/or excessive exercise.
3. Develop the ability to control the impulse to overeat.
4. Learn and demonstrate constructive strategies to cope with dysphoric moods.
5. Replace negative, self-defeating addictive thinking about food and body image with more realistic, self-enhancing self-talk.
6. Implement a program of addiction recovery that reduces the impact of the eating disorder on sobriety.

—. _____

_____

—. _____

_____

—. _____

_____

SHORT-TERM OBJECTIVES	THERAPEUTIC INTERVENTIONS
1. Describe the history and current status of dysfunctional eating patterns. (1, 2)	1. Explore the client's history and current status of his/her eating disorder. *RP: _____ _____
2. List five occasions when the eating disorder has been triggered. (3, 4, 5)	2. Confront minimization and denial of the eating disorder behavior and its related distorted thinking. RP: _____ _____
3. Keep a daily feelings journal. (6)	
4. Identify distorted, negative thoughts that lead to eating disorder behavior. (7, 8)	3. Help the client to see how negative feelings increase
5. Keep a daily record of five negative, self-defeating thoughts that lead to feel-	

_____

*RP = responsible professional.

ings of failure and increase eating disorder behavior. (7, 8, 9)

6. Make a list of 10 positive, accurate self-statements to use in daily positive self-talk. (7, 10)

7. Implement self-enhancing, realistic thoughts to replace distorted, self-defeated thinking. (10, 11)

8. Draw an outline of own body, and ask for feedback about the accuracy of body image. (12)

9. Develop a written plan to decrease the frequency of impulsive eating that is related to dysphoric moods. (3, 5, 13, 14, 15)

10. Verbalize an understanding of how fear of abandonment is expressed in eating disorders and addictive behavior. (16, 17)

11. Identify situations that easily trigger feelings of fear about weight and body image. (16, 17, 18)

12. Verbalize five negative consequences of eating disorder behavior. (2, 19)

13. Verbalize alternative, constructive ways to cope with feelings of anger, sadness, or fear. (11, 15, 20, 21, 22)

14. Make a written plan to modify an impulsive abnormal eating behavior. (15, 20, 21, 22, 23)

the probability of dysfunctional eating and addictive behavior.

RP: _____

_____

4. Explore the specific circumstances that increase the probability of the client's eating disorder behaviors being triggered.

RP: _____

_____

5. Review several eating disorder behaviors (e.g., gorging, purging, use of laxatives, and excessive exercise) that occurred under stress, and help the client to discover what he/she could have done to cope more effectively than to use food dysfunctionally in each situation.

RP: _____

_____

6. Assign the client to write a daily journal of what emotions were experienced, why the feelings developed, and what actions resulted from those feelings.

RP: _____

_____

7. Help the client to differentiate between distorted, self-defeating thoughts and self-enhancing, realistic thinking.

RP: _____

_____

15. Five times this week, talk calmly to someone when feeling upset. (21, 22, 24)

16. Cooperate with a complete physical exam. (25, 26)

17. Submit to a dental exam. (27)

18. Cooperate with admission to inpatient treatment if a fragile medical condition necessitates such treatment. (25, 26, 28)

19. Attain and maintain balanced fluids and electrolytes, as well as resumption of reproductive functions. (25, 26, 29, 30, 31)

20. Meet with a physician to be evaluated for the need for pharmacological treatment. (32)

21. Take medications as prescribed, and report any side effects to the appropriate professionals. (33, 34)

22. Practice the healthy communication skills of listening to others, the use of "I" statements, and sharing feelings. (35, 36)

23. Verbalize five ways in which a higher power can assist in resolving fears of being fat. (37)

24. Acknowledge how perfectionism leads to fear of rejection. (38, 39)

25. Make a list of 10 positive body characteristics. (40)

8. Use cognitive techniques to help the client identify his/her negative, self-defeating thoughts and how they lead to eating disorders and other addictive behaviors.
   RP: _____
   _____

9. Assign the client to keep a daily record of distorted, self-defeating thoughts.
   RP: _____
   _____

10. Assist the client in building a list of 10 positive reinforcing statements to use daily for self-enhancement.
    RP: _____
    _____

11. Use cognitive techniques to help the client to correct self-defeating thinking and to replace self-derogatory thinking with positive, self-enhancing statements.
    RP: _____
    _____

12. Teach the client about his/her distorted, negative body image, and ask him/her to draw an outline of his/her body. Give feedback as to the accuracy or distortion of his/her drawing.
    RP: _____
    _____

13. Help the client to develop and practice coping skills to

26. Practice relaxation techniques two times a day for 10 to 20 minutes. (20, 41)

27. Exercise at least three times a week for at least 20 minutes. (20, 42, 43)

28. Write an aftercare program that lists resources that will be used when feeling frightened, abandoned, or depressed, rather than reverting to eating disorder or other addictive behavior. (23, 44, 45)

29. Attend a support group for people with eating disorders. (45)

___. _____

      _____

___. _____

      _____

___. _____

      _____

deal with dysphoric moods rather than engaging in disordered eating.

RP: _____

    _____

14. Teach the client how negative thinking, feeling, and acting lead to negative consequences. Then, teach how positive thinking leads to positive consequences.

RP: _____

    _____

15. Teach the client self-control strategies (e.g., "stop, look, listen, think, and plan") to control the impulse to engage in eating disorders and other addictive behavior.

RP: _____

    _____

16. Probe the relationship between the client's feelings of anger, sadness, or fear of abandonment and the eating disorder and other addictive behavior.

RP: _____

    _____

17. Assist the client in identifying triggers for the fear of abandonment and possible historical causes for these feelings being so predominant.

RP: _____

    _____

18. Assist the client in identifying situations that trigger

fear regarding weight and body image.

RP: _____

_____

19. Help the client to understand the self-defeating, alienating consequences of being obsessed with weight.

RP: _____

_____

20. Develop with the client a list of constructive reactions to feelings of anger or fear (e.g., writing about his/her feelings, talking to a counselor, delaying expression for 24 hours, tracing his/her feelings to his/her own background, substituting a physical exercise for an outlet, practicing a relaxation exercise, etc.) that reduce impulsive acting out of feelings.

RP: _____

_____

21. Use role playing and modeling to teach the client to verbalize anger in a controlled, respectful manner, delaying the response, if necessary, to gain more control.

RP: _____

_____

22. Help the client to make a list of the people to call or visit when he/she becomes upset. Then, role-play several situations in which the

client discusses a problem
calmly.
RP: _____

_____

23. Assign the client to develop
a written plan to control impulsive eating; process the
plan.
RP: _____

_____

24. Assign the client the task of
talking to someone calmly
when feeling sad, angry,
fearful, or depressed.
RP: _____

_____

25. Refer the client to a physician for a physical exam.
RP: _____

_____

26. Stay in close consultation
with the physician as to the
client's medical condition
and nutritional habits.
RP: _____

_____

27. Refer the client to a dentist
for a dental exam.
RP: _____

_____

28. Refer the client for hospitalization, as necessary, if
his/her weight loss becomes
severe and physical health
is jeopardized.
RP: _____

_____

29. Establish a minimum daily calorie intake for the client.
RP: _____

_____

30. Assist the client in meal planning.
RP: _____

_____

31. Refer the client back to the physician at regular intervals if fluids and electrolytes need monitoring due to poor nutritional habits.
RP: _____

_____

32. Refer the client to a physician to evaluate if psychopharmacological intervention is warranted.
RP: _____

_____

33. Monitor the client's response as the physician prescribes and adjusts medication to maximize effectiveness and reduce side effects.
RP: _____

_____

34. Staff to administer medications as ordered by physician and monitor for compliance, effectiveness, and side effects.
RP: _____

_____

35. Teach the client how to listen, use "I" statements, and share feelings.
   RP: _____

   _____

36. Assign the client to implement listening skills and "I"-message communication in daily life; monitor, review, reinforce, and redirect as indicated.
   RP: _____

   _____

37. Teach the client about the higher-power concept in Alcoholics Anonymous/Narcotics Anonymous (AA/NA), and give examples about how the patient can turn problems over to the higher power in recovery.
   RP: _____

   _____

38. Assist the client in understanding how the need to be perfect leads to feelings of inadequacy, helping him/her see positive and negative traits in himself/herself.
   RP: _____

   _____

39. Challenge the extremes of the client's thinking about how he/she needs to be perfect to be loved.
   RP: _____

   _____

40. Assign the client the task of listing 10 positive charac-

teristic of his/her body. Process the list.

RP: _____

_____

41. Teach the client relaxation techniques (e.g., progressive relaxation, deep breathing, and/or imagery).

RP: _____

_____

42. Help the client to develop an exercise program that will help in reducing stress levels.

RP: _____

_____

43. Recommend that the client read and implement programs from *Exercising Your Way to Better Mental Health* (Leith).

RP: _____

_____

44. Assist the client in developing a structured aftercare program that lists resources he/she can use when feeling sad, angry, anxious, abandoned, or depressed.

RP: _____

_____

45. Refer the client to a support group for people with eating disorders.

RP: _____

_____

—.   _____

     _____

RP: _____

     _____

—.   _____

     _____

RP: _____

     _____

—.   _____

     _____

RP: _____

     _____

DIAGNOSTIC SUGGESTIONS

Axis I:	307.1	Anorexia Nervosa
	307.51	Bulimia Nervosa
	307.50	Eating Disorder NOS
	300.7	Body Dysmorphic Disorder
	296.xx	Major Depressive Disorder
	300.4	Dysthymic Disorder
	309.81	Posttraumatic Stress Disorder
	313.82	Identity Problem
	_____	_____
	_____	
Axis II:	301.83	Borderline Personality Disorder
	301.50	Histrionic Personality Disorder
	301.81	Narcissistic Personality Disorder
	301.6	Dependent Personality Disorder
	301.4	Obsessive-Compulsive Personality Disorder
	_____	_____
	_____	_____

FAMILY CONFLICTS

BEHAVIORAL DESCRIPTIONS

1. Use of addictive behavior to cope with feelings of anger, alienation, or depression related to conflict within the family.
2. A pattern of family conflicts leading to dysfunctional relationships.
3. Repeated family physical fights, verbal arguments, or unresolved disputes.
4. Poor communication skills leading to an inability to solve family problems.
5. Physical or verbal abuse of family members.
6. Long-term unresolved conflicts between family members leading to distrust and alienation within the family.
7. Long periods of noncommunication between family members due to unresolved conflicts.
8. A family that is not supportive to the client's recovery.
9. Addiction in family members leading to a poor recovery environment for the client.

__. _____
   _____

__. _____
   _____
   _____

__. _____
   _____

LONG-TERM GOALS

1. Maintain a program of recovery that is free of addiction and family conflict.

2. Learn and demonstrate healthy communication and conflict resolution skills leading to harmony within the family.
3. Forgive family members' past misdeeds, and begin a life of harmony with each family member.
4. Resolve family conflicts, and elicit the aid of family members in working a stable program of recovery.
5. Terminate addictive behavior, and implement more healthy coping behaviors to deal with the conflicts within the family.
6. Begin to emancipate from the parents in a healthy way by making reasonable arrangements for independent living.
7. Learn and demonstrate healthy family interaction.
8. Forgive family members for the past, and begin a life with each family member working his or her own program of recovery.

—. _____
   _____
   _____

—. _____
   _____

—. _____

SHORT-TERM OBJECTIVES

THERAPEUTIC INTERVENTIONS

1. Verbalize the powerlessness and unmanageability that have resulted from using addictive behavior to cope with family conflicts. (1, 3)

2. Identify the nature and history of current family conflicts. (2)

3. Verbalize an understanding of how family conflicts lead to addiction and how addiction leads to family conflicts. (3)

4. Verbalize how current family conflicts relate to conflicts in the family of origin,

1. Help the client to see the powerlessness and unmanageability that have resulted from using addiction to cope with family conflicts.
    *RP: _____
    _____

2. Explore the client's history to identify the nature of and causes for the current family conflicts.
    RP: _____
    _____

3. Assist the client in understanding the vicious cycle

*RP = responsible professional.

which were experienced as a child. (4)

5. Acknowledge that attempts to seize power and control within the family lead to unhealthy interpersonal relationships. (4, 5, 6)

6. Family members give individual perspectives on current conflicts. (7)

7. Family members identify and implement changes that each one must make to reduce conflict. (8, 9, 10)

8. In a family session, verbalize how addiction fosters misunderstanding and conflict and how conflict fosters addiction. (7, 11)

9. Write a letter to each family member taking responsibility for past misdeeds, stating remorseful feelings, and asking for support from each member during recovery. (12, 13)

10. Family members read letters sharing how they feel and stating what behavior they would like from the client during his/her recovery. (14)

11. List and implement conflict resolution skills to be used during a family argument. (15, 16)

12. List five ways in which a higher power can assist in recovery from family conflicts and addiction. (17)

13. Practice the assertive communication formula "I

that results from reacting to family conflicts with addictive behaviors.
RP: _____

_____

4. Help the client to see the relationship between the family-of-origin childhood conflicts and current family conflicts. Assign him/her to write a detailed account of how the two are related.
RP: _____

_____

5. Teach the client about respect for independence and autonomy in a healthy family, and help the client to see how power struggles led to unresolved family conflict.
RP: _____

_____

6. Assist the client in identifying how he/she has attempted to seize power and control within the family.
RP: _____

_____

7. In a family session, make a list of current family conflicts from each member's perspective.
RP: _____

_____

8. Assist each family member in identifying what he/she could do to reduce family

feel . . . When you. . . . I would prefer it if. . . ." (18, 19)

14. List instances when feelings, wishes, and wants were shared calmly in a respectful manner. (18, 19)

15. Verbalize the negative effects of passive or aggressive behaviors, and list the positive effects of using assertive skills. (18, 19, 20)

16. Increase the level of independent functioning (i.e., finding and keeping a job, socializing with positive friends, finding own housing, etc.). (21, 22, 23)

17. Agree to continue to work on family conflict and addiction issues by regularly attending recovery groups and family therapy in aftercare. (24)

18. Family members verbalize a connection between family conflicts and addictive behavior. (25)

19. Family members verbalize what each can do to assist the client in recovery. (26, 27)

__. _____
   _____

__. _____
   _____
   _____

__. _____
   _____

conflict and heal wounds of the past.
RP: _____
    _____

9. Develop a written contract that outlines what each family member will do to resolve family conflict.
RP: _____
    _____

10. Review the family members' implementation of changes to reduce conflict. Reinforce success, confront projection, and redirect for failures.
RP: _____
    _____

11. Help family members to understand how family conflict increases the probability of addictive behavior and how addictive behavior increases the probability of family conflict.
RP: _____
    _____

12. Confront the client when he/she blames others and does not accept responsibility for his/her own role in the family conflict.
RP: _____
    _____

13. Help the client to write a letter to each family member, taking responsibility for problems in the past, sharing his/her feelings, and asking for what he/she would like from each family

member to support his/her
recovery.

RP: _____

_____

14. Help each family member
    to write a letter to the
    client, stating how they feel
    and asking for what they
    would like from him/her
    during the recovery. Ask
    each member to read the
    letter to the client in a
    family session.

    RP: _____

    _____

15. Using modeling, role play-
    ing, and behavior rehearsal,
    teach the client what to do
    when he/she is in a family
    conflict (e.g., call someone;
    go to a meeting; use "I"
    messages; accept the re-
    sponsibility for his/her own
    behavior; don't blame; turn
    it over to a higher power;
    stop, look, listen, think, and
    plan before acting, etc.).

    RP: _____

    _____

16. Review the client's imple-
    mentation of conflict resolu-
    tion skills. Reinforce
    success, confront the projec-
    tion of blame, and redirect
    him/her for failure.

    RP: _____

    _____

17. Teach the client about the
    12-step recovery program's
    concept of a higher power
    and how this power can

be used to assist in resolving family conflicts and addiction.

RP: _____

_____

18. Teach the client the assertive communication formula "I feel. . . . When you. . . . I would prefer it if. . . . ," then practice the formula five times in role-playing current problem situations.

RP: _____

_____

19. Using modeling, role playing, and behavior rehearsal, teach the client how to share feelings, wishes, and wants calmly in several difficult situations. Assign implementation with family members.

RP: _____

_____

20. Teach the client the difference between passive, aggressive, and assertive behavior; assign him/her to list the negative effects of passivity and aggression and the positive effects of assertiveness.

RP: _____

_____

21. Probe the client's fears surrounding emancipation.

RP: _____

_____

22. Confront emotional dependence and avoidance of economic responsibility that promote a continuing pattern of living dependently off others.

RP: _____

_____

23. Develop a structured written plan for the client's emancipation that includes steady employment, paying his/her own expenses, and independent housing.

RP: _____

_____

24. Help the client develop an aftercare program that includes regular attendance at recovery groups and the family therapy that is necessary to resolve family conflicts and maintain abstinence from addictive behavior.

RP: _____

_____

25. Discuss with family members the connection between borderline traits and addictive behavior.

RP: _____

_____

26. In a family session, review what each member can do to assist the client in recovery.

RP: _____

_____

27. Provide the family members with information about family conflicts and the steps that the client must take to recover successfully.

RP: _____

_____

___. _____

_____

RP: _____

_____

___. _____

_____

RP: _____

_____

___. _____

_____

RP: _____

_____

DIAGNOSTIC SUGGESTIONS

Axis I:	313.81	Oppositional Defiant Disorder
	312.8	Conduct Disorder
	V61.20	Parent-Child Relational Problem
	V61.1	Partner Relational Problem
	V61.8	Sibling Relational Problem
	V62.81	Relational Problem NOS
	V71.01	Adult Antisocial Behavior
	V71.02	Child or Adolescent Antisocial Behavior
	_____	_____
	_____	_____
Axis II:	301.83	Borderline Personality Disorder
	301.70	Antisocial Personality Disorder
	301.6	Dependent Personality Disorder
	_____	_____
	_____	_____

GAMBLING

BEHAVIORAL DEFINITIONS

1. Repeated unsuccessful attempts to stop or cut down on gambling, despite the verbalized desire to do so and the many negative consequences that continued gambling brings.
2. Denial that gambling is a problem despite feedback from significant others that it is negatively affecting them and others.
3. Maintains a distorted belief that more gambling will certainly result in a windfall of profit that will more than equal previous financial losses.
4. Persistent physical, legal, financial, vocational, social, or relationship problems that are directly caused by gambling.
5. Suspension of important social, recreational, or occupational activities because they interfere with gambling.
6. Restlessness and irritability when attempting to stop gambling.
7. Frequent loss of time when gambling.
8. Physical withdrawal symptoms (i.e., shaking, nausea, headaches, sweating, anxiety, insomnia, and/or depression) when going without gambling for any length of time.
9. Arrests for gambling-related offenses (e.g., bad checks, forgery, embezzlement, theft, etc.).
10. Large investment in money, time, and activities to gamble.
11. Gambling greater amounts and for longer periods than intended.
12. Concurrent substance abuse.
13. Underlying unresolved emotional issues that contribute to use of gambling as an escape.

—. _____

_____

—. _____
   _____
   _____

—. _____
   _____

LONG-TERM GOALS

1. Accept the powerlessness and unmanageability over gambling, and participate in a recovery-based program.
2. Accept the problem with gambling, and begin to actively participate in a recovery program.
3. Establish a sustained recovery, free from gambling and other addictive behaviors.
4. Acquire the necessary skills to maintain long-term abstinence from gambling.
5. Improve quality of life by maintaining an ongoing abstinence from all gambling.
6. Develop financial planning that will allow repayment of losses and established financial stability.
7. Withdraw from gambling emotionally, and learn a new program of recovery free from excessive stress and addictive behavior.
8. Successfully resolve emotional issues that underlie the pathological gambling.

—. _____
   _____

—. _____
   _____

—. _____
   _____

SHORT-TERM OBJECTIVES

1. Provide honest and complete information regarding gambling history. (1)

2. Verbalize an increased knowledge of addiction and the process of recovery. (2, 3, 4, 5)

3. Attend group therapy sessions to share thoughts and feelings associated with reasons for, consequences of, feelings about, and alternatives to gambling. (6, 7)

4. List 10 negative consequences resulting from or exacerbated by gambling. (7, 8)

5. Verbally admit to powerlessness over gambling. (9)

6. Verbalize a recognition that gambling was used as the primary coping mechanism to escape from stress or emotional pain and resulted in negative consequences. (10, 11, 12)

7. List three negative emotions that were caused by or exacerbated by gambling. (12)

8. Develop a list of the social, emotional, and family factors that contributed to gambling. (1, 13)

9. List 10 reasons to work on a plan for recovery from gambling. (14)

THERAPEUTIC INTERVENTIONS

1. Complete a thorough family and personal biopsychosocial history that has a focus on the client's gambling.
   *RP: _____
   _____

2. Assign the client to attend a gambling didactic series to increase his/her knowledge of the patterns and effects of gambling.
   RP: _____
   _____

3. Ask the client to identify several key points attained from attending each didactic; process these points.
   RP: _____
   _____

4. Ask the client to read a pamphlet on cross-tolerance (i.e., one drug or addictive behavior causes tolerance to develop for another) and process with the therapist five key points gained from the reading.
   RP: _____
   _____

5. Require the client to read the Gamblers Anonymous (GA) *Combo Book* and gather five key points

---

*RP = responsible professional.

10. List 10 lies used to hide gambling behavior. (15)

11. Verbalize five ways in which a higher power can assist in recovery. (16)

12. Practice turning problems over to a higher power each day. Record each event and share these with the primary therapist. (17)

13. Practice healthy communication skills to reduce stress and increase positive social interaction. (18)

14. Practice problem-solving skills. (19)

15. List the reasons for gambling and the ways in which needs can be met in an adaptive manner. (10, 20)

16. Identify underlying emotional issues that contributed to gambling as an escape behavior. (10, 20, 21)

17. Follow through on obtaining treatment for underlying emotional issues. (22, 23, 24)

18. Develop a written leisure skills program to decrease stress and improve health. (25)

19. Verbalize that there are options to gambling in dealing with stress and in finding pleasure or excitement in life. (25, 26, 27)

20. Practice stress management skills to reduce overall stress levels and attain a

from it to process with the therapist.
RP: _____
_____

6. Assign the client to attend group therapy that is focused on gambling and other addictions.
RP: _____
_____

7. Direct group therapy that facilitates the sharing of causes for, consequences of, feelings about, and alternatives to gambling.
RP: _____
_____

8. Ask the client to make a list of the ways in which gambling has negatively impacted his/her life and to process the list with the therapist or group.
RP: _____
_____

9. Assign the client to complete a GA first-step paper admitting to powerlessness over gambling behavior and any other addictions, and present it in group therapy or to the therapist for feedback.
RP: _____
_____

10. Assess the client's history for depression, abuse, neglect, or other traumas that

feeling of relaxation and comfort. (26, 27)

21. Exercise at a training heart rate for at least 20 minutes at least three times per week. (27)

22. Complete a fourth-step inventory and share with a clergy person or someone else in the GA program. (28)

23. List the triggers (persons, places, and things) that may precipitate relapse. (29)

24. Make a written plan to cope with each high-risk or trigger situation. (29, 30, 31)

25. Write a personal recovery plan that includes regular attendance at recovery group meetings, aftercare, getting a sponsor, and helping others in recovery. (32, 33)

26. Take a personal inventory at the end of each day, listing the problems in recovery, the plans to address the problems, and five things to be grateful for that day. (34)

27. Enter the continuum of care treatment setting that is necessary to maintain abstinence and maximize chances for recovery. (35)

28. Family members verbalize an understanding of their role in the gambling problem and the process of recovery. (36, 37, 38)

contribute to underlying emotional pain.

RP: _____

_____

11. Explore how gambling was used to escape from stress, emotional pain, and/or boredom. Confront the negative consequences of this pattern of escapism.

RP: _____

_____

12. Probe the sense of shame, guilt, and low self-worth that has resulted from gambling and its consequences.

RP: _____

_____

13. Using the biopsychosocial history, assist the client in understanding the familial, emotional, and social factors that contributed to the development of problem gambling.

RP: _____

_____

14. Assign the client to write a list of 10 reasons to be abstinent from gambling.

RP: _____

_____

15. Help the client to see the dishonesty that goes along with gambling. Have him/her list 10 lies that he/she told to hide gambling. Then, teach him/her

29. Family members decrease the frequency of enabling the gambler after verbally identifying their enabling behaviors. (37, 39, 40)

30. Acknowledge the abuse of mind-altering drugs and/or alcohol. (41)

31. Accept a referral for treatment for chemical dependence. (42)

__. _____
   _____
__. _____
   _____
__. _____
   _____

why honesty is essential to recovery.
RP: _____
   _____

16. Teach the client about the GA concept of a higher power and how this can assist in recovery.
RP: _____
   _____

17. Using an GA step-three exercise, teach the client about the GA concept of *turning it over*, then assign turning over problems to the higher power each day. Have the client record the event and discuss the results.
RP: _____
   _____

18. Teach the client healthy communication skills (i.e., using "I" messages, reflecting, active listening, empathy, being reinforcing, sharing, etc.).
RP: _____
   _____

19. Using modeling, role playing, and behavior rehearsal, teach the client how to solve problems in an organized fashion (i.e., write the problem, think accurately, list the options of action, evaluate alternatives, act, monitor results).
RP: _____
   _____

20. Assist the client in clarifying why he/she was gambling, and help him/her to identify healthier ways to get satisfaction of these needs.

    RP: _____

    _____

21. Assess the depth of the client's underlying depression and whether the depression predates the gambling problem.

    RP: _____

    _____

22. Refer the client to a physician for an evaluation of the need for antidepressant medication.

    RP: _____

    _____

23. Monitor the client for medication prescription compliance, effectiveness, and side effects.

    RP: _____

    _____

24. Recommend to the client that he/she obtain counseling to resolve underlying emotional issues that contribute to gambling behavior. Make referrals, if necessary.

    RP: _____

    _____

25. Assign the client to list the pleasurable activities that he/she plans to use in recov-

ery to take the place of
gambling.
RP: _____

_____

26. Using progressive relax-
    ation, guided imagery, or
    biofeedback, teach the
    client how to relax, then as-
    sign him/her to relax twice
    a day for 10 to 20 minutes.
    RP: _____

    _____

27. Considering the client's cur-
    rent physical fitness levels
    (clear strenuous exercise
    with the client's physician),
    direct him/her to exercise
    three times a week, then in-
    crease the exercise by 10
    percent a week, until he/she
    is exercising at a training
    heart rate for at least 20
    minutes at least three times
    a week.
    RP: _____

    _____

28. Assign the client to complete
    a fourth-step inventory, then
    make arrangements for
    him/her to share this with a
    clergy person or someone
    else in recovery.
    RP: _____

    _____

29. Using a GA relapse preven-
    tion exercise, help the client
    to uncover his/her triggers
    for relapse.
    RP: _____

    _____

30. Teach the client about high-risk situations (i.e. negative emotions, social pressure, interpersonal conflict, positive emotions, and test personal control). Assist the client in making a written plan to cope with each high-risk situation.
RP: _____

_____

31. Using modeling, role playing, and behavior rehearsal, teach the client how to say no to gambling and other addictive behaviors. Then, practice saying no in high-risk situations.
RP: _____

_____

32. Help the client to develop a personal recovery plan that includes regular attendance at recovery group meetings, aftercare, getting a sponsor, and helping others in recovery.
RP: _____

_____

33. Help the client to see the necessity for working a personalized program of recovery every day to maintain abstinence from gambling.
RP: _____

_____

34. Encourage the client to take a personal inventory each night, listing the problems that he/she had that day, making a plan to deal with

any problems, and then listing five things for which
he/she was grateful that day.
RP: _____

_____

35. Discuss continuum of care
options with the client (i.e.,
regular recovery meetings,
therapy, halfway house,
group home, therapeutic
community, etc.).
RP: _____

_____

36. Direct the client's family to
attend GA meetings.
RP: _____

_____

37. Educate the client's family
in the dynamics of enabling
and tough love.
RP: _____

_____

38. Ask the client's family to attend the family education
component of the treatment
program.
RP: _____

_____

39. Monitor the client's family
for enabling behaviors, and
redirect them in the family
session as appropriate.
RP: _____

_____

40. Assist the client's family
members in implementing
and sticking with tough-
love techniques.
RP: _____

_____

41. Explore and assess the
     client's use and abuse of
     mind-altering drugs and
     alcohol.

     RP: _____

     _____

42. Refer the client for treat-
     ment of a concommitant
     chemical dependence
     problem.

     RP: _____

     _____

—.   _____

     _____

     RP: _____

     _____

—.   _____

     _____

     RP: _____

     _____

—.   _____

     _____

     RP: _____

     _____

DIAGNOSTIC SUGGESTIONS

Axis I:	312.31	Pathological Gambling
	312.30	Impulse-Control Disorder NOS
	296.xx	Bipolar I Disorder
	296.3x	Major Depressive Disorder, Recurrent
	_____	_____
	_____	_____
Axis II:	301.7	Antisocial Personality Disorder
	_____	_____
	_____	_____

GRIEF/LOSS UNRESOLVED

BEHAVIORAL DEFINITIONS

1. Unresolved bereavement resulting in addictive behavior to cope with the grief.
2. Constant thoughts of the lost loved one resulting in an inability to move forward in life with new plans or other relationships.
3. Depression centered around a deceased loved one.
4. Excessive and unreasonable feelings of responsibility for the loss of a significant other, including feeling guilty about not doing enough to prevent the person's death.
5. Feelings of guilt about being a survivor when loved ones have died.
6. Avoidance of talking about the death of a loved one on anything more than a superficial level.
7. Vegetative symptoms of depression (lack of appetite, weight loss, sleep disturbance, anhedonia, lack of energy).
8. Feels that life is barely worth, or not worth, living since the loss of the loved one.
9. Does not fulfill responsibilities to relationships, usual tasks, or personal interests due to being preoccupied with the pain of loss.

—. _____
_____
—. _____
_____
—. _____
_____

LONG-TERM GOALS

1. Resolve feelings of anger, sadness, guilt, and/or abandonment surrounding the loss of the loved one and make plans for the future.
2. Accept the loss of the loved one and increase social contact with others and investments in all of life's responsibilities.
3. Develop a plan for life that includes renewing old relationships and making new ones.
4. Maintain a program of recovery that is free from addiction and unresolved grief.
5. Let go of the deceased person and give him/her over to a higher power.

—. _____

_____

—. _____

_____

—. _____

_____

SHORT-TERM OBJECTIVES

1. Tell the story of the lost relationship. (1)
2. Discuss the positive and negative aspects of the lost relationship. (1, 2)
3. Verbalize the feelings of anger, guilt, sadness, and/or abandonment that are felt because of the loss. (3, 4, 5)
4. Verbalize how the loss of the loved one led to addictive behavior to avoid painful feelings. (6)
5. List several negative consequences that resulted from

THERAPEUTIC INTERVENTIONS

1. Encourage the client to share the entire story of the relationship with the lost person, possibly using pictures or mementos that are connected to the deceased loved one.
   *RP: _____

   _____

2. Help the client to see both the positive and negative aspects of the lost relationship, keeping him/her from

———————————

*RP = responsible professional.

using addiction to cope with grief and loss. (6, 7)

6. Verbalize a resolution of guilt about the loss. (5, 8)

7. Terminate the blame of others for the loss. (9)

8. Verbalize an understanding of how the dependence on the lost person and dependence on addictive behavior are similar. (10)

9. Make a written plan to live a more independent life. (11)

10. Make a written plan to increase social interaction with old friends and make new ones. (12, 13)

11. List five ways in which a higher power can assist in recovery from grief and addiction. (14, 15)

12. Verbalize an understanding of how someone's death can be a part of a higher power's plan. (14, 15)

13. Practice prayer and meditation each day, seeking only God's will as to how to live without the loved one and the power to carry that out. (14, 16)

14. Write a letter of good-bye to the lost loved one, sharing feelings and thoughts. (3, 4, 5, 9, 17)

15. Make contact with a 12-step recovery program temporary sponsor and share plans for recovery. (13, 18)

overidealizing the relationship.

RP: _____

_____

3. Assist the client in expressing and clarifying the painful emotions that are associated with the loss and the life changes that have resulted from this loss.

RP: _____

_____

4. Help the client to identify the feelings of hurt, loss, abandonment, and anger that are felt because of the loss.

RP: _____

_____

5. Explore with the client feelings of guilt and blame of himself/herself or others surrounding the loss.

RP: _____

_____

6. Explore with the client the role that addictive behavior has had in avoidance of facing and working through the loss.

RP: _____

_____

7. Show the client how addictive behavior has led to more pain and unresolved feelings.

RP: _____

_____

16. Encourage at least one person in recovery each day. (19)

17. Develop a written aftercare plan to resolve addiction and grief. (13, 20)

18. Family members verbalize a connection between unresolved grief/loss and addictive behavior. (21)

19. Family members verbalize what each can do to assist the client in recovery. (22, 23)

—. _____
   _____

—. _____
   _____

—. _____
   _____

8. Using logic and reasoning, help the client to see that he/she is not responsible for the loss.
   RP: _____
   _____

9. Teach the client about the destructive consequences of holding on to anger and blame toward others for the loss.
   RP: _____
   _____

10. Help the client to see the common elements in the dependency on the deceased individual and on addictive behavior.
    RP: _____
    _____

11. Help the client to make a written plan to help him/her to live a more active and independent life (i.e., make plans for social life, hobbies, financial security, job, recovery, sponsor, a grief group, a singles' group, etc.)
    RP: _____
    _____

12. Assign the client to write a plan to improve social contact with old friends and make new ones.
    RP: _____
    _____

13. Teach the client about the importance of regularly attending recovery groups,

getting a sponsor, and helping others in recovery.

RP: _____

_____

14. Teach the client about the
    12-step recovery program's
    concept of a higher power,
    and help him/her to see how
    this can assist in recovery
    from grief and addiction.

    RP: _____

    _____

15. Assign the client to read
    page 449 in the *Big Book*
    (Alcoholics Anonymous),
    and discuss how the loss of
    a loved one could be a part
    of the higher power's plan.

    RP: _____

    _____

16. Using a 12-step recovery
    program's step-eleven exer-
    cise, teach the client how to
    pray and meditate. Then,
    assign him/her to contact
    his/her higher power each
    day about his/her grief.

    RP: _____

    _____

17. Assign the client to write a
    letter to the lost individual,
    sharing the unresolved feel-
    ings. Process the letter in
    group or individual session.

    RP: _____

    _____

18. Assign the client to make
    contact with a 12-step re-
    covery program temporary

sponsor and discuss recovery plans.

RP: _____

_____

19. To improve self-worth and self-esteem, assign the client to encourage one person in recovery each day.

RP: _____

_____

20. Help the client to develop a written aftercare plan that specifically outlines a recovery plan (e.g., 12-step recovery program meetings to attend, aftercare sessions, continued therapy, sponsor, turn it over daily, pray and meditate, etc.).

RP: _____

_____

21. Discuss with family members the connection between borderline traits and addictive behavior.

RP: _____

_____

22. In a family session, review what each member can do to assist the client in recovery.

RP: _____

_____

23. Provide the family members with information about borderline syndrome and the steps that the client must take to recover successfully.

RP: _____

_____

—. _____

_____

RP: _____

_____

—. _____

_____

RP: _____

_____

—. _____

_____

RP: _____

_____

DIAGNOSTIC SUGGESTIONS

Axis I:	296.2x	Major Depressive Disorder, Single Episode
	296.3x	Major Depressive Disorder, Recurrent
	311	Depressive Disorder NOS
	308.3	Acute Stress Disorder
	V62.82	Bereavement
	309.0	Adjustment Disorder With Depressed Mood
	309.3	Adjustment Disorder With Disturbance of Conduct
	309.24	Adjustment Disorder With Anxiety
	309.28	Adjustment Disorder With Mixed Anxiety and Depressed Mood
	309.4	Adjustment Disorder With Mixed Disturbance of Emotions and Conduct
	_____	_____
	_____	_____

IMPULSIVITY

BEHAVIORAL DEFINITIONS

1. A tendency to act too quickly without careful deliberation, resulting in numerous negative consequences.
2. Difficulty with being patient, particularly waiting for someone or waiting in line.
3. A pattern of impulsive addictive behavior.
4. Loss of control over aggressive impulses resulting in assault, self-destructive behavior, or damage to property.
5. Desires to be satisfied almost immediately—decreased ability to delay pleasure or gratification.
6. A history of acting out in at least two areas that are potentially self-damaging (e.g., spending money, sexual activity, reckless driving, addictive behavior).
7. Overreactivity to mildly aversive or pleasure-oriented stimulation.
8. A sense of tension or affective arousal before engaging in the impulsive behavior (e.g., kleptomania or pyromania).
9. A sense of pleasure, gratification, or release at the time of committing the ego-dystonic, impulsive act.

__. _____
   _____
__. _____
   _____
__. _____
   _____

LONG-TERM GOALS

1. Maintain a program of recovery that is free from impulsive and addictive behavior.
2. Reduce the frequency of impulsive behavior, and increase the frequency of behavior that is carefully thought out.
3. Reduce thoughts that trigger impulsive behavior, and increase self-talk that controls behavior.
4. Learn to stop, look, listen, think, and plan before acting.
5. Learn to reinforce self rather than depend upon others for reward.

—. _____

   _____

—. _____

   _____

—. _____

   _____

SHORT-TERM OBJECTIVES

1. Verbalize an understanding of the powerlessness and unmanageability that result from impulsivity and addiction. (1)
2. Identify specific instances of impulsivity. (2)
3. Discuss how impulsivity and addiction meet the 12-step recovery program's criteria for *insanity*. (3)
4. Identify the negative consequences that are caused by impulsivity. (4, 5, 6)
5. Verbally identify several times when impulsive action led to addictive behav-

THERAPEUTIC INTERVENTIONS

1. Using a 12-step recovery program's step-one exercise, help the client to understand how impulsivity and addictive behavior lead to powerlessness and unmanageability.

   *RP: _____

   _____

2. Review the client's behavior pattern to assist him/her in clearly identifying, without minimization, denial, or projection of blame, his/her pattern of impulsivity.

   RP: _____

   _____

_____

*RP = responsible professional.

ior and subsequent negative consequences. (4, 7)

6. Increase the frequency of reviewing behavioral decisions with a trusted friend or family member for feedback regarding consequences before the decision is enacted. (8, 9)

7. Verbalize the biopsychosocial elements that cause or exacerbate impulsivity and addictive behavior. (10)

8. Comply with a physician's evaluation regarding the necessity for psychopharmacological intervention. (11)

9. Take all medications as prescribed and report as to effectiveness and side effects. (11, 12, 13)

10. Identify the thoughts that trigger impulsive behavior, then replace each thought with a thought that is accurate, positive, self-enhancing, and adaptive. (14, 15)

11. Develop a list of accurate, positive, self-enhancing statements to read each day, particularly when feeling upset. (15)

12. List the inappropriate behaviors that are displayed when feeling anxious and uncomfortable, and replace each behavior with an action that is positive and adaptive. (2, 16)

3. Using a 12-step recovery program's step-two exercise, help the client to see that doing the same things over and over again and expecting different results meets the 12-step program definition of *insanity*.
   RP: _____
   _____

4. Assist the client in making connections between his/her impulsivity and the negative consequences for himself/herself and others resulting from it.
   RP: _____
   _____

5. Assign the client to write a list of the negative consequences that occurred because of impulsivity.
   RP: _____
   _____

6. Help the client to see how dangerous it is to act impulsively (i.e., you don't have time to think, you can't plan effectively, etc.)
   RP: _____
   _____

7. Explore times when the client acted too quickly on impulses, resulting in addictive behavior.
   RP: _____
   _____

8. Conduct a session with the spouse, significant other, sponsor, or family member

13. List new ways to reinforce self without depending upon others for reward. (17)

14. Practice a relaxation exercise twice a day for 10 to 20 minutes; then, practice relaxing when feeling upset or uncomfortable. (18)

15. Practice the assertive formula, "I feel . . . When you. . . . I would prefer it if. . . ." (19)

16. Identify situations where assertiveness has been implemented, and identify the resulting consequences. (20)

17. Practice stopping, looking, listening, thinking, and planing before acting. (21)

18. List instances where "stop, look, listen, think, and plan" has been implemented, citing the positive consequences. (21, 22)

19. Verbalize an understanding of a 12-step recovery program's step-three regarding the role of a higher power and how this step can be used in recovery from impulsivity and addictive behavior. (23, 24)

20. Write an autobiography detailing the exact nature of wrong behavior by others and self. (25)

21. Relate how each wrong behavior identified in the step-four exercise can be related to impulsivity and addiction. (26)

and the client to develop a contract for the client to receive feedback prior to his/her engaging in impulsive acts.

RP: _____

_____

9. Review the client's implementation of reviewing with significant others decisions to act before engaging in impulsive actions; reinforce success and redirect for failure.

RP: _____

_____

10. Probe the client's biopsychosocial history and help the client to see the contributing factors to his/her impulsivity and addictive behavior (e.g., family models of impulsivity or addictive behavior, anxiety that energizes impulsivity, failure to learn delay of gratification in childhood, etc.).

RP: _____

_____

11. Physician will examine the client, order medications as indicated, titrate medications, and monitor for side effects and effectiveness.

RP: _____

_____

12. Staff will administer the medications as ordered by the physician.

RP: _____

_____

22. Develop and write a continuing care program that includes the recovery group meetings and any further therapy that is necessary for recovery. (27)
23. Share with family members the journey through impulsivity, addiction, and recovery. (28)
24. Family members verbalize a connection between impulsivity and addictive behavior. (29)
25. Family member verbalize what each can do to assist the client in recovery. (30, 31)

__. _____
_____

__. _____
_____

__. _____
_____

13. Monitor for the client's psychotropic medication's side effects and effectiveness.
RP: _____
_____

14. Help the client to uncover dysfunctional thoughts that lead to impulsivity; then, replace each thought with a thought that is accurate, positive, self-enhancing, and adaptive.
RP: _____
_____

15. Help the client to develop a list of positive, accurate, self-enhancing thoughts to read to himself/herself each day, particularly when feeling upset, anxious, or uncomfortable.
RP: _____
_____

16. Probe the client's anxious, impulsive behaviors, and then use modeling, role playing, and behavior rehearsal to teach the client new behaviors that are positive and adaptive (i.e., talking to someone about the problem, taking a time-out, calling the sponsor, going to a meeting, exercising, relaxing, etc.).
RP: _____
_____

17. Help the client to see the importance of rewarding himself/herself, not depending on others for reward

(i.e., hobbies, relaxation, games, sports, social activities, meetings, etc.).

RP: _____

_____

18. Teach the client relaxation techniques, such as progressive relaxation, self-hypnosis or biofeedback; assign him/her to relax whenever he/she feels uncomfortable.

RP: _____

_____

19. Using modeling, role playing, and behavior rehearsal, teach the client the assertive formula, "I feel . . . When you. . . . I would prefer it if. . . ." to be used in difficult situations that the client is facing.

RP: _____

_____

20. Review the client's implementation of assertiveness, his/her feelings about it, as well as the consequences of it; reinforce success and redirect for failure.

RP: _____

_____

21. Using modeling, role playing, and behavior rehearsal, teach the client to use "stop, look, listen, think, and plan before acting" in several current situations.

RP: _____

_____

22. Review the use of "stop, look, listen, think, and plan" in day-to-day living and identify the positive consequences.

    RP: _____

    _____

23. Teach the client about the 12-step recovery program's concept of a higher power, and discuss how he/she can use a higher power effectively in recovery.

    RP: _____

    _____

24. Using a 12-step recovery program's step-three exercise, teach the client how to turn his/her will and life over to the care of the higher power, and discuss how this step can be beneficial in recovery.

    RP: _____

    _____

25. Using a 12-step recovery program's step-four exercise, assign the client to write an autobiography of the exact nature of his/her wrongs and relate these wrongs.

    RP: _____

    _____

26. Assist the client in acknowledging the relationship between the wrongful behavior identified in a step-four exercise and

his/her impulsivity and
addiction.
RP: _____

_____

27. Help the client to develop
an aftercare plan that includes regular recovery
groups, getting a sponsor,
and any further therapy
that is necessary to recover
from impulsivity and
addiction.
RP: _____

_____

28. Encourage the client to
share with family members
the journey through im-
pulsivity, addiction, and
recovery.
RP: _____

_____

29. Discuss with family members the connection between
impulsive behavior and addictive behavior.
RP: _____

_____

30. In a family session, review
what each member can do to
assist the client in recovery.
RP: _____

_____

31. Provide the family members
with information about impulsive behavior and the
steps that the client must
take to recover successfully.
RP: _____

_____

—. _____

_____

RP: _____

_____

—. _____

_____

RP: _____

_____

—. _____

_____

RP: _____

_____

DIAGNOSTIC SUGGESTIONS

Axis I: 312.80   Conduct Disorder
313.81   Oppositional Defiant Disorder
309.3   Adjustment Disorder With Disturbance of
Conduct
312.34   Intermittent Explosive Disorder
314.01   Attention-Deficit/Hyperactivity Disorder,
Predominantly Hyperactive-Impulsive
312.9   Disruptive Behavior Disorder NOS
312.30   Impulse-Control Disorder NOS
V71.01   Adult Antisocial Behavior
V71.02   Child or Adolescent Antisocial Behavior

_____   _____

_____   _____

Axis II: 301.70   Antisocial Personality Disorder
301.83   Borderline Personality Disorder
301.81   Narcissistic Personality Disorder

_____   _____

_____   _____

LEGAL PROBLEMS

BEHAVIORAL DEFINITIONS

1. Legal charges pending adjudication.
2. History of repeated violations of the law, many of which occurred while under the influence of drugs or alcohol.
3. Unresolved legal problems complicating recovery from addictive behavior.
4. Fears of the legal system adjudicating current problems.
5. History of repeated violations of the law when buying, selling, or using illegal substances.
6. Court-ordered treatment for chemical dependence.
7. Pending divorce with resulting anger, resentment, and fear of abandonment.
8. Chemical dependency that has resulted in several arrests.
9. Fear of loss of freedom due to current legal charges.

__. _____
   _____

__. _____
   _____
   _____

__. _____
   _____

LONG-TERM GOALS

1. Maintain a program of recovery that is free from addictive behavior and legal conflicts.
2. Accept the responsibility for legal problems without blaming others.

3. Consult with legal authorities (i.e., attorney, probation officer, police, court official, etc.) to make plans for adjudicating legal conflicts.

4. Understand the need to maintain abstinence from the addictive behavior to remain free of negative consequences, which include legal problems.

—. _____

_____

—. _____

_____

—. _____

_____

SHORT-TERM OBJECTIVES

1. Verbalize the powerlessness and unmanageability that result from legal conflicts and addiction. (1, 2, 3)

2. Identify the nature and history of legal problems. (2)

3. Verbalize an acceptance of the responsibility for legal problems without blaming others. (3, 4)

4. Acknowledge the connection between legal problems and addictive behavior. (5, 6)

5. Write a plan that outlines the changes needed in behavior, attitude, and associates to protect self from harmful legal consequences. (7)

6. Identify the negative, distorted thoughts that were

THERAPEUTIC INTERVENTIONS

1. Help the client to understand the relationship between addictive behavior and legal conflicts and how these problems result in powerlessness and unmanageability.

   *RP: _____

   _____

2. Gather a history of the client's illegal behavior and his/her experience with the legal system.

   RP: _____

   _____

3. Help the client to identify and accept responsibility for the many decisions that he/she made that resulted

_____

*RP = responsible professional.

associated with illegal activity and addictive behavior. (8)

7. Replace distorted thoughts with realistic, positive cognitions. (9)

8. Meet with an attorney to make plans for resolving legal conflicts. (10)

9. Contact the probation or parole officer and agree in writing to meet the conditions of probation or parole. (11)

10. Verbalize ways to meet social, emotional, and financial needs in recovery without illegal activity or addiction. (12)

11. Identify the antisocial behaviors and attitudes that contributed to legal conflicts and learn prosocial behaviors. (13)

12. Verbalize the importance of obeying the laws of society to maintain abstinence and work a program of recovery. (13, 14)

13. Identify the criminal thinking that led to legal conflicts and addiction. (13, 14, 15)

14. Verbalize the importance of helping others to maintain recovery. (16)

15. Verbalize the importance of a higher power in recovery, and list five ways in which a higher power can assist in recovery. (17)

in legal problems without blaming others.
RP: _____

_____

4. Confront the client for avoidance of his/her responsibility for the legal problems.
RP: _____

_____

5. Teach the client the relationship between his/her legal problems and his/her addictive behavior; solicit the client's acknowledgment of this relationship.
RP: _____

_____

6. Assign the client to write how each legal conflict has been related to addictive behavior.
RP: _____

_____

7. Help the client to make a plan to honestly protect himself/herself from possible adverse consequences of legal problems by living within the law and associating with law-abiding people.
RP: _____

_____

8. Probe the client's distorted thoughts and feelings that surround addictive behavior and legal problems.
RP: _____

_____

16. Develop an aftercare program that includes regular attendance at recovery groups and any other necessary therapy. (18)

17. Verbalize the importance of resolving legal issues honestly. (10, 11, 19)

18. Family members verbalize a connection between legal problems and addictive behavior. (20)

19. Family members verbalize what each can do to assist the client in recovery. (21, 22)

__. _____
    _____

__. _____
    _____

__. _____
    _____

9. Assist the client in identifying positive, realistic thoughts to replace dysfunctional thinking that leads to addictive and illegal behaviors.
   RP: _____
   _____

10. Encourage and facilitate the client meeting with an attorney to discuss plans for resolving legal conflicts.
   RP: _____
   _____

11. Encourage and facilitate the client meeting with his/her probation or parole officer, and assign him/her to agree in writing to meet all conditions of probation or parole.
   RP: _____
   _____

12. Help the client to develop a plan to meet social, emotional, and financial needs in recovery without resorting to criminal activity or addictive behavior.
   RP: _____
   _____

13. Teach the client the difference between antisocial and prosocial behaviors, helping to identify his/her antisocial behaviors and attitudes. Then, help develop prosocial plans in recovery (i.e., respect for the law, helping others, honesty, reliability, regular attendance at work,

recovery groups, aftercare, halfway house, etc.).

RP: _____

_____

14. Help the client to understand why he/she needs to obey the law in order to maintain abstinence from addictive behavior.

RP: _____

_____

15. Teach the client about criminal thinking (e.g., rationalization, denial, superoptimism, blaming others, etc.). Assist him/her in identifying his/her criminal thinking, correcting each criminal thought with a thought that is honest and respectful of others.

RP: _____

_____

16. Help the client to understand the importance of helping others in recovery in order to replace an attitude of taking with an attitude of giving and self-sacrifice.

RP: _____

_____

17. Teach the client about the 12-step recovery program's concept of a higher power and how a higher power can assist him/her in recovery from legal conflicts and addiction.

RP: _____

_____

18. Help the client to develop
    an aftercare program that
    has all of the elements that
    are necessary to maintain
    abstinence and resolve legal
    conflicts.

    RP: _____

    _____

19. Help the client to under-
    stand the importance of re-
    solving legal conflicts
    honestly and legally.

    RP: _____

    _____

20. Discuss with family mem-
    bers the connection between
    legal problems and addic-
    tive behavior.

    RP: _____

    _____

21. In a family session, review
    what each member can do to
    assist the client in recovery.

    RP: _____

    _____

22. Provide the family members
    with information about
    legal problems and the
    steps that the client must
    take to recover successfully.

    RP: _____

    _____

—.   _____

      _____

RP: _____

      _____

—.   _____

      _____

RP: _____

      _____

—.   _____

      _____

RP: _____

      _____

DIAGNOSTIC SUGGESTIONS

Axis I: 312.80   Conduct Disorder
               313.81   Oppositional Defiant Disorder
               309.3   Adjustment Disorder With Disturbance of
                         Conduct
               312.34   Intermittent Explosive Disorder
               V71.01   Adult Antisocial Behavior
               V71.02   Child or Adolescent Antisocial Behavior

               _____   _____

Axis II: _____   _____
               301.70   Antisocial Personality Disorder
               301.83   Borderline Personality Disorder
               301.81   Narcissistic Personality Disorder

               _____   _____

               _____   _____

LIVING ENVIRONMENT DEFICIENCY

BEHAVIORAL DEFINITIONS

1. Currently living in an environment in which there is a high risk for relapse to addictive behavior.
2. Lives with an individual who practices addictive behavior regularly.
3. Social life is characterized by significant social isolation or withdrawal.
4. Living in an environment in which there is a high risk of physical, sexual, or emotional abuse.
5. Friends or relatives practice addictive behavior patterns.
6. Family is angry with the client and not supportive of a recovery program.
7. Financially destitute and needs assistance for adequate food and shelter.
8. Peer group members regularly practice addictive behavior.
9. Lives in a neighborhood that has a high incidence of addictive behavior.

__. _____
   _____

__. _____
   _____

__. _____
   _____

LONG-TERM GOALS

1. Maintain a program of recovery that is free from addiction and the negative impact of the deficient environment.
2. Improve the social, occupational, financial, and living situations sufficiently to increase the probability of a successful recovery from addictive behavior.
3. Understand the negative impact of the current environment on recovery from addictive behavior.
4. Develop a peer group that is supportive of recovery.
5. Accept the importance of working a program of recovery that necessitates attendance at recovery groups and helping others.
6. Family members support the client's recovery.

—. _____

_____

—. _____

_____

—. _____

_____

SHORT-TERM OBJECTIVES

1. Verbalize the sense of powerlessness and unmanageability that results from a deficient environment and addiction. (1, 2, 3, 4)
2. Identify specific living environment problems and how they negatively affect recovery. (2, 3, 4)
3. List several times that the living environment deficit led to negative consequences and addiction. (3)

THERAPEUTIC INTERVENTIONS

1. Using a 12-step program's step-one exercise, help the client see the powerlessness and unmanageability that result from addiction and a deficient environment.
   *RP: _____

   _____

2. Help the client to identify problems with the living environment and the negative impact that they have on recovery.
   RP: _____

   _____

_____

*RP = responsible professional.

4. Verbalize an understanding of why the current peer or family group increases the risk for relapse. (3, 4)

5. List the specific living environment problems, and make a written plan to address each one in recovery. (2, 3, 5)

6. List alternatives to living in the current high-risk environment. (6)

7. Identify the current social, occupational, and financial needs, and make a plan to meet each need in recovery. (7, 8)

8. List 10 reasons why there is a need to become involved in a new peer group that is supportive of recovery. (4, 8)

9. Meet with a 12-step program contact person and discuss plans for recovery. (9)

10. Write a personal recovery plan detailing the recovery groups, aftercare, and further treatment that will be needed in recovery. (10, 11)

11. Make a written plan as to how to develop relationships with people who attend recovery meetings. (11, 12)

12. List the ways in which a higher power can assist in recovery from a deficient living environment and addiction. (13, 14)

13. Practice turning over to a higher power the living en-

3. Help the client to list specific instances when living environment problems led to negative consequences and addiction.
RP: _____

_____

4. Help the client to see how his/her current social and/or family environment is a high-risk situation.
RP: _____

_____

5. Help the client to develop a written plan for addressing each living environment problem in recovery.
RP: _____

_____

6. Discuss the alternatives that are available for moving out of the current living situation that promotes ongoing addiction.
RP: _____

_____

7. Help the client to identify his/her social, occupational, and financial needs, and make a written plan to meet each need in recovery.
RP: _____

_____

8. Teach the importance of a supportive peer group, and assign the client to list 10 reasons why he/she needs a

vironment problems and urges to engage in addictive behavior. (13, 14, 15)

14. Verbalize a plan to continue spiritual growth within a community of believers. (13, 14, 15, 16)

15. Implement refusal behavior in high-risk situations. (17)

16. Write a letter to each significant other, discussing the problems with the living environment and share plans for recovery. (18, 19)

17. Develop a written plan as to how to react to family members who are addicted. (20)

18. Family members verbalize a connection between living environment deficiencies and addictive behavior. (21, 22)

19. Family members verbalize what each can do to assist the client in recovery. (23)

—. _____

_____

—. _____

_____

—. _____

_____

new peer group to maintain abstinence.

RP: _____

_____

9. Facilitate the client meeting with a 12-step program contact person, and encourage him/her to discuss recovery plans.

RP: _____

_____

10. Help the client to develop a personal recovery plan that has all of the elements necessary to recover from addictive behavior and the deficient living environment.

RP: _____

_____

11. Encourage the client's attendance at 12-step recovery program meetings as a means of developing a supportive peer group.

RP: _____

_____

12. Assign the client to write at least five steps that he/she will take to initiate new relationships with recovering people.

RP: _____

_____

13. Teach the client about the 12-step program's concept of a higher power, and show him/her how the higher power can assist in recovery.

RP: _____

_____

14. Using a 12-step recovery program's step-three exercise, teach the client how to turn his/her will and life over to a higher power.
RP: _____

_____

15. Monitor the client's implementation of a 12-step recovery program's step-three exercise; reinforce his/her success and redirect for failure.
RP: _____

_____

16. Assist the client in developing a plan to continue his/her spiritual growth (i.e., church, recovery groups, counseling, meeting with a pastor, spiritual reading material, etc.).
RP: _____

_____

17. Using modeling, role playing, and behavior rehearsal, teach the client how to say no to addictive behavior in high-risk situations.
RP: _____

_____

18. Help the client to write a letter to each significant other sharing his/her problem with addiction, how the living environment has fostered the addiction, and the plan for recovery.
RP: _____

_____

19. Meet with family members to teach them about addiction, discuss the living environment deficiencies, and make plans for support of the client's recovery.

    RP: _____

    _____

20. Help the client to develop a plan as to how to deal with family members who are addicted.

    RP: _____

    _____

21. Discuss with family members the connection between living environment deficiencies and addictive behavior.

    RP: _____

    _____

22. In a family session, review what each member can do to assist the client in recovery.

    RP: _____

    _____

23. Provide the family members with information about living environmental deficiencies and the steps that the client must take to recover successfully.

    RP: _____

    _____

—. _____

_____

RP: _____

_____

—. _____

_____

RP: _____

_____

—. _____

_____

RP: _____

_____

DIAGNOSTIC SUGGESTIONS

Axis I: V61.20   Parent-Child Relational Problem
V61.10   Partner Relational Problem
V61.8   Sibling Relational Problem
V62.81   Relational Problem NOS
V61.21   Physical Abuse of Child
V61.21   Sexual Abuse of Child
V61.21   Neglect of Child
V61.12   Sexual Abuse of Adult (*by partner*)
V62.83   Sexual Abuse of Adult (*by person other than partner*)
V62.20   Occupational Problem
V62.89   Religious or Spiritual Problem
V62.4   Acculturation Problem

_____   _____
_____   _____

Axis II:

_____   _____
_____   _____

MANIA/HYPOMANIA

BEHAVIORAL DEFINITIONS

1. A distinct period of persistently elevated or irritable mood lasting at least four days.
2. Inflated sense of self-esteem and an exaggerated, euphoric belief in capabilities that denies any self-limitations or realistic obstacles but sees others as standing in the way.
3. Decreased need for sleep.
4. More talkative than normal—pressured speech.
5. Racing thoughts.
6. Poor attention span and susceptibility to distraction.
7. An increase in initiating projects at home, work, or school but without completion of tasks.
8. Excessive activities that are potentially self-damaging (e.g., buying sprees, sexual acting out, or foolish business investments).
9. Impulsive engagement in addictive behavior to an exaggerated level without regard for consequences.
10. Verbal and/or physical aggression coupled with tantrum-like behavior (e.g., breaking things explosively) if wishes are blocked, which is in contrast to an earlier pattern of restraint.

__. _____
    _____
__. _____
    _____
__. _____
    _____

LONG-TERM GOALS

1. Maintain a program of recovery that is free of manic/hypomanic behavior and addiction.
2. Increase control over impulses, reduce the energy level, and stabilize the mood.
3. Reduce agitation, irritability, and pressured speech.
4. Increase rational thinking and behavior.
5. Understand the relationship between manic/hypomanic states and addictive behavior.
6. Moderate mood and increase goal-directed behavior.
7. Understand the biopsychosocial aspects of manic/hypomanic states and addiction, and accept the need for continued treatment.
8. Terminate addictive behavior and take medications for mania on a consistent basis.

—. _____

_____

—. _____

_____

—. _____

_____

SHORT-TERM OBJECTIVES

1. Verbalize an understanding of the signs and symptoms of mania/hypomania and how bipolar disease is related to addictive behavior. (1, 2)

2. List several specific instances that manic/hypomanic states led to addictive behavior. (2, 3)

3. Verbalize an acceptance of the powerlessness and unmanageability that result

THERAPEUTIC INTERVENTIONS

1. Teach the client about the signs and symptoms of mania/hypomania and how it can foster addictive behavior.

   *RP: _____

   _____

2. Explore the client's pattern of manic/hypomanic behavior.

   RP: _____

   _____

---

*RP = responsible professional.

from mania/hypomania and using addictive behavior to cope with the impulsivity and mood swings. (2, 3, 4)

4. Verbalize an understanding of the biopsychosocial correlates of mania/hypomania and addiction. (5)

5. List several negative consequences that resulted from untreated mania/hypomania and addictive behavior. (6)

6. Verbalize an understanding that manic/hypomanic states and addiction meet the 12-step program's criteria for *insanity*. (7)

7. Verbalize five ways in which a higher power can assist in recovery from manic/hypomanic states and addictive behavior. (8, 9)

8. Practice turning over at least one problem to the higher power each day. Record the situation and discuss it with the primary therapist. (9, 10)

9. Meet with the physician to see if psychopharmacological intervention is warranted, and take all medication as directed. (11, 12)

10. Report as to effectiveness and side effects of the medication. (12, 13)

11. Verbalize an acceptance of the necessity for continued medical monitoring for

3. Explore the client's addictive behavior history, and identify instances in which manic/hypomanic states led to addictive behavior.
RP: _____
_____

4. Using a 12-step program's step-one exercise, help the client to see the powerlessness and unmanageability that result from mania/hypomania symptoms and the use of addictive behavior to cope with these symptoms.
RP: _____
_____

5. Teach the client about the biopsychosocial correlates of mania/hypomania and addictive behavior.
RP: _____
_____

6. Help the client to identify the negative consequences of mania/hypomania and addictive behavior.
RP: _____
_____

7. Teach the client about the 12-step recovery program's concept of *insanity*, helping him/her understand how manic/hypomanic states and addiction meet the 12-step program's criteria for insanity.
RP: _____
_____

manic/hypomanic symptoms. (11, 12, 13, 14)

12. Achieve mood stability by becoming slower to react with anger, less expansive, and more socially appropriate and sensitive. (11, 13, 15, 16)

13. Decrease grandiose statements and express self more realistically. (11, 15, 16)

14. Terminate self-destructive impulsive behaviors such as promiscuity, addictive behavior, and the expression of overt hostility or aggression. (11, 16, 17, 18)

15. Accept the limits set on manipulative and hostile behaviors that attempt to control others. (11, 15, 19)

16. Speak more slowly and be more subject-focused. (11, 20, 21)

17. Dress and groom in a less attention-seeking manner. (17, 22)

18. Identify positive traits and behaviors that build genuine self-esteem. (23)

19. Develop a personal recovery plan that includes all of the elements necessary to control mania/hypomania and to recover from addiction. (24, 25)

20. Write a 12-step program's fourth-step inventory, and share with someone in recovery. (26)

8. Teach the client about the 12-step program's concept of a higher power and how a higher power can help restore him/her to sanity.
   RP: _____

   _____

9. Using a 12-step program's step-three exercise, teach the client how to turn problems over to the higher power.
   RP: _____

   _____

10. Review the client's implementation of turning problems over to a higher power; reinforce success and redirect for failure.
    RP: _____

    _____

11. Physician examine the client, order medications as indicated, titrate medications, and monitor for effectiveness and side effects.
    RP: _____

    _____

12. Staff administer medications as ordered by the physician.
    RP: _____

    _____

13. Monitor the client's use of prescribed psychotropic medication for side effects and effectiveness.
    RP: _____

    _____

21. Verbalize the importance of consistently attending recovery groups and of helping others in recovery. (27)

22. Meet with a 12-step program contact person, and discuss manic/hypomanic states and addiction. (28)

23. Have the family members meet with the physician to discuss medication and side effects. (29)

24. Make a written contract with family members to comply with all aftercare. (30)

25. Family members verbalize a connection between mania/hypomania and addictive behavior. (31, 32)

26. Family members verbalize what each can do to assist the client in recovery. (33)

__. _____

   _____

__. _____

   _____

__. _____

   _____

14. Help the client to understand the importance of consistent medical management of manic/hypomanic illness.
    RP: _____

    _____

15. Confront gently but firmly the client's grandiosity and demandingness.
    RP: _____

    _____

16. Reinforce the client's increased mood stability, social appropriateness, and reduced impulsivity.
    RP: _____

    _____

17. Repeatedly focus on the consequences of behavior to reduce thoughtless impulsivity.
    RP: _____

    _____

18. Facilitate impulse control by using role play, behavior rehearsal, and role reversal to increase sensitivity to the consequences of behavior.
    RP: _____

    _____

19. Set limits on manipulation or acting out by making rules and establishing clear consequences for breaking them.
    RP: _____

    _____

20. Provide structure and focus for the client's thoughts and actions by regulating the direction of conversation and establishing plans for behavior.

RP: _____

_____

21. Verbally reinforce slower speech and more deliberate thought processes.

RP: _____

_____

22. Encourage and reinforce appropriate dress and grooming.

RP: _____

_____

23. Assist the client in identifying strengths and assets to build his/her self-esteem and confidence.

RP: _____

_____

24. Outline with the client the essential components for managing manic/hypomanic states and addiction (i.e., taking medication, complying with medical monitoring, continuing therapy, attending recovery groups regularly, using the higher power, getting a sponsor, helping others in recovery, etc.).

RP: _____

_____

25. Discuss discharge planning
and help the client to decide
what environment he/she
needs in early recovery.
RP: _____

_____

26. Using a 12-step program's
fourth-step inventory, assign the client to write an
autobiography and then to
share it with someone in
recovery.
RP: _____

_____

27. Teach the client the importance of working a program
of recovery that includes
attending recovery group
meetings regularly and
helping others.
RP: _____

_____

28. Arrange for the client to
meet a 12-step program
contact person, and assign
him/her to talk about
manic/hypomanic states
and addiction.
RP: _____

_____

29. Physician will meet with
the family to discuss medication and side effects.
RP: _____

_____

30. Have the client make a
written contract with the
family to attend all after-

care plans and to take medication as prescribed.

RP: _____

_____

31. Discuss with family members the connection between mania/hypomania and addictive behavior.

RP: _____

_____

32. In a family session, review what each member can do to assist the client in recovery.

RP: _____

_____

33. Provide the family members with information about mania/hypomania and the steps that the client must take to recover successfully.

RP: _____

_____

__. _____

_____

RP: _____

_____

__. _____

_____

RP: _____

_____

__. _____

_____

RP: _____

_____

DIAGNOSTIC SUGGESTIONS

Axis I: 296.xx   Bipolar I Disorder
               296.89   Bipolar II Disorder
               301.13   Cyclothymic Disorder
               295.70   Schizoaffective Disorder
               296.80   Bipolar Disorder NOS
               310.10   Personality Change Due to (*Axis III Disorder*)

    _____   _____

    _____   _____

MEDICAL ISSUES

BEHAVIORAL DEFINITIONS

1. Diagnosed with biomedical problems that complicate recovery from addictive behavior.
2. Medical problems requiring monitoring of medications or assistance with mobility.
3. Use of mood-altering chemicals has resulted in organic brain syndrome, which compromises learning.
4. Incapable of self-administering prescribed medications.
5. Chronic pain syndrome places the client at high risk for relapse into substance dependence.
6. Biomedical problems require medical/nursing assistance.
7. Use of mood-altering chemicals to self-medicate medical problems.
8. Negative emotions surrounding medical illness lead to addictive behavior.
9. Medical problems are so severe that concentration on recovery is compromised.

—. _____
   _____

—. _____
   _____

—. _____
   _____

LONG-TERM GOALS

1. Maintain a program of recovery that is free of addiction and the negative effects of medical issues.

2. Resolve medical problems and return to a normal level of functioning.
3. Understand the relationship between medical issues and addictive behavior.
4. Reduce the impact of medical problems on recovery and relapse potential.
5. Improve the coping skills with organic brain syndrome to allow for a self-directed program of recovery.

—. _____
   _____

—. _____
   _____

—. _____
   _____

SHORT-TERM OBJECTIVES

1. Verbalize an acceptance of the powerlessness and unmanageability that result from using addictive behavior to cope with medical problems. (1, 2)

2. Identify the medical problems and how these relate to addiction. (2)

3. Verbalize an acceptance of the seriousness of medical problems and addictive behavior. (3)

4. Verbalize an understanding of the medical problem and the need for medical management. (3, 4, 5)

5. List the negative consequences that resulted from

THERAPEUTIC INTERVENTIONS

1. Using a 12-step program's step-one exercise, help the client to see the powerlessness and unmanageability that result from medical issues and addiction.

   *RP: _____
   _____

2. Help the client to see the relationship between his/her medical problems and addictive behavior.

   RP: _____
   _____

3. Teach the client about the medical issues and addiction and how each of these

_____

*RP = responsible professional.

using addictive behavior to cope with medical problems. (2, 6)

6. Visit with the physician for an examination of the medical condition and cooperate with treatment plan. (7, 8)

7. Verbalize an understanding of the medical condition, the treatment options, and prognosis. (5, 9, 10)

8. Participate in decisions regarding the medical management of biomedical problems. (9, 10)

9. Verbalize an understanding of how addictive behavior has been a contributing causal factor in the development of the medical problem. (2, 11)

10. Make a commitment to follow through with medical treatment. (12)

11. List 10 things to do to improve physical functioning. (13)

12. Cooperate with a psychological assessment. (14)

13. Implement relaxation exercises as a pain management technique. (15)

14. Accept and follow through on a referral to a pain management clinic. (16)

15. Discuss with family members the medical problems and addiction, and make plans for family members to obtain supportive services. (17)

illnesses poses a serious risk to his/her welfare.
RP: _____

_____

4. Help the client to understand his/her medical problem and the need to cooperate with medical management.
RP: _____

_____

5. Provide the client with references to literature or other informational resources regarding his/her medical condition.
RP: _____

_____

6. Help the client to develop a list of 10 negative consequences that occurred because of using addictive behavior to cope with medical problems.
RP: _____

_____

7. Physician examine the client, and make recommendations as indicated to treat the medical condition and alleviate symptoms.
RP: _____

_____

8. Medical staff monitor treatment plan as ordered by the physician, and follow up with the client as needed.
RP: _____

_____

16. List five ways in which a higher power can assist in recovery from medical issues and addiction. (18, 19)

17. Pray and meditate each day, asking the higher power for will and the power to carry that out. (18, 19)

18. Write a personal recovery plan that includes regular attendance at recovery groups and any medical treatment that is necessary to control the medical issues and addiction. (20)

19. Family members verbalize a connection between medical issues and addictive behavior. (21, 22)

20. Family members verbalize what each can do to assist the client in recovery. (23)

—. _____
   _____
—. _____
   _____
—. _____
   _____

9. Medical personnel teach the client about his/her medical condition and discuss the treatment plan and prognosis.
   RP: _____
   _____

10. Teach the client assertiveness skills and encourage the implementation of assertiveness in obtaining information about and becoming involved in the management of his/her medical treatment.
    RP: _____
    _____

11. Educate the client regarding the negative impact of addictive behavior on bodily functioning and systems.
    RP: _____
    _____

12. Help the client to understand the importance of medical management and follow-up in aftercare.
    RP: _____
    _____

13. After a discussion with the medical staff, help the client to list 10 actions that he/she can take to improve physical functioning (e.g., take medications, maintain abstinence, practice relaxation, implement proper diet, rest and exercise, keep regular follow-up ap-

pointments with the physician, etc.).

RP: _____

_____

14. Arrange for a psychological assessment with recommendations for treatment.

RP: _____

_____

15. Teach deep muscle relaxation and guided imagery to be used by the client in pain management.

RP: _____

_____

16. Refer the client to a pain clinic for medical and psychological management of pain.

RP: _____

_____

17. In a family session, discuss the medical issues and addiction, and make recommendations for family members to obtaining supportive services (e.g., Alanon, Alateen, medical support group, etc.).

RP: _____

_____

18. Teach the client the 12-step recovery program's concept of a higher power, and help him/her to see how the higher power can be helpful in recovery.

RP: _____

_____

19. Teach the client about step eleven and how this step can be used daily in recovery.
    RP: _____

    _____

20. Help the client to develop a personal recovery plan that details what he/she is going to do in recovery to remain abstinent and treat biomedical issues (attend recovery groups regularly, make medical visits regularly, take medication as indicated, get a sponsor, attend aftercare, help others, etc.).
    RP: _____

    _____

21. Discuss with family members the connection between medical issues and addictive behavior.
    RP: _____

    _____

22. In a family session, review what each member can do to assist the client in recovery.
    RP: _____

    _____

23. Provide the family members with information about medical issues and the steps that the client must take to recover successfully.
    RP: _____

    _____

—. _____

_____

RP: _____

_____

—. _____

_____

RP: _____

_____

—. _____

_____

RP: _____

_____

DIAGNOSTIC SUGGESTIONS

Axis I: 307.89   Pain Disorder Associated With Both
                         Psychological Factors and [*Axis III Disorder*]
               307.80   Pain Disorder Associated With Psychological
                         Factors
               300.7   Hypochondriasis
               300.81   Somatization Disorder
               316   Personality Traits Affecting (*Axis III Disorder*)
               316   Maladaptive Health Behaviors Affecting (*Axis
                         III Disorder*)
               316   Psychological Symptoms Affecting (*Axis III
                         Disorder*)
               307.23   Tourette's Disorder
               293.0   Delirium Due to . . . [*Axis III Disorder*]
               290   Dementia

               ____   _____

               ____   _____

NARCISSISTIC TRAITS

BEHAVIORAL DEFINITIONS

1. A grandiose sense of self-importance and self-worth.
2. Fantasies of unlimited power, success, intelligence, or beauty.
3. Believes that he/she is special and only other special people can appreciate him/her.
4. A powerful need to be recognized, admired, and adored.
5. Becomes angry and resentful when people do not immediately meet his/her wishes, wants and needs, or expectations.
6. Lacks empathy for others.
7. Often envious of others or feels others are envious of him/her.
8. Brags about achievements, exaggerated abilities, and body image.
9. Interpersonally manipulative and exploitive.

—. _____
   _____
   _____
—. _____
   _____
   _____
—. _____
   _____

LONG-TERM GOALS

1. Maintain a program of recovery that is free of addiction and the negative effects of narcissistic traits.
2. Develop a realistic sense of self without narcissistic grandiosity, exaggeration, or sense of entitlement.
3. Understand the relationship between narcissistic traits and addiction.

4. Understand narcissistic traits and how the sense of omnipotence is a risk for relapse.
5. Develop empathy for other people, particularly victims of his/her narcissism.

—. _____

_____

—. _____

_____

—. _____

_____

SHORT-TERM OBJECTIVES

1. Verbalize the powerlessness and unmanageability that result from narcissistic traits and addiction. (1, 2)
2. Verbalize an identification of several narcissistic traits, and state how they contribute to addictive behavior. (2, 3)
3. List specific times when narcissistic traits led to addiction and the negative consequences that resulted from it. (2, 3)
4. Verbalize a commitment to honesty and humility that can form the basis for a program of recovery. (4, 5, 6)
5. Verbalize an understanding of how manipulating others leads to interpersonal frustration and loneliness. (5, 7, 8)

THERAPEUTIC INTERVENTIONS

1. Using a 12-step recovery program's step-one exercise, help the client to see that narcissistic traits and addictive behavior lead to a state of powerlessness and unmanageability.
   *RP: _____

   _____

2. Assist the client in identifying his/her narcissistic traits and how they can lead to addictive behavior.
   RP: _____

   _____

3. Help the client to identify 10 times when narcissistic traits and addictive behavior led to negative consequences.
   RP: _____

   _____

_____

*RP = responsible professional.

6. List 10 lies that were told to exaggerate accomplishments and seek acceptance and recognition. (7)

7. List several narcissistic strategies that were used to manipulate others in relationships. (8)

8. Identify with the vulnerable revelations of other people by sharing similar experiences, feelings, and thoughts. (9, 10, 13, 14)

9. Share situations from the family of origin that resulted in emotional pain. (11)

10. Identify a pattern of narcissism (anxious, fearful thoughts followed by exaggerated thoughts of power and importance), and replace that pattern with confident but realistic self-talk. (12, 14)

11. Verbalize how the dynamics of the family of origin led to a poor self-image and a sense of rejection and failure. (11, 12)

12. Acknowledge that low self-esteem and fear of failure or rejection are felt internally in spite of the external facade of braggadocio. (11, 12, 13, 14)

13. List five ways in which a higher power can assist in recovery from narcissistic traits and addiction. (15, 16)

14. Verbalize a commitment to helping others as essential

4. Teach the client how a 12-step program can assist in recovery from narcissistic traits and addiction.
   RP: _____
   _____

5. Teach the client that honesty is essential for real intimacy and how lies lead to interpersonal frustration and loneliness.
   RP: _____
   _____

6. Discuss why resolution of narcissistic traits, especially the tendency toward dishonesty and feeling superior and all-powerful, is essential in maintaining abstinence.
   RP: _____
   _____

7. Assign the client to list 10 common lies that are told to exaggerate accomplishments and bolster self-image. Then, show why the self-defeating lies eventually led to the rejection from others that he/she fears.
   RP: _____
   _____

8. Assist the client in listing 10 ways in which he/she uses narcissistic traits to control and manipulate others. Then, explain how narcissistic behaviors are counterproductive to inter-

to recovery from narcissistic traits and addiction. (9, 14, 17)

15. Practice stopping, looking, listening, thinking, and planning before acting impulsively and without regard for others' rights and feelings. (14, 18)

16. Practice honesty and realistic humility in communication with others. (13, 14, 19)

17. Write a personal recovery plan that details the regular recovery groups and further treatment that are needed to recover from narcissistic traits and addiction. (20)

18. Family members verbalize a connection between narcissistic traits and addictive behavior. (21, 22)

19. Family members verbalize what each can do to assist the client in recovery. (23)

—. _____
_____

—. _____
_____

—. _____
_____

personal acceptance and respect.

RP: _____
_____

9. Conduct or refer the client for group therapy sessions that focus on developing empathy by asking him/her to share with the group members his/her similar vulnerable, anxious experiences, feelings and thoughts.

RP: _____
_____

10. Use role playing, modeling, and behavior rehearsal to teach the client self-disclosure of feelings of vulnerability.

RP: _____
_____

11. Probe the client's family of origin for experiences of criticism, emotional abandonment or rejection, and abuse or neglect that led to feelings of low self-esteem covered by narcissism.

RP: _____
_____

12. Probe the client's narcissistic thoughts (e.g., grandiosity, the sense of entitlement, tendency to blame others, the need to exaggerate achievements in search of acceptance, etc.). Show the client how these thoughts are based in low self-esteem and an expectation of rejection, then replace this pat-

tern with confident, realistic self-talk.

RP: _____

_____

13. Confront the client's expressions of entitlement and
braggadocio, interpreting
them as a cover for feelings
of fear and low self-esteem

RP: _____

_____

14. Reinforce the client's social
interactions that are characterized by humility, empathy, honesty, and
compassion.

RP: _____

_____

15. Teach the client about the
12-step program's concept of
a higher power and how
this can be used in recovery.

RP: _____

_____

16. Using a 12-step recovery
program's step-three exercise, teach the client how to
turn problems over to the
higher power.

RP: _____

_____

17. Teach the client that helping others will give them a
genuine sense of self-
worth, which is essential to
working a good program of
recovery.

RP: _____

_____

18. Using modeling, role playing, and behavior rehearsal,
teach the client the impulse
control skills of stopping,
looking, listening, thinking,
and planning before acting.
RP: _____

_____

19. Using modeling, role playing, and behavior rehearsal,
teach the client healthy interpersonal communication
skills (i.e., honesty, ask for
what you want, share how
you feel, care for what the
other person wants, active
listening, and the use of "I"
messages).
RP: _____

_____

20. Help the client to develop a
personal recovery plan that
will detail what he/she is
going to do for further treatment in recovery (e.g., regular attendance at recovery
groups, get a sponsor, further treatment or therapy,
etc.).
RP: _____

_____

21. Discuss with family members the connection between
narcissistic traits and addictive behavior.
RP: _____

_____

22. In a family session, review
what each member can

do to assist the client in recovery.

RP: _____

_____

23. Provide the family members with information about narcissistic traits and the steps that the client must take to recover successfully.

RP: _____

_____

__. _____

_____

RP: _____

_____

__. _____

_____

RP: _____

_____

__. _____

_____

RP: _____

_____

DIAGNOSTIC SUGGESTIONS

Axis I:	296.xx	Bipolar I Disorder
	296.89	Bipolar II Disorder
	301.13	Cyclothymic Disorder
	310.1	Personality Change due to (*Axis III Disorder*)
	_____	_____
	_____	_____
Axis II:	301.81	Narcissistic Personality Disorder
	301.83	Borderline Personality Disorder
	301.50	Histrionic Personality Disorder
	301.4	Obsessive-Compulsive Personality Disorder
	_____	_____
	_____	_____

NICOTINE DEPENDENCE

BEHAVIORAL DEFINITIONS

1. A maladaptive pattern of tobacco use manifested by increased use, tolerance, and withdrawal.
2. Inability to stop or reduce the use of tobacco, despite the verbalized desire to do so and the negative consequences that continued use brings.
3. Physical indicators (e.g., chronic obstructive lung disease, bronchitis, lung or oral cancer, etc.) that reflect the results of a pattern of heavy tobacco use.
4. Denial that nicotine dependence is a problem despite feedback from significant others that the use of tobacco is negatively affecting him/her and others.
5. Continued tobacco use despite the knowledge of experiencing persistent physical, legal, financial, vocational, social, or relationship problems that are directly caused by the use of nicotine.
6. Withdrawal symptoms (e.g., tobacco craving, anxiety, insomnia, irritability, depression, etc.) when going without nicotine for any length of time.
7. Continued use of tobacco after being told by a physician that its use is causing health problems.
8. Nicotine dependence is concurrent with other addictive behaviors, and their practice reinforces one another.

__. _____
   _____

__. _____
   _____

__. _____
   _____

LONG-TERM GOALS

1. Withdraw from nicotine, stabilize physically and emotionally, and then establish a supportive recovery plan.
2. Accept the powerlessness over nicotine and participate in a recovery-based program of abstinence.
3. Establish and maintain total abstinence from tobacco products while increasing knowledge of the addiction and the process of recovery.
4. Acquire the necessary skills to maintain long-term sobriety from all mood-altering substances.

—. _____

_____

—. _____

_____

—. _____

_____

SHORT-TERM OBJECTIVES

1. Cooperate with medical assessment and an evaluation of the necessity for pharmacological intervention. (1, 2)
2. Take prescribed medications as directed by the physician. (2, 3)
3. Report any acute withdrawal symptoms. (4)
4. Provide honest and complete information for a nicotine dependence biopsychosocial history. (5)
5. Attend didactic sessions and read assigned material in order to increase knowl-

THERAPEUTIC INTERVENTIONS

1. Physician perform a physical exam and write treatment orders, including, if necessary, prescription of medications to facilitate withdrawal from nicotine and maintenance of abstinence.

   *RP: _____

   _____

2. Physician monitor the side effects and effectiveness of medication, titrating as necessary.

   RP: _____

   _____

———————————

*RP = responsible professional.

edge of nicotine dependence and the process of recovery. (6, 7, 8, 9)

6. Attend group therapy sessions to share thoughts and feelings that are associated with reasons for, consequences of, feelings about, and alternatives to tobacco abuse. (10, 11)

7. List 10 negative consequences resulting from or exacerbated by nicotine dependence. (12, 13)

8. Verbally admit to powerlessness over the mood-altering substances. (12, 13, 14)

9. Verbalize a recognition that tobacco use was used as the primary coping mechanism to escape from stress or pain and resulted in negative consequences. (13)

10. List five negative emotions that were caused by or exacerbated by nicotine dependence. (14)

11. Develop a list of three social, emotional, and family factors that contributed to tobacco dependence. (5, 15)

12. List 10 reasons to work on a plan for recovery from tobacco abuse. (5, 12, 14, 16)

13. List 10 lies used to hide tobacco dependence. (17)

14. Verbalize five ways in which a higher power can assist in recovery. (18, 19)

3. Monitor prescribed medications for client's compliance, side effects, and effectiveness.
   RP: _____
   _____

4. Assess and monitor the client's condition during withdrawal from nicotine.
   RP: _____
   _____

5. Complete a thorough family and personal biopsychosocial history that has a focus on nicotine dependence and any other addictions.
   RP: _____
   _____

6. Assign the client to attend a nicotine dependence didactic series to increase knowledge of the patterns and negative effects of tobacco dependence.
   RP: _____
   _____

7. Require the client to attend all nicotine dependence didactics; ask him/her to identify several key points attained from each didactic and to process these points with the therapist.
   RP: _____
   _____

8. Ask the client to read literature on nicotine dependence etiology and its negative social, emotional, and medical consequences; process with

15. Practice turning problems over to a higher power each day, recording each event. (19)

16. Practice healthy communication skills to reduce interpersonal stress and increase positive social interaction. (20, 21)

17. Practice problem-solving skills. (22)

18. List the reasons for tobacco use and the ways the same things can be attained in an adaptive manner. (23, 24, 25)

19. Practice stress management and relaxation skills to reduce overall stress levels and attain a feeling of relaxation and comfort. (25, 26)

20. Exercise at a training heart rate for at least 20 minutes at least three times per week. (26)

21. List the triggers (persons, places, and things) that may precipitate relapse. (13, 27, 28)

22. Make a written plan to cope with each high-risk or trigger situation. (28, 29)

23. Practice saying no to tobacco, alcohol, and drugs. (29)

24. Write a personal recovery plan that includes attending recovery group meetings regularly, aftercare, getting a sponsor, and helping others in recovery. (30, 31)

the therapist five key points gained from the reading.
RP: _____
_____

9. Assign the client to attend group therapy that focuses on nicotine dependence recovery issues.
RP: _____
_____

10. Direct group therapy that facilitates the sharing of causes for, consequences of, feelings about, and alternatives to nicotine dependence.
RP: _____
_____

11. Assign the client to complete a 12-step program's first-step paper admitting to powerlessness over tobacco, and present it in group therapy or to the therapist for feedback.
RP: _____
_____

12. Ask the client to make a list of the ways in which nicotine dependence has negatively impacted his/her life, and process the list with the therapist or group.
RP: _____
_____

13. Explore how tobacco abuse was used to escape from stress, physical and emotional pain, and boredom.

25. Take a personal inventory at the end of each day listing the problems in recovery, the plans to address the problems, and five things to be grateful for that day. (32)

26. Enter the continuing care treatment setting that is necessary to maintain abstinence and maximize chances for recovery. (33)

27. Family members decrease the frequency of enabling the nicotine-dependent person after verbally identifying their enabling behaviors. (34, 35, 36, 37)

28. Identify rewards for nicotine abstinence. (38)

29. Implement a structured behavior modification program for nicotine abstinence. (39, 40, 41)

__. _____
   _____

__. _____
   _____

__. _____
   _____

Confront the negative consequences of this pattern.
RP: _____
   _____

14. Probe the sense of powerlessness, shame, guilt, and low self-worth that has resulted from tobacco abuse and its consequences.
RP: _____
   _____

15. Using the biopsychosocial history, assist the client in understanding the familial, emotional, and social factors that contributed to the development of nicotine dependence (e.g., modeling effects of older adults, peer pressure and anxiety, etc.).
RP: _____
   _____

16. Assign the client to write a list of 10 reasons to be abstinent from nicotine dependence.
RP: _____
   _____

17. Help the client see the dishonesty that goes along with nicotine dependence. Have him/her list 10 lies that he/she told to hide tobacco use, and then teach him/her why honesty is essential to recovery.
RP: _____
   _____

18. Teach the client about the concept of a higher power

and how this can assist in recovery.

RP: _____

_____

19. Using a step-three exercise, teach the client about the concept of "turning it over," then assign turning over problems to the higher power each day. Have the client record the event and discuss the results.

RP: _____

_____

20. Teach the client healthy communication skills (i.e., using "I" messages, reflecting, active listening, empathy, being reinforcing, sharing, etc.)

RP: _____

_____

21. Refer the client for or teach him/her social interaction skills to reduce interpersonal anxiety that triggered tobacco use.

RP: _____

_____

22. Using modeling, role playing, and behavior rehearsal, teach the client how to solve problems in an organized fashion (i.e., write the problem, think accurately, list the options of action, evaluate alternatives, act, monitor, and evaluate results.)

RP: _____

_____

23. Assist the client in clarifying why he/she was using tobacco, and help him/her to identify adaptive ways to obtain the sought-after result (e.g., relaxation).
RP: _____
_____

24. Assign the client to list five pleasurable activities that he/she plans to use in recovery.
RP: _____
_____

25. Using progressive relaxation or biofeedback, teach the client how to relax, then assign him/her to relax twice a day for 10 to 20 minutes.
RP: _____
_____

26. Using current physical fitness levels, help the client to exercise three times a week. Then, increase the exercise by 10 percent a week, until he/she is exercising at a training heart rate for at least 20 minutes at least three times a week.
RP: _____
_____

27. Using a relapse prevention exercise, help the client uncover his/her triggers for relapse into tobacco use.
RP: _____
_____

28. Teach the client about high-risk situations (e.g., negative emotions, social pressure, interpersonal conflict, positive emotions, testing personal control, etc.); assist the client in making a written plan to cope with each high-risk situation.
RP: _____
_____

29. Using modeling, role playing, and behavior rehearsal, teach the client how to say no to tobacco, alcohol, or drugs, then practice saying no in high-risk situations.
RP: _____
_____

30. Help the client to develop a personal recovery plan that includes regular attending recovery group meetings regularly, aftercare, getting a sponsor, and helping others in recovery.
RP: _____
_____

31. Help the client to see the necessity for working on a personalized program of recovery every day to maintain abstinence.
RP: _____
_____

32. Encourage the client to take a personal inventory each night, listing the problems that he/she had that day, making a plan to deal with any problems, and

then listing five things for
which he/she was grateful
that day.
RP: _____

_____

33. Discuss continuing care options with the client (e.g.,
attending recovery group
meetings regularly, taking
daily inventory, attending
counseling, etc.).
RP: _____

_____

34. Monitor the client's family
for enabling behaviors, and
redirect them in the family
session as appropriate.
RP: _____

_____

35. Educate the client's family
in the dynamics of enabling
and tough love.
RP: _____

_____

36. Assist the client's family
members in implementing
and sticking with tough-
love techniques.
RP: _____

_____

37. Ask the client's family to attend the family education
component of the treatment
program.
RP: _____

_____

38. Assist the client in identifying reinforcing events that

could be used in rewarding abstinence from nicotine.

RP: _____

_____

39. Design with the client a behavior modification program that targets tobacco abuse and reinforces periods of abstinence.

RP: _____

_____

40. Assign implementation of a behavior modification program that stipulates rewards for nicotine abstinence.

RP: _____

_____

41. Review, process, and redirect the behavior modification to maximize success rates.

RP: _____

_____

__. _____

_____

RP: _____

_____

__. _____

_____

RP: _____

_____

__. _____

_____

RP: _____

_____

DIAGNOSTIC SUGGESTIONS

Axis I: 305.10   Nicotine Dependence
                 292.0   Nicotine Withdrawal
                 304.90   Other (or Unknown) Substance Dependence
                 _____   _____
                 _____   _____

OCCUPATIONAL PROBLEMS

BEHAVIORAL DEFINITIONS

1. Rebellion against and/or conflicts with authority figures in the employment situation.
2. Underemployed or unemployed due to the negative effect of addictive behavior on work performance and attendance.
3. Work environment is too stressful, leading to addictive behavior to escape.
4. Job jeopardy due to addictive behavior.
5. Anxiety related to perceived or actual job jeopardy.
6. Feelings of inadequacy, fear, and failure secondary to severe business losses.
7. Coworkers are alcohol/drug abusers and supportive of addiction, increasing the risk for relapse.
8. Employer does not understand addiction or what is required for recovery.
9. Retirement has led to feelings of loneliness, lack of meaning to life, and addictive behavior.

—. _____
   _____
—. _____
   _____
   _____
—. _____
   _____

LONG-TERM GOALS

1. Maintain a program of recovery that is free of addiction and occupational problems.
2. Change occupation in order to maximize the chances of recovery.
3. Communicate with coworkers and management to obtain support for treatment and recovery.
4. Make a contract with management that details the recovery plan and the consequences of relapse.
5. Fill life with new interests so retirement or job change can be appreciated.
6. Engage in job-seeking behaviors consistently and with a reasonably positive attitude.

—. _____
   _____
   _____

—. _____
   _____
   _____

—. _____
   _____

SHORT-TERM OBJECTIVES

1. Identify the occupational problems and how they relate to addiction. (1, 2, 6, 7)
2. Identify own role in the conflict with coworkers or supervisor. (3, 4, 5)
3. Identify own behavioral changes that would help resolve conflict with coworkers or supervisors. (3, 4, 5, 6)
4. List five times that addiction led to occupational problems. (7)

THERAPEUTIC INTERVENTIONS

1. Take a history of the client's occupational problems, and determine how they relate to addiction.
   *RP: _____
   _____

2. Teach the client how the occupational problems led to his/her addiction.
   RP: _____
   _____

3. Confront the client's projection of responsibility for

---

*RP = responsible professional.

5. List five ways in which occupational problems led to addiction. (2, 8)

6. Verbalize why current employment increases the risk for relapse. (2, 8, 9)

7. Verbalize feelings of fear, anger, and helplessness that are associated with the vocational stress. (10)

8. Identify distorted cognitive messages that are associated with the perception of job stress. (11)

9. Develop healthier, more realistic cognitive messages that promote harmony with others, self-acceptance, and self-confidence. (12, 13)

10. Replace projection of responsibility for conflict, feelings, or behavior with acceptance of responsibility for behavior, feelings, and role in conflict. (3, 14)

11. Develop a written plan to resolve occupational problems and maximize chances for recovery in the workplace. (15)

12. Meet with the employer to discuss occupational stress and to gain support for treatment and recovery. (16, 17)

13. Implement the assertiveness skills that are necessary to be honest with coworkers about addiction and recovery. (17, 18, 19)

14. List the skills or changes that will help in coping with

his/her behavior and feelings onto others.

RP: _____

_____

4. Assist the client in identifying his/her patterns of interpersonal conflict that occur beyond the work setting; relate these patterns to current occupational problems.

RP: _____

_____

5. Probe family-of-origin history for how the client may have learned dysfunctional relationship patterns; relate these patterns to current coworker/supervisor conflicts.

RP: _____

_____

6. Assist the client in listing behavioral changes that he/she could make to resolve conflicts with coworkers and supervisors.

RP: _____

_____

7. Help the client to list five times when addictive behavior led to problems at work.

RP: _____

_____

8. Assign the client to list five ways that occupational problems led to addictive behavior.

RP: _____

_____

the stress of the current occupation. (19, 20)

15. List five ways in which working a program of recovery will improve occupational problems. (18, 21)

16. Make written plans to change employment to a job that will be supportive to recovery. (22)

17. List five ways in which a higher power can assist in recovery from occupational problems and addictive behavior. (23, 24)

18. Turn the stress of the occupational problems and the urge for addictive behavior over to a higher power at least once a day. (23, 24)

19. Honestly acknowledge the negative impact that addiction has had on work performance. (7, 25)

20. Share with the employer a written personal recovery plan that includes regular attendance at recovery group meetings and any treatment that is necessary to recover from addiction and occupational problems. (15, 26)

21. Discuss the grief over retirement, and make written plans to replace addictive behavior with specific constructive activities. (27)

22. Family members verbalize a connection between occupational problems and addictive behavior. (28, 29)

9. Help the client to see why his/her current employment is a high risk for relapse (e.g., coworkers' addictions, job dissatisfaction, supervisor conflict, work hours too long, absence from his/her family due to travel, ethical conflicts, etc.).
   RP: _____
   _____

10. Probe and clarify emotions surrounding the client's vocational situation.
    RP: _____
    _____

11. Assess and make the client aware of his/her cognitive messages and the schema that is connected with vocational stress.
    RP: _____
    _____

12. Train the client in the development of more realistic, healthy cognitive messages that relieve anxiety and depression.
    RP: _____
    _____

13. Confront catastrophizing the situation leading to immobilizing anxiety.
    RP: _____
    _____

14. Reinforce acceptance of responsibility for personal feelings and behavior.
    RP: _____
    _____

23. Family members verbalize what each can do to assist the client in recovery. (30)

—. _____
　　_____

—. _____
　　_____

—. _____
　　_____

15. Help the client to develop a written plan to resolve occupational problems and maximize recovery (e.g., regular attendance at recovery groups, regular drug testing, management monitors recovery plan, honesty with management and coworkers, etc.).
RP: _____

_____

16. Meet with the client and his/her employer to educate the supervisor about addiction and to gain support for treatment and recovery.
RP: _____

_____

17. Using modeling, role playing, and behavior rehearsal, have the client practice telling his/her coworkers and employer the truth about his/her addictive behavior and plans for recovery.
RP: _____

_____

18. Help the client to learn the skills that are necessary to remain abstinent in his/her current work environment (e.g., honesty with management and coworkers, regular recovery group meetings, using a sponsor, eliciting the support of management, continued treatment, etc.).
RP: _____

_____

19. Use role playing, behavior rehearsal, and modeling to teach the client assertiveness skills.

    RP: _____

    _____

20. Help the client to develop the skills to reduce job stress and improve employment satisfaction (e.g., time management; relaxation; exercise; assertiveness; reducing responsibilities, work hours, and travel time; realistic expectations of work performance, etc.).

    RP: _____

    _____

21. Teach the client how working a 12-step recovery program will improve occupational problems.

    RP: _____

    _____

22. Help the client to accept the need to change jobs to employment that will be more supportive to recovery.

    RP: _____

    _____

23. Teach the client about the 12-step program's concept of a higher power and how this can assist in recovery.

    RP: _____

    _____

24. Using a 12-step recovery program's step-three exercise, teach the client how to turn problems over to the

higher power. Assign him/her to practice turning problems over to a higher power at least once a day.
RP: _____

_____

25. Help the client to be honest with himself/herself, coworkers, and management about the negative impact of addictive behavior on job performance; list the negative consequences of addictive behavior on employment.
RP: _____

_____

26. Use role playing, modeling, and behavior rehearsal to teach the client to share his/her personal recovery plan with the employer.
RP: _____

_____

27. Help the client to work through the grief of retirement, and then make plans to engage in constructive activities (e.g., volunteering, hobbies, exercise, social contacts, special-interest groups, 12-step recovery program meetings, continuing education, religious involvement, etc.).
RP: _____

_____

28. Discuss with family members the connection between

occupational problems and addictive behavior.

RP: _____

_____

29. In a family session, review what each member can do to assist the client in recovery.

RP: _____

_____

30. Provide the family members with information about the client's occupational problems and the steps that he/she must take to recover successfully.

RP: _____

_____

__. _____

_____

RP: _____

_____

__. _____

_____

RP: _____

_____

__. _____

_____

RP: _____

_____

DIAGNOSTIC SUGGESTIONS

Axis I: V62.81   Relational Problem NOS
             V62.2   Occupational Problem
             V62.89   Phase of Life Problem
             300.02   Generalized Anxiety Disorder
             311   Depressive Disorder NOS
             296.xx   Major Depressive Disorder

             _____   _____

             _____   _____

Axis II: 301.7   Antisocial Personality Disorder
             301.0   Paranoid Personality Disorder

             _____   _____

             _____   _____

OPPOSITIONAL DEFIANT BEHAVIOR

BEHAVIORAL DEFINITIONS

1. History of explosive, aggressive outbursts.
2. Often argues with authority figures over requests or rules.
3. Deliberately annoys people as a means of gaining control.
4. Tendency to blame others rather than accept the responsibility for own problems.
5. Angry overreaction to perceived disapproval, rejection, or criticism.
6. Passively withholds feelings, then explodes in a violent rage.
7. Abuses substances to cope with angry feelings and relinquish responsibility for aggression.
8. Persistent pattern of challenging or disrespecting authority figures.
9. Body language of tense muscles (e.g., clenched fists or jaw, glaring looks, or refusal to make eye contact).
10. Views aggression as a means to achieve needed power and control.
11. Use of verbally abusive language.
12. Harbors deep resentments toward authority figures.

—. _____
_____

—. _____
_____

—. _____
_____

LONG-TERM GOALS

1. Maintain a program of recovery that is free of addiction and oppositional defiant behavior.

2. Decrease the frequency of the occurrence of angry thoughts, feelings, and behaviors.
3. Follow family rules without opposition or complaint.
4. Stop blaming others for problems, and begin to accept responsibility for own feelings, thoughts, and behaviors.
5. Learn and implement stress management skills to reduce the level of stress and the irritability that accompanies it.
6. Understand the relationship between angry feelings and the feelings of hurt and worthlessness that are experienced in the family of origin.
7. Learn the assertiveness skills that are necessary to reduce angry feelings and solve problems in a less aggressive and more constructive manner.

—. _____
_____

—. _____
_____

—. _____
_____

SHORT-TERM OBJECTIVES

1. Keep a daily anger log. (1)
2. Identify and verbalize the pain and hurt of past and current life that fuels oppositional defiant behavior. (2, 3, 10)
3. Verbalize an understanding of how family dynamics lead to oppositional defiant behavior. (2, 3, 10)
4. Reduce the frequency and severity of temper outbursts and other aggressive behaviors. (4, 5, 6)

THERAPEUTIC INTERVENTIONS

1. Assign the client to keep a daily anger log, writing down each situation that produced angry feelings, the thoughts associated with the situation. Then, rate the level of anger on a scale from 1 to 100; process the anger log and assist in uncovering the dysfunctional thoughts that trigger anger.
   *RP: _____
   _____

_____

*RP = responsible professional.

5. Increase the frequency of assertive behaviors while reducing the frequency of aggressive behaviors. (5, 6)

6. Verbalize regret and remorse for the harmful consequences of oppositional defiant behavior, as well as the steps that are necessary to forgive self and react more constructively. (7)

7. Decrease the frequency of blaming others, and increase the frequency of positive, self-enhancing self-talk. (8, 9)

8. Verbalize an understanding of the relationship between the feelings of worthlessness and hurt that are experienced in the family of origin and the current feelings of anger. (2, 9, 10)

9. Report a termination of assuming to know the negative thoughts, intentions, and feelings of others, and start asking others for more information. (10)

10. Verbalize an understanding of the need for and process of forgiving others to reduce oppositional defiant behavior. (2, 11, 16)

11. Verbalize an understanding of how angry thoughts and feelings can lead to the increased risk of addiction. List instances when oppositional defiant behavior has resulted in addiction. (12, 13)

2. Assign the client to list experiences of life that have hurt and lead to oppositional defiant behavior.
RP: _____
_____

3. Probe the family dynamics that lead to the oppositional defiant behavior.
RP: _____
_____

4. Teach the client how anger blocks the awareness of pain, discharges uncomfortable feelings, erases guilt, and places the blame for problems on someone else.
RP: _____
_____

5. Teach the client the impulse control skill of "stop, look, listen, think, and plan" before acting.
RP: _____
_____

6. Teach assertiveness and its benefits through role playing and modeling, assigning appropriate reading material (e.g., *Your Perfect Right* by Alberti and Emmons), or participating in an assertiveness training group.
RP: _____
_____

7. Use modeling and role reversal to make the client more aware of the negative consequences that his/her oppositional defiant behavior has had on others who

12. List five reasons why angry thoughts, feelings, and behaviors increase the risk of relapse into addiction. (13, 14)

13. Make a list of the thoughts that trigger hurt or angry feelings, and replace each thought with a more positive and accurate thought that is supportive to self and recovery. (1, 13, 14, 16)

14. Practice relaxation skills twice a day for 10 to 20 minutes. (15)

15. Report instances of the implementation of the stress management skills of prayer to a higher power, relaxation, sharing feelings, regular exercise, and healthy self-talk. (15, 16, 17, 18)

16. Implement proactive steps to meet the needs of self without expecting other people to meet those needs, and angrily blaming them when they fail to do so. (6, 19)

17. Report the implementation of stopping the impulsive angry reaction, opening the hands, relaxing the muscles, using reassuring self-talk, and speaking in a soft voice when feeling angry. (20)

18. Parents will verbalize an understanding of positive and negative rewards and use them effectively in setting rules. (21)

have been the target or witness to the oppositional defiant behavior.
RP: _____
_____

8. Help the client to develop a list of positive, self-enhancing statements to use daily in building a positive and accurate self-image. Use role playing and modeling to demonstrate implementation of positive self-talk.
RP: _____
_____

9. Probe the patterns of violence, anger, and suspicion in the family of origin, and help the client to see how these problems lead to a tendency to scc people and situations as dangerous and threatening.
RP: _____
_____

10. Teach the client about the tendency to read malicious intent into the words and actions of others. Then, use modeling, role playing, and behavior rehearsal to show the client how to ask other people what they think and feel.
RP: _____
_____

11. Assist the client in identifying who he/she needs to forgive, and educate client as to the long-term process

19. Parents write a plan for dealing with the client's suicidal threats, violent behavior, running away, and poor school performance. (21, 22)

20. Parents develop a written plan for nurturing each family member through positive interaction and positive events each week. (21, 23)

21. Practice the time-out technique five times with the therapist and significant other. Keep a record of the utilization of the technique in daily interaction. (20, 24)

22. Develop an aftercare program that details what to do when feeling angry or frustrated. (17, 24, 25, 26)

—. _____
   _____

—. _____
   _____

—. _____
   _____

that is involved in forgiveness versus a magical single event. Recommend reading *Forgive and Forget* by Smedes.
RP: _____
_____

12. Educate the client about the tendency to use addictive behavior as a means of relieving uncomfortable feelings. Develop a list of several instances of this occurrence.
RP: _____
_____

13. Teach the client about the high-risk situations of strong negative emotions, social pressure, interpersonal conflict, strong positive emotions, and testing personal control. Discuss how anger, as a strong negative emotion, places them at high risk for addiction.
RP: _____
_____

14. Assist the client in identifying five reasons why anger increases the risk of relapse.
RP: _____
_____

15. Assist the client in identifying his/her distorted thoughts that trigger anger; teach him/her to replace these thoughts with realistic, positive thoughts.
RP: _____
_____

16. Teach the client how to turn perpetrators of pain over to his/her higher power for judgment and punishment.
RP: _____

_____

17. Teach the client progressive relaxation skills, and encourage their utilization twice a day for 10 to 20 minutes.
RP: _____

_____

18. Teach the client the stress management skills of regular exercise and positive self-talk and their benefits.
RP: _____

_____

19. Teach the client the importance of actively attending Alcoholics Anonymous/Narcotics Anonymous (AA/NA) meetings, getting a sponsor, reinforcing people around him/her, sharing feelings, and developing pleasurable leisure activities.
RP: _____

_____

20. Assist the client in developing a list of his/her own needs and wishes, and then the personal actions that are necessary to attain these rather than being angry with others for not meeting his/her needs and wishes.
RP: _____

_____

21. Using modeling, role playing, and behavior rehearsal,
show the client how to stop
the impulse to react with
anger; relax the muscles;
use positive, comforting
self-talk; and speak softly in
frustrating, threatening, or
hurtful situations.
RP: _____

_____

22. Using modeling and behavior rehearsal, help the parents to role-play their
response to oppositional defiant behavior; teach them
the use of positive and negative consequences, as well as
consistent rule enforcement.
RP: _____

_____

23. Teach the parents how to
deal with suicidal threats,
violent behavior, running
away, and poor school performance; then, role-play
each situation.
RP: _____

_____

24. Help the parents to develop
a written plan for how to
nurture family members by
doing positive things with
each child each week.
RP: _____

_____

25. Develop a time-out contract
between the client and
his/her significant other.

Role-play the technique with five different situations.

RP: _____

_____

26. Help the client to develop a list of what adaptive action they are going to take when they feel angry in recovery (e.g., calling a sponsor, being assertive rather than aggressive, taking a time-out, praying to a higher power, etc.) to avoid relapse.

RP: _____

_____

__. _____

_____

RP: _____

_____

__. _____

_____

RP: _____

_____

__. _____

_____

RP: _____

_____

DIAGNOSTIC SUGGESTIONS

Axis I: 313.81   Oppositional Defiant Disorder
312.8   Conduct Disorder
296.xx   Bipolar I Disorder
296.89   Bipolar II Disorder
312.34   Intermittent Explosive Disorder
312.30   Impulse-Control Disorder NOS

	309.4	Adjustment Disorder With Mixed Disturbance of Emotions and Conduct
	V71.02	Child or Adolescent Antisocial Behavior
	—————	————————————————————
	—————	————————————————————
Axis II:	301.0	Paranoid Personality Disorder
	301.70	Antisocial Personality Disorder
	301.83	Borderline Personality Disorder
	301.9	Personality Disorder NOS
	301.81	Narcissistic Personality Disorder
	—————	————————————————————
	—————	————————————————————

PARENT-CHILD RELATIONAL PROBLEM

BEHAVIORAL DEFINITIONS

1. A parent's pattern of addiction and dishonesty leading to a child's anger and resentment toward that parent.
2. A parent's verbal or physical abuse toward the child.
3. Frequent arguing and a feeling of emotional distance between the parent and child.
4. A parent's pattern of addictive behavior leads to his/her social isolation and withdrawal.
5. The child has a pattern of oppositional defiance.
6. Poor communication between the parent and child.
7. Parent-child relationship stress triggers addictive behavior, which, in turn, exacerbates the relationship conflicts.
8. A child's involvement in his/her peer group to the exclusion of the parents and family members.
9. All family members have an inability to establish and maintain meaningful, intimate family relationships.

—. _____
_____

—. _____
_____

—. _____
_____

LONG-TERM GOALS

1. Maintain a program of recovery that is free from addiction and parent-child conflicts.

2. Terminate addictive behavior and resolve the parent-child relationship conflicts.
3. Understand the relationship between addictive behavior and parent-child conflicts.
4. Learn and demonstrate healthy communication skills.
5. Decrease parent-child conflict, and increase mutually supportive and pleasurable interaction.
6. Terminate all abusive behavior toward the children.

—. _____
   _____
   _____
—. _____
   _____
   _____
—. _____
   _____

SHORT-TERM OBJECTIVES

1. Verbalize the powerlessness and unmanageability that result from parent-child conflicts and addiction. (1, 2)

2. List five times when addictive behavior led to parent-child relational conflicts. (2, 3, 6)

3. List five occasions when relationship conflicts triggered addictive behavior. (2, 4, 6)

4. Verbalize an acceptance of responsibility for own role in parent-child relationship problems and in choosing addictive behavior as a

THERAPEUTIC INTERVENTIONS

1. Using a step-one exercise (from a 12-step program of recovery), help the client to see how parent-child relational conflicts and addiction lead to powerlessness and unmanageability.
   *RP: _____
   _____

2. Help the client to see how addiction has caused relationship conflicts and how relationship conflicts have precipitated addictive behavior.
   RP: _____
   _____

_____

*RP = responsible professional.

means of coping with the relationship conflicts. (3, 5, 7)

5. Listen to and verbalize acceptance of the perspective
of all family members on
the nature of and causes for
the relational conflicts.
(5, 6, 7)

6. Acknowledge that the child
has been the victim of
abuse. (6, 7, 8, 9, 10)

7. Identify five positive and
five negative aspects of the
current parent-child relationship. (11)

8. Identify three causes for
past and present conflicts
within the parent-child relationship. (5, 7, 12)

9. List three changes that
each family member must
make to restore the rela-
tionship. (7, 9, 13)

10. Each family member list
the changes that he/she believes each person must
make to restore the rela-
tionship. (6, 14)

11. Sign a written plan as to
behaviors that each family
member will change to im-
prove the relationship.
(13, 14, 15)

12. Discuss the problems that
exist in the parent-child relationship, and initiate activities that verbally and
nonverbally promote inti-
macy. (16, 17)

13. Learn and demonstrate
healthy communication
skills. (18, 19, 20)

3. Ask the client to list five instances when addictive behavior led to parent-child
relationship conflicts.
RP: _____
_____

4. Ask the client to list five occasions when relationship
conflicts triggered addictive
behavior.
RP: _____
_____

5. Help the client to accept the
responsibility for his/her
role in the relationship
problems and for choosing
addiction as a reaction to
the conflicts.
RP: _____
_____

6. In a family session, take a
history of the parent-child
relational conflicts; solicit
input from all family members.
RP: _____
_____

7. Confront the client's denial
of responsibility for the parent-child conflict and the
client's projection of all responsibility onto the child.
RP: _____
_____

8. Assess the nature and
severity of the client's abusive behaviors toward the
child; follow through on

14. Make a written plan to increase the quality and frequency of healthy communication with each family member. (19, 20)

15. Make written plans to increase pleasurable activities spent with the parent and child. (21, 22)

16. Write a letter to each family member sharing feelings toward them, and suggest what enjoyable activities they could engage in during recovery. (22)

17. Write a plan for meeting social and emotional needs during aftercare. (21, 23)

18. Develop a personal recovery plan that includes attending recovery groups regularly, getting a sponsor, and any other therapy that is necessary to recover from parent-child relational conflicts and addiction. (24, 25)

19. Encourage each family member to work his/her own program of recovery. (25, 26)

__. _____
   _____

__. _____
   _____

__. _____
   _____

mandatory reporting of any child abuse.
RP: _____
_____

9. Facilitate the immediate protection of the child from any further abuse (e.g., notifying legal authorities of the abuse, temporary placement of the child with other family or a friend, removal of the abusive parent from the home, etc.).
RP: _____
_____

10. Refer the abusive parent to a domestic violence treatment program.
RP: _____
_____

11. Ask the client to list the positive and negative aspects of the parent-child relationship.
RP: _____
_____

12. Assist the client in identifying the causes for past and present conflicts.
RP: _____
_____

13. Assign the client the task of listing the behavioral changes that he/she needs to make and the changes that he/she believes each family member needs to

make to restore the rela-
tionship.

RP: _____

_____

14. Assign each family member
the task of listing the behavioral changes that
he/she needs to make and
the changes that he/she believes the other family
members need to make to
restore the relationship.

RP: _____

_____

15. In a family session, obtain a
written commitment from
each member as to what behaviors each will attempt to
change.

RP: _____

_____

16. In a family session, facilitate a discussion of the parent-child problems, and
make plans to improve intimacy, nurturing, and com-
munication.

RP: _____

_____

17. Using modeling, role playing, and behavior rehearsal,
teach the family members
how to show verbal and
nonverbal affection to each
other (e.g., going for a walk
together, sharing feelings,
doing fun things together,
giving hugs, giving each

other compliments and
praise, etc.).

RP: _____

_____

18. Using modeling, role playing, and behavior rehearsal,
teach the client healthy
communication skills (e.g.,
active listening, reflecting,
sharing feelings, using "I"
messages, etc.)

RP: _____

_____

19. Facilitate a family session
with the focus on teaching
and improving communica-
tion skills.

RP: _____

_____

20. Assign the client to develop
a written plan as to the
time, place, and amount of
time that will be devoted to
private, one-to-one communication with each family
member each day.

RP: _____

_____

21. Help the family to make a
list of the pleasurable activities that they would like to
do together. Help them to
make plans to become in-
volved in at least one activity each week.

RP: _____

_____

22. Assign the client to write a
letter to each family member sharing how he/she

feels and suggesting pleasurable activities that they could engage in together during recovery.
RP: _____

_____

23. Encourage and support the client in building new social relationships that will meet his/her emotional needs, increase satisfaction with life, replace addictive behavior, and reinforce social skills.
RP: _____

_____

24. Help the client to develop a written personal recovery plan that includes attending recovery group meetings regularly, getting a sponsor, and any other therapy that is necessary to recover from parent-child relational problems and addiction.
RP: _____

_____

25. Teach the client and the family about twelve-step recovery groups (Alanon, Narcanon, Alateen, etc.)
RP: _____

_____

26. Teach the family the importance of each family member working his/her own program of recovery.
RP: _____

_____

—. _____

_____

RP: _____

_____

—. _____

_____

RP: _____

_____

—. _____

_____

RP: _____

_____

DIAGNOSTIC SUGGESTIONS

Axis I: V61.20   Parent-Child Relational Problem
              V62.81   Relational Problem NOS
              V61.21   Physical Abuse of Child
              V61.21   Sexual Abuse of Child
              V61.21   Neglect of Child

              _____   _____

              _____   _____

Axis II: 301.70   Antisocial Personality Disorder
              301.20   Schizoid Personality Disorder
              301.81   Narcissistic Personality Disorder

              _____   _____

              _____   _____

PARTNER RELATIONAL CONFLICTS

BEHAVIORAL DEFINITIONS

1. Relationship stress that provides an excuse for addiction and addictive behavior that exacerbates the relationship conflicts.
2. Lack of communication with spouse or significant other.
3. Marital separation due to addictive behavior.
4. Pending divorce.
5. A pattern of superficial or lack of communication, frequent arguing, infrequent sexual enjoyment, and a feeling of emotional distance from partner.
6. A pattern of substance use leading to social isolation and withdrawal.
7. A pattern of verbal or physical abuse that is present in the relationship.
8. Involvement in multiple superficial relationships, often with sexual intercourse, but without commitment or meaningful intimacy.
9. Inability to establish and maintain meaningful, intimate interpersonal relationships.

__. _____
_____

__. _____
_____

__. _____
_____

LONG-TERM GOALS

1. Maintain a program of recovery that is free of addiction and partner relational conflicts.
2. Terminate addictive behavior and resolve the relationship conflicts that increase the risk of relapse.
3. Understand the relationship between addictive behavior and partner relational conflicts.
4. Accept termination of the relationship, and make plans to move forward in life.
5. Decrease partner relational conflict, and increase mutually supportive pleasurable interaction.
6. Develop the skills that are necessary to maintain open, effective communication, sexual intimacy, and enjoyable time together.

—. _____

_____

—. _____

_____

—. _____

_____

SHORT-TERM OBJECTIVES

1. Verbalize the powerlessness and unmanageability that result from partner relational conflicts and addiction. (1, 2)
2. List five times when addictive behavior led to partner relational conflicts. (2, 3, 6)
3. List five occasions when relationship conflicts led to addictive behavior. (2, 4, 6)
4. Verbalize an acceptance of the responsibility for own

THERAPEUTIC INTERVENTIONS

1. Using a 12-step recovery program's step-one exercise, help the client to see how partner relational conflicts and addictive behavior led to powerlessness and unmanageability.

   *RP: _____

   _____

2. Help the client to see how addictive behavior has caused relationship conflicts and how relationship

---

*RP = responsible professional.

role in relationship problems and in choosing addictive behavior as a means of coping with the relationship conflicts. (3, 5)

5. Meet with the significant other or spouse to listen to and accept his/her perspective on the causes for the relational conflicts. (6, 7)

6. Partner and the client identify the positive and negative aspects of the current relationship. (6, 7)

7. Identify the causes for past and present conflicts within the relationship. (6, 7, 8)

8. List the changes that each partner must make to restore the relationship. (6, 7, 8, 9)

9. Spouse or significant other to list the changes that each partner must make to restore the relationship. (6, 7, 10)

10. Develop a plan as to behaviors that each partner will change to improve the relationship. (9, 10, 11)

11. Discuss the sexual problems that exist in the relationship. (12)

12. Both partners list changes that the other could make to improve mutual sexual satisfaction. (13)

13. Demonstrate the ability to show affection verbally and nonverbally. (14)

conflicts have precipitated addictive behavior.
RP: _____
   _____

3. Ask the client to list five instances when addictive behavior led to relationship conflict.
RP: _____
   _____

4. Ask the client to list five occasions when relationship conflicts led to addictive behavior.
RP: _____
   _____

5. Help the client to accept the responsibility for his/her role in the relationship problems and for choosing addictive behavior as a reaction to the conflicts.
RP: _____
   _____

6. In a conjoint session, take a history of the partner relational conflicts; solicit perspective from each partner on each issue.
RP: _____
   _____

7. Ask the client and the partner to list the positive and negative aspects of the relationship.
RP: _____
   _____

14. Learn and demonstrate healthy communication skills. (14, 15, 17, 18)

15. Verbalize a commitment to continued therapy to improve the relationship and maintain gains. (16)

16. Make a written plan to increase the quality and the frequency of healthy communication with the partner. (14, 15, 17, 18)

17. Grieve the loss of the relationship and make plans to move forward in life. (19, 20)

18. Make written plans to increase pleasurable activities spent with the spouse or significant other. (21, 22)

19. Write a letter to the spouse or significant other sharing feelings and asking for support in recovery. (22)

20. Write a plan for meeting social and emotional needs during separation and divorce. (19, 22, 23)

21. Develop a personal recovery plan that includes attending recovery groups regularly, getting a sponsor, and any other therapy that is necessary to recover from partner relational conflicts and addiction. (16, 24)

22. Encourage the significant other or spouse to work his/her own program of recovery. (25)

23. Family members verbalize a connection between part-

8. Assist the client in identifying the causes for past and present conflicts.
   RP: _____
   _____

9. Assign the client the task of listing the behavioral changes that he/she needs to make and the changes that he/she believes the spouse or significant other needs to make to restore the relationship.
   RP: _____
   _____

10. Assign the spouse or significant other the task of listing the behavioral changes that he/she needs to make and the changes that he/she believes the partner needs to make to restore the relationship.
    RP: _____
    _____

11. In a conjoint session, obtain a commitment from each partner as to what behaviors each will attempt to change to improve the relationship.
    RP: _____
    _____

12. In a conjoint session, facilitate a discussion of the sexual problems.
    RP: _____
    _____

13. Solicit input from each partner as to changes that the partner could make

ner relational conflicts and addictive behavior. (26, 27)

24. Family member verbalize what each can do to assist the client in recovery. (28)

__. _____
   _____

__. _____
   _____

__. _____
   _____

to increase mutual sexual satisfaction.

RP: _____
_____

14. Using modeling, role playing, and behavior rehearsal, teach the partners how to show verbal and nonverbal affection to each other (e.g., going for a walk together, talking intimately, holding hands, hugging, dancing, giving each other compliments and praise, etc.).

RP: _____
_____

15. Using modeling, role playing, and behavior rehearsal, teach the client healthy communication skills (e.g., active listening, reflecting, sharing feelings, using "I" messages, etc.).

RP: _____
_____

16. Help the couple to see the importance of continued therapy to improve the relationship and maintain gains.

RP: _____
_____

17. Assign the client to develop a written plan as to the time, place, and amount of time that will be devoted to private, one-to-one communication with his/her partner each day.

RP: _____
_____

18. Facilitate a conjoint session with the focus on improving communication skills.

    RP: _____

    _____

19. Encourage the client to share the grief of losing the significant other or spouse, and help him/her make a written plan to increase social interaction and improve old relationships.

    RP: _____

    _____

20. Encourage and support the client in building new social relationships.

    RP: _____

    _____

21. Help the couple to make a list of the pleasurable activities that they would like to do together. Then, help them to make plans to become involved in one activity each week.

    RP: _____

    _____

22. Assign the client to write a letter to the partner, sharing how he/she feels and suggesting pleasurable activities that they could engage in together during recovery.

    RP: _____

    _____

23. Assist the client in identifying potential sources of emotional and social sup-

port during the stressful time of separation and divorce.

RP: _____

_____

24. Help the client to develop a written personal recovery plan that includes attending recovery group meetings regularly, getting a sponsor, and any other therapy that is necessary to recover from partner relational problems and addictive behavior.

RP: _____

_____

25. Teach the client and the significant other or spouse about 12-step recovery groups (Alanon, Narcanon, etc.) and other support groups for people in the middle of divorce.

RP: _____

_____

26. Discuss with family members the connection between partner relational conflicts and addictive behavior.

RP: _____

_____

27. In a family session, review what each member can do to assist the client in recovery.

RP: _____

_____

28. Provide the family members with information about partner relational conflicts and the steps that the client

must take to recover suc-
cessfully.

RP: _____

_____

___. _____

_____

RP: _____

_____

___. _____

_____

RP: _____

_____

___. _____

_____

RP: _____

_____

DIAGNOSTIC SUGGESTIONS

Axis I:	V61.1	Partner Relational Problem
	V62.81	Relational Problem NOS
	V61.12	Physical Abuse of Adult (*by partner*)
	V62.83	Physical Abuse of Adult (*by person other than partner*)
	V61.12	Sexual Abuse of Adult (*by partner*)
	V62.83	Sexual Abuse of Adult (*by person other than partner*)
	995.81	Physical Abuse of Adult (*victim*)
	_____	_____
	_____	_____
Axis II:	301.7	Antisocial Personality Disorder
	301.20	Schizoid Personality Disorder
	301.81	Narcissistic Personality Disorder
	_____	_____
	_____	_____

PEER GROUP NEGATIVITY

BEHAVIORAL DEFINITIONS

1. Many friends and relatives are chemically dependent and encourage the client to join them in addictive behavior.
2. Peers are involved in the sale of illegal substances and encourage the client to join them.
3. Peer group is not supportive of recovery from addiction.
4. Involved in a gang that is supportive of criminal activity and addictive behavior.
5. Peers laugh and joke about recovery and continue to engage in addictive behavior.
6. Peers engage in and encourage gambling.

—. _____

_____

—. _____

_____

_____

—. _____

_____

LONG-TERM GOALS

1. Maintain a program of recovery that is free of addiction and the negative influence of peers.
2. Understand that continuing to associate with the current peer group increases the risk for relapse.
3. Develop a new peer group that is free from addictive behavior and supportive of working a program of recovery.
4. Educate family members about addiction and the need for recovery.

5. Learn the skills that are necessary to make new friends who are not addicts.

—. _____

_____

—. _____

_____

—. _____

_____

SHORT-TERM OBJECTIVES

1. Verbalize the powerlessness and unmanageability that result from peer group negativity and addictive behavior. (1, 2)

2. Identify several times when peer group negativity led to addiction. (2, 3, 4)

3. Verbalize an acceptance of the need for breaking ties with the current peer group. (2, 3, 4)

4. Verbalize how peer group negativity and addiction meets the 12-step recovery program's concept of *insanity*. (2, 5)

5. Accept the 12-step recovery program's step two by verbalizing how a higher power can restore self to sanity. (5, 6)

6. List five times when peer group negativity lead to criminal activity. (2, 3, 7)

THERAPEUTIC INTERVENTIONS

1. Using a 12-step recovery program's step-one exercise, help the client to see the powerlessness and unmanageability that result from peer group negativity and addiction.
   *RP: _____

   _____

2. Help the client to see the relationship between his/her peer group and addictive behavior, particularly how often the peer group encouraged the addictive behavior.
   RP: _____

   _____

3. Assign the client to list instances when peers encouraged addictive behavior.
   RP: _____

   _____

4. Reinforce the client's verbalized intent to break ties with

---

*RP = responsible professional.

7. List 10 reasons why the peer group has to be changed to maintain abstinence. (4, 8)

8. Verbalize grief over the loss of the peer group, and make plans for meeting new people in recovery. (4, 9)

9. Verbalize why obeying the law is essential for working a program of recovery. (7, 10)

10. List five ways in which a higher power can assist in recovery from peer group negativity and addiction. (6, 11)

11. Turn one problem over to a higher power each day. Keep a journal of this behavior, and discuss it with the primary therapist. (6, 11, 12)

12. Make a written plan as to how to increase social interaction with a new peer group that is supportive of recovery. (13)

13. Attend regular recovery group meetings, and stay for coffee and conversation after each meeting. (13, 14)

14. Write an autobiography detailing the exact nature of the wrongs committed and how these relate to the negative peer group and addiction. (15)

15. Practice to engage in addictive behavior in high-risk situations. (16)

the current peer group; empathize with the difficulty in leaving friends behind and making new friends.

RP: _____

_____

5. Using a 12-step recovery program's step-two exercise, help the client to see how peer group negativity and addiction meet the 12-step program concept of *insane*.

RP: _____

_____

6. Teach the client about the 12-step recovery program's concept of a higher power and how this power can restore the client to sanity.

RP: _____

_____

7. Assign the client to list five times when the peer group lead him or her into criminal activity.

RP: _____

_____

8. Help the client to see the reasons why continuing to associate with the current peer group increases the risk for relapse.

RP: _____

_____

9. Help the client to grieve the loss of the old peer group and make plans to develop new friends in recovery.

RP: _____

_____

16. Meet with a temporary sponsor and make plans to attend recovery group meetings. (13, 14, 17)

17. Make a list of peers who are positive and negative to recovery efforts. (18)

18. Family members indicate who in the client's peer group needs to be avoided in recovery. (19)

19. Family members verbalize a connection between peer group negativity and addictive behavior. (20, 21)

20. Family members verbalize what each can do to assist the client in recovery. (22)

—. _____
   _____

—. _____
   _____

—. _____
   _____

10. Teach the client about the 12-step recovery program's concept of rigorous honesty and why obeying the law is essential in working a program of recovery.
RP: _____
   _____

11. Assist the client in identifying the ways that a higher power can assist him/her.
RP: _____
   _____

12. Using a 12-step recovery program's step-three exercise, teach the client about turning problems over to the higher power each day; then, assign him or her to use this step at least once a day. Have the client keep a record of using step three and discuss how it worked.
RP: _____
   _____

13. Assign the client to make a written plan about how he/she plans to increase social contact with a new peer group that is positive toward recovery.
RP: _____
   _____

14. Encourage the client to stay for coffee and conversation after each 12-step recovery program meeting to increase social skills and make new, positive friends.
RP: _____
   _____

15. Using a 12-step recovery program's step-four inventory, assign the client to write an autobiography detailing the exact nature of his/her wrongs and how these relate to the negative peer group and addictive behavior.
RP: _____

_____

16. Using modeling, role playing, and behavior rehearsal, teach the client refusal to engage in addictive behavior, then practice refusal in the high-risk situations for relapse (e.g., negative emotions, social pressure, interpersonal conflict, positive emotions, and testing personal control).
RP: _____

_____

17. Encourage and facilitate the client meeting his/her 12-step program temporary sponsor, and discuss plans for recovery.
RP: _____

_____

18. Help the client to make a list of all peers who are positive or negative toward recovery.
RP: _____

_____

19. In a family session, have the family members indicate which peers need to

be avoided in recovery and why.

RP: _____

_____

20. Discuss with family members the connection between peer group negativity and addictive behavior.

RP: _____

_____

21. In a family session, review what each member can do to assist the client in recovery.

RP: _____

_____

22. Provide the family members with information about peer group negativity and the steps that the client must take to recover successfully.

RP: _____

_____

__. _____

_____

RP: _____

_____

__. _____

_____

RP: _____

_____

__. _____

_____

RP: _____

_____

244 THE ADDICTION TREATMENT PLANNER

DIAGNOSTIC SUGGESTIONS

Axis I:	312.82	Conduct Disorder, Adolescent Onset Type
	309.4	Adjustment Disorder With Mixed Disturbance of Emotions and Conduct
	309.3	Adjustment Disorder With Disturbance of Conduct
	V62.81	Relational Problem NOS
	V71.01	Adult Antisocial Behavior
	V71.02	Child or Adolescent Antisocial Behavior
	_____	_____
	_____	_____
Axis II:	301.70	Antisocial Personality Disorder
	301.83	Borderline Personality Disorder
	301.81	Narcissistic Personality Disorder
	301.82	Avoidant Personality Disorder
	_____	_____
	_____	_____

POSTTRAUMATIC STRESS
DISORDER (PTSD)

BEHAVIORAL DEFINITIONS

1. Past experience with a traumatic event that involved actual or threatened death or serious injury and caused a reaction of intense fear or helplessness.
2. Recurrent intrusive memories or dreams of the event.
3. Acting or feeling as if the trauma were recurring.
4. Intense distress when exposed to reminders of the trauma.
5. Avoidance of activities, places, or people that are associated with the event.
6. Avoidance of feelings, thoughts, or conversations about the trauma.
7. Periods of disassociation or inability to remember parts of the trauma.
8. Persistent symptoms of increased autonomic arousal (e.g., difficulty sleeping, irritability, difficulty concentrating, hypervigilance, or exaggerated startle response).
9. Verbally and/or physically violent threats or behavior.
10. A pattern of intimate relationship, coworker, and authority conflict.
11. Engages in addictive behavior as an escape from pain that is associated with the trauma.

__. _____

_____

__. _____

_____

_____

__. _____

_____

LONG-TERM GOALS

1. Maintain a program of recovery that is free of addiction and post-traumatic stress.
2. Resolve the emotional effects of the past trauma, and terminate the negative impact on current behavior.
3. Terminate the destructive behaviors that serve to maintain escape and denial, while implementing behaviors that promote healing, acceptance of the past events, and responsible living.
4. Learn the coping skills that are necessary to bring posttraumatic stress and addiction under control.
5. Understand posttraumatic stress symptoms and how they led to addiction in a self-defeating attempt to cope.

—. _____

_____

—. _____

_____

—. _____

_____

SHORT-TERM OBJECTIVES	THERAPEUTIC INTERVENTIONS
1. Verbalize the powerlessness and unmanageability that result from posttraumatic stress and addictive behavior. (1)	1. Using a 12-step recovery program's step-one exercise, help the client to see that posttraumatic stress and addictive behavior lead to powerlessness and unmanageability.
2. Describe the traumatic events and the resultant feelings and thoughts in the past and present. (2)	*RP: _____ _____
3. List 10 times that posttraumatic stress symptoms led to addictive behavior. (3)	2. Explore the past traumatic event(s) that the client has experienced and the associated feelings and thoughts.
4. List the ways in which a 12-step recovery program	RP: _____ _____

_____

*RP = responsible professional.

can assist in recovery from posttraumatic stress and addictive behavior. (4)

5. List the feelings that lead to disassociation. (2, 5)

6. Visit the physician to see if psychopharmacological intervention is warranted. (6)

7. Take psychotropic medications as directed, and report as to their effectiveness and side effects. (7, 8)

8. Verbalize five ways in which a higher power can assist in recovery from posttraumatic stress and addiction. (9)

9. Turn posttraumatic stress and addiction over to a higher power each day. Log this behavior, and discuss it with the primary therapist. (9, 10)

10. Practice relaxation skills twice a day for at least 10 to 20 minutes. (11)

11. Cooperate with systematic desensitization sessions using imagery of the past trauma and current triggers for anxiety. (12)

12. Identify negative self-talk and catastrophizing that is associated with past trauma and current stimulus triggers for anxiety. (2, 13)

13. Approach actual stimuli in vivo that trigger memories and feelings associated with past trauma. Stay

3. Assign the client to list 10 times when symptoms of posttraumatic stress led to addictive behavior.
RP: _____
_____

4. Teach the client about the 12-step recovery program, and discuss how it can assist in his/her recovery.
RP: _____
_____

5. Help the client to uncover the feelings that revolve around the past traumatic event and lead to dissociation.
RP: _____
_____

6. Physician examine the client, order psychotropic medications as indicated, titrate medications, and monitor for side effects and effectiveness.
RP: _____
_____

7. Medical staff administer medications as ordered by the physician.
RP: _____
_____

8. Monitor the client for psychotropic prescription compliance, side effects, and effectiveness.
RP: _____
_____

calm using relaxation techniques and positive self-talk. (11, 12, 13, 14)

14. Practice turning perpetrators of painful trauma over to a higher power. (9, 10, 15)

15. Sleep without being disturbed by dreams of the trauma. (11, 12, 16)

16. Express anger without rage, aggressiveness, or intimidation. (17, 18)

17. Practice stress management skills to reduce overall stress levels and craving. (10, 11, 19)

18. Develop a written personal recovery plan that details the steps to follow to maintain abstinence from addictive behavior and recover from posttraumatic stress. (20)

19. Verbalize five reasons why working on a program of recovery is essential to recover from posttraumatic stress and addictive behavior. (20, 21)

20. Family members verbalize a connection between posttraumatic stress and addictive behavior. (22, 23)

21. Family members verbalize what each can do to assist the client in recovery. (24)

—. _____

_____

9. Teach the client about the 12-step recovery program's concept of a higher power and how this can be used in recovery.
RP: _____

_____

10. Using a 12-step recovery program's step-three exercise, teach the client how to turn problems over to a higher power. Have the client keep a record of this, and then discuss how he/she felt using the step.
RP: _____

_____

11. Using progressive relaxation, biofeedback, or hypnosis, teach the client how to relax. Assign him/her to relax twice a day for 10 to 20 minutes.
RP: _____

_____

12. Using imaginal systematic desensitization, have the client experience the past trauma and current triggers for anxiety until the anxious avoidance reaction is terminated.
RP: _____

_____

13. Explore the client's negative self-talk that is associated with the past trauma and the predictions of un-

—. _____
    _____
—. _____
    _____

successful coping or catastrophizing.

RP: _____

   _____

14. Encourage the client to ap-
    proach actual stimuli that
    have been avoided, which
    trigger thoughts and feel-
    ings associated with the
    past trauma. Urge the use
    of relaxation, deep breath-
    ing, and positive self-talk.

    RP: _____

       _____

15. Encourage the client to turn
    perpetrators of pain over to
    a higher power.

    RP: _____

       _____

16. Monitor the client's sleep
    pattern, and encourage the
    use of relaxation and posi-
    tive imagery as aids to in-
    duce sleep.

    RP: _____

       _____

17. Review triggers to anger
    outbursts, and teach the
    negative consequences of
    loss of control.

    RP: _____

       _____

18. Use role playing and be-
    havior rehearsal to teach
    assertive, respectful expres-
    sion of angry feelings.

    RP: _____

       _____

19. Teach the client stress management skills (e.g., relaxation exercises, physical exercise, talking about problems, going to meetings, getting a sponsor, etc.) to reduce the level of anxiety and increase a sense of mastery over the environment.
RP: _____

_____

20. Help the client to develop a personal recovery plan that includes attending recovery group meetings regularly, getting a sponsor, taking medications as directed, follow-up visits with therapist or doctor.
RP: _____

_____

21. Assist the client in listing reasons why he/she should faithfully adhere to a recovery plan.
RP: _____

_____

22. Discuss with family members the connection between posttraumatic stress disorder (PTSD) and addictive behavior.
RP: _____

_____

23. In a family session, review what each member can do to assist the client in recovery.
RP: _____

_____

24. Provide the family members
with information about
PTSD and the steps that
the client must take to recover successfully.

RP: _____

_____

___. _____

_____

RP: _____

_____

___. _____

_____

RP: _____

_____

___. _____

_____

RP: _____

_____

DIAGNOSTIC SUGGESTIONS

Axis I:
309.81	Posttraumatic Stress Disorder
300.14	Dissociative Identity Disorder
300.6	Depersonalization Disorder
300.15	Dissociative Disorder NOS
309.xx	Adjustment Disorder
995.54	Physical Abuse of Child (*victim*)
V61.21	Sexual Abuse of Child
V61.12	Sexual Abuse of Adult (*by partner*)
V62.83	Sexual Abuse of Adult (*by person other than partner*)
308.3	Acute Stress Disorder
_____	_____
_____	_____

Axis II:
301.83	Borderline Personality Disorder
301.9	Personality Disorder NOS
_____	_____
_____	_____

PSYCHOSIS

BEHAVIORAL DEFINITIONS

1. Bizarre content of thought (delusions of grandeur, persecution, reference, influence, control, somatic sensations, or infidelity).
2. Illogical form of thought/speech (loose association of ideas in speech, incoherence; illogical thinking; vague, abstract, or repetitive speech; neologisms, perseverations, and clanging).
3. Perception disturbance (hallucinations, primarily auditory but occasionally visual or olfactory).
4. Disturbed affect (blunted, none, flattened, or inappropriate).
5. Lost sense of self (loss of ego boundaries, lack of identity, blatant confusion).
6. Volition diminished (inadequate interest, drive, or ability to follow a course of action to its logical conclusion; pronounced ambivalence or cessation of goal-directed activity).
7. Relationship withdrawal (withdrawal from involvement with the external world and a preoccupation with egocentric ideas and fantasies, alienation feelings).
8. Psychomotor abnormalities (marked decrease in reactivity to environment; various catatonic patterns such as stupor, rigidity, excitement, posturing, or negativism; unusual mannerisms or grimacing).
9. Inability to adequately care for own basic physical needs.
10. Potentially harmful to self or others.
11. Engages in substance abuse, which exacerbates psychotic symptoms.

__. _____
    _____
    _____

__. _____
    _____
    _____

__. _____

LONG-TERM GOALS

1. Control or eliminate active psychotic symptoms such that supervised functioning is positive and medication is taken consistently.
2. Significantly reduce or eliminate hallucinations and/or delusions.
3. Eliminate acute, reactive, psychotic symptoms and return to normal functioning in affect, thinking, and relating.
4. Stabilize functioning adequate to allow treatment in outpatient
   settings.
5. Develop adaptive methods to cope with symptoms and seek treatment when necessary.
6. Terminate substance abuse.

__. _____

__. _____

__. _____

SHORT-TERM OBJECTIVES	THERAPEUTIC INTERVENTIONS
1. Accept and understand that distressing symptoms are due to a mental illness and addictive behavior. (1, 2, 3)	1. Determine if the client's psychosis is of a brief, reactive nature or chronic with prodromal and reactive elements.
2. Cooperate with a psychiatric evaluation to assess the need for psychotropic medication. (4)	*RP: _____ _____
3. Take antipsychotic medications consistently as ordered by physician. (5, 6, 7)	

---
*RP = responsible professional.

4. Understand the necessity for taking antipsychotic medications, and agree to cooperate with prescribed care. (7, 8)

5. Comply with an examination to evaluate for brain tumors, dementia, or other contributing organic factors. (9, 42)

6. Describe auditory and visual hallucinations to staff, and accept a reality-based perception from others. (8, 10, 12, 13)

7. Verbalize delusional thoughts regarding irrational fear of harm from others or other distortions of reality regarding powers or traits of self or others. (11, 12, 13)

8. Verbalize a trust of others that is contrary to earlier beliefs of persecution or plotting of harm to self. (12, 13, 14)

9. Demonstrate reduction in thought disturbance by reporting less frequent and less severe hallucinations. (7, 13, 14, 15, 16)

10. Verbalize a cessation of hallucinations. (7, 13, 14, 15, 16)

11. Terminate bizarre behavior. (5, 7, 14, 16, 17)

12. Discuss progress toward reality orientation, appropriate affect, organized thought, and improved relational skills. (16, 17, 18)

2. Explore the client's family history for serious mental illness.
   RP: _____
   _____

3. Evaluate the severity of the client's disturbance of reality perception and frequency of intrusive irrational thoughts; refer him/her for inpatient care, if necessary.
   RP: _____
   _____

4. Psychiatrist evaluate the client to determine the need for antipsychotic medications.
   RP: _____
   _____

5. Psychiatrist prescribe medication to the client and adjust dosage as necessary to increase effectiveness and reduce side effects.
   RP: _____
   _____

6. Staff to administer psychotropic medication to the client.
   RP: _____
   _____

7. Monitor the client's prescribed psychotropic medication for compliance, effectiveness, and side effects.
   RP: _____
   _____

13. Begin to show limited social functioning by responding appropriately to friendly encounters. (14, 19)

14. Initiate contact with others, and report feeling comfortable (not threatened) by the interaction. (14, 19, 20)

15. Engage in social interaction that is reality-based, coherent, and characterized by appropriate affect, subject-focused, logical, and organized. (7, 14, 19, 20)

16. Tend to own basic needs of dress, hygiene, feeding self, grooming, and toileting without direction from others. (21, 22)

17. Verbalize or write a plan for constructive activities for the day, and follow through on implementation of the plan. (22, 23, 24)

18. Attend a therapy group and share thoughts and feelings that are organized, logical, and appropriate. (25, 26, 27)

19. Attend a therapy group and demonstrate appropriate social skills (no interruption, logical sequence to remarks within a group conversation, comprehension of abstract comments). (25, 27, 28)

20. Replace pacing and other agitation behaviors with calm, appropriate sitting and a relaxed demeanor. (7, 29, 30)

8. Urge the client to take medication consistently.
RP: _____
_____

9. Physician provide physical exam to the client to evaluate for organic factors that may contribute to psychosis.
RP: _____
_____

10. Gently provide an alternative, reality-based perception to the client when hallucinations are described.
RP: _____
_____

11. Ask the client to verbalize irrational beliefs and assess their content.
RP: _____
_____

12. Calmly and matter-of-factly confront delusional thoughts, offering a reality-based explanation without debating it.
RP: _____
_____

13. Encourage the client to focus on the reality of external world versus his/her distorted perceptions and beliefs.
RP: _____
_____

14. Reinforce the client for calm, normal appearance, behavior, and speech; gently confront bizarre behaviors (e.g., talking to himself/her-

21. Attend recreational therapy activities and follow the rules of interaction while reporting feeling nonthreatened. (31, 32)

22. Attend an occupational therapy group and participate with actions that show initiative, logic, follow-through, and abstract reasoning. (20, 27, 33)

23. Utilize various art media to express and identify feelings of alienation, fear, and isolation. Engage in an art therapy group discussion to identify feelings, enhance reality focus, and increase social contact. (34, 35)

24. Sleep in a normal pattern of 6 to 9 hours per night without agitation, fears, or disruption. (36)

25. Family to verbalize an understanding that the client's bizarre behavior and irrational thoughts are due to mental illness. (37, 38, 39)

26. Family to increase the frequency of statements of positive support of the client to reduce chances of acute exacerbation of client's psychotic episode. (39, 40)

27. Cooperate with psychological testing to evaluate thought disturbance severity. (41)

28. Cooperate with a neuropsychological assessment to evaluate the presence of organicity. (9, 42)

self, laughing or crying inappropriately, posturing, facial grimaces, incoherent speech, blank staring, etc.).
RP: _____

_____

15. Reduce the level of the client's stress and stimulation in the milieu by speaking calmly, keeping noise levels low, maintaining a structure and routine that are predictable, and engaging him/her in simple tasks that distract him/her from internal focus.
RP: _____

_____

16. Demonstrate acceptance to the client through a calm, nurturing manner; consistent eye contact; and active listening.
RP: _____

_____

17. Conduct an individual therapy session to assess the client's progress toward the reduction of thought disturbance.
RP: _____

_____

18. Provide supportive therapy to alleviate the client's fears and reduce feelings of alienation.
RP: _____

_____

19. Encourage others to engage the client in social interac-

29. Verbalize an understanding and acceptance of the need for a structured, supervised living situation after discharge from intensive treatment. (43)

30. Verbalize an awareness of symptom levels that are indicative of decompensation and methods to contact staff, clinician, and/or family/significant other if the symptoms increase in intensity. (44, 45)

31. Verbalize an understanding of the need for current medications, the importance of compliance and correct dosage, and the identification of side effects and benefits. (7, 8, 46)

32. Family members verbalize a connection between psychosis and addictive behavior. (47, 48)

33. Family members verbalize what each can do to assist the client in recovery. (49)

__. _____
    _____

__. _____
    _____

__. _____
    _____

tion and to give feedback as to the appropriateness of social skills.
RP: _____
    _____

20. Reinforce the client for initiating appropriate social interaction with others.
RP: _____
    _____

21. Prompt the client to complete activities of daily living (ADLs) to promote caring for own basic needs.
RP: _____
    _____

22. Reinforce the client's independent performance of ADLs.
RP: _____
    _____

23. Assign the client the task of daily preparing a list of activities that are planned.
RP: _____
    _____

24. Reinforce the client for implementing a plan of daily activities.
RP: _____
    _____

25. Direct the client to attend group therapy, and then ask for a report on the content of the group and his/her contribution.
RP: _____
    _____

26. Therapist lead group therapy and draw the client into interaction.
RP: _____

_____

27. Therapist reinforce the client for logical, coherent participation in group process.
RP: _____

_____

28. Group therapist reinforce the client for calm acceptance of social interaction without becoming agitated, bizarre, or distrustful.
RP: _____

_____

29. Gently confront the client's agitation behavior, and calmly reassure him/her of his/her safety.
RP: _____

_____

30. Reinforce the client for a more relaxed demeanor and sitting calmly and normally.
RP: _____

_____

31. Direct the client to attend recreational therapy activities that are nonthreatening, simple to master, and encourage a low level of social interaction.
RP: _____

_____

32. Reinforce the client for appropriate participation in a recreational activity.

    RP: _____

    _____

33. Direct occupational therapy activity that diverts the client from internal cognitive focus and provides for structured social interaction and a sense of accomplishment on the completion of a task.

    RP: _____

    _____

34. Conduct an art therapy group in which the client is encouraged to express feelings through various art media.

    RP: _____

    _____

35. Lead a group discussion in which the client is encouraged to share the meaning of his/her artwork.

    RP: _____

    _____

36. Direct the client to sleep at expected times, and reinforce him/her for compliance.

    RP: _____

    _____

37. Arrange family therapy sessions to educate family members regarding the

client's illness, treatment, and prognosis.

RP: _____

_____

38. Within a family therapy session, encourage family members to share their feelings of frustration, guilt, fear, or grief surrounding the client's mental illness and behavior patterns.

RP: _____

_____

39. Hold family therapy sessions to reduce the atmosphere of criticism and hostility toward the client and to promote compassion, empathy, and support for him/her.

RP: _____

_____

40. Assist the family in replacing double-bind messages that are inconsistent and contradictory, resulting in increased anxiety, confusion, and psychotic symptoms in the client, with clear, direct, concrete communication.

RP: _____

_____

41. Perform psychological testing to evaluate the pervasiveness of the client's thought disturbance.

RP: _____

_____

42. Perform neuropsychological testing to evaluate the client for organicity.

    RP: _____

    _____

43. Arrange for an appropriate level of supervised, residential care for the client.

    RP: _____

    _____

44. Educate the client regarding critical symptoms that are indicative of decompensation, and urge initiation of clinical contact if intense positive symptoms of psychosis appear and interfere with daily functioning.

    RP: _____

    _____

45. Provide the client with written instructions and phone numbers to use if the symptoms become intense.

    RP: _____

    _____

46. Educate the client and/or the family/significant other about the importance of medication compliance, proper dosage, refilling prescriptions, safety factors, and side effect recognition.

    RP: _____

    _____

47. Discuss with family members the connection between psychosis and addictive behavior.
   RP: _____

   _____

48. In a family session, review what each member can do to assist the client in recovery.
   RP: _____

   _____

49. Provide the family members with information about psychosis and the steps that the client must take to recover successfully.
   RP: _____

   _____

__. _____

   _____

   RP: _____

   _____

__. _____

   _____

   RP: _____

   _____

__. _____

   _____

   RP: _____

   _____

DIAGNOSTIC SUGGESTIONS

Axis I:

291.x	Alcohol-Induced Psychotic Disorder
292.xx	Other (or Unknown) Substance–Induced Disorder
295.xx	Schizophrenia
296	Major Depressive Disorder
296.xx	Bipolar I Disorder
296.89	Bipolar II Disorder
297.1	Delusional Disorder
298.8	Brief Psychotic Disorder
295.40	Schizophreniform Disorder
310.1	Personality Change Due to (*Axis III Disorder*)
_____	_____
_____	_____

RELAPSE PRONENESS

BEHAVIORAL DEFINITIONS

1. History of multiple treatment attempts and relapse.
2. Frequent emotions increase the risk for relapse and continued addiction.
3. Friends or family members engage in addictive behavior.
4. Interpersonal conflicts increase the risk for relapse.
5. Social pressure encourages substance use.
6. Never has worked a program of recovery long enough to maintain abstinence.
7. Mental illness increases the risk for relapse.

__. _____
   _____
__. _____
   _____
__. _____
   _____

LONG-TERM GOALS

1. Develop coping skills to use when experiencing high-risk situations and/or craving.
2. Practice a program of recovery that includes consistent attendance at recovery group meetings, working with a sponsor, and helping others in recovery.
3. Develop a new peer group that is supportive of recovery.
4. Resolve interpersonal conflicts and learn healthy communication skills.

5. Learn refusal skills for being tempted into addictive behavior.
6. Understand the reason for the medications and take all of them as ordered by the physician.
7. Obtain ongoing treatment for mental illness, as well as practicing a program of recovery from addictive behavior.

—. _____

_____

—. _____

_____

—. _____

_____

SHORT-TERM OBJECTIVES

1. Write a detailed chemical use history, describing treatment attempts and the specific situations surrounding relapse. (1)
2. Verbalize an understanding of why the client continues to relapse. (2, 3)
3. Verbalize the powerlessness and unmanageability that result from addiction and relapse. (3, 4)
4. Verbalize an acceptance of the powerlessness over alcohol/drugs. (3, 4, 5)
5. Verbalize that continued alcohol/drug use meets the 12-step recovery program concept of insanity. (4, 5, 6)
6. Verbalize five reasons why it is essential to work a

THERAPEUTIC INTERVENTIONS

1. Assign the client to write a chemical use history, describing his/her attempts at recovery and the situations surrounding relapse.
   *RP: _____

   _____

2. Teach the client the high-risk situations that lead to relapse (e.g., negative emotions, social pressure, interpersonal conflict, positive emotions, tests of personal control).
   RP: _____

   _____

3. Help the client to understand why he/she keeps relapsing (e.g., failure to work a daily program of recovery, failure to go to

---

*RP = responsible professional.

daily program of recovery to maintain abstinence. (3, 7)

7. List five reasons for failure of the program of recovery. (3, 7, 8)

8. Turn problems over to a higher power each day, praying only for its will and the power to carry that out. Record each of these events and discuss them with the primary therapist. (9)

9. List five ways in which a higher power can assist in recovery from addiction. (9, 10)

10. Verbalize reasons for not continuing to attend 12-step recovery program meetings long enough to maintain abstinence. (3, 8, 11)

11. Make a written plan to increase reinforcement when attending recovery group meetings. (12)

12. Develop a new peer group that is supportive of recovery. (12, 13)

13. Develop a written plan to deal with each situation that represents a high risk for relapse. (14)

14. Practice healthy communication skills. (15)

15. Implement the application of conflict resolution skills to interpersonal conflicts. (16)

16. Practice refusal skills in the face of enticement to engage in addictive behavior. (17)

meetings, poor coping skills for high-risk situations, mental illness, interpersonal problems, poor recovery environment, etc.)
RP: _____

_____

4. Using a 12-step recovery program's step-one exercise, help the client to see the powerlessness and unmanageability that result from addiction and relapse.
RP: _____

_____

5. Using the client's chemical use history, help him/her to accept his/her powerlessness over alcohol/drugs.
RP: _____

_____

6. Using a 12-step recovery program's step-two exercise, help the client to see the insanity of his/her disease, then teach him/her that a higher power can restore him/her to sanity.
RP: _____

_____

7. Help the client to understand why it is essential to implement a daily program of recovery to maintain abstinence.
RP: _____

_____

8. Using the client's relapse history, help him/her to understand the reasons why

17. Visit with the physician to see if pharmacological intervention is warranted. (18)

18. Take all medication as directed, and report as to effectiveness and side effects. (19, 20)

19. Make an emergency card that has the phone numbers to call when in a high-risk situation. (21)

20. Agree to enter the structured continuing care treatment setting that is necessary to maintain abstinence. (22)

21. Develop a written personal recovery plan that includes honesty, attending recovery group meetings regularly, getting a sponsor, and any other treatment that is needed to maintain abstinence. (23)

22. Family members verbalize a connection between relapse proneness and addictive behavior. (24, 25)

23. Family members verbalize what each can do to assist the client in recovery. (26)

__. _____
   _____

__. _____
   _____

__. _____
   _____

his/her recovery program failed.
RP: _____
    _____

9. Teach the client how to use the 12-step recovery program's step three, and assign him/her to practice turning problems over to a higher power each day. Have the client record each situation and discuss these with the primary therapist.
RP: _____
    _____

10. Teach the client how the higher power can assist in recovery.
RP: _____
    _____

11. Probe the reasons why the client discontinues going to 12-step recovery program meetings consistently.
RP: _____
    _____

12. Help the client to develop a plan that will increase the rewards obtained at recovery groups (e.g., concentrate on helping others, go for coffee and pie after the meeting, socialize, stick with the winners, etc.).
RP: _____
    _____

13. Assign the client a 12-step recovery program contact person, and begin to attend recovery group meetings

with him/her regularly. Encourage both individuals to make the outing fun rather than a boring obligation.
RP: _____

_____

14. Help the client to make a written plan to carry with him/her at all times that details the coping skills (e.g., go to a meeting, call the sponsor, call the 12-step recovery program hot line, call the counselor/doctor or treatment center, talk to someone about the problem, etc.) to use when in a high-risk situation (e.g., negative emotions, social pressure, interpersonal conflict, positive emotions, test of personal control).
RP: _____

_____

15. Teach the client healthy communication skills (e.g., active listening, using "I" messages, reflecting, sharing feelings, etc.)
RP: _____

_____

16. Teach the client conflict resolution skills. Using modeling, role playing, and behavior rehearsal, have him/her practice handling conflict in high-risk situations.
RP: _____

_____

17. Using modeling, role play-
    ing, and behavior rehearsal,
    teach the client how to say
    no to alcohol/drugs, and
    then practice refusal in sev-
    eral high-risk situations.
    RP: _____

    _____

18. Physician will examine the
    client, order medications as
    indicated, titrate medica-
    tions, and monitor for side
    effects.
    RP: _____

    _____

19. Staff administer medica-
    tions as ordered by the
    physician.
    RP: _____

    _____

20. Monitor the client's psy-
    chotropic medications for
    compliance, effectiveness,
    and side effects.
    RP: _____

    _____

21. Help the client to make an
    emergency card to carry at
    all times that has the phone
    numbers of the people to
    call when he/she is at high
    risk for relapse.
    RP: _____

    _____

22. Help the client to decide on
    the aftercare placement that
    is structured enough to help
    him/her maintain absti-
    nence (e.g., halfway house,
    group home, outclient treat-

ment, day care, partial hospitalization, etc.).

RP: _____

_____

23. Help the client to develop a written continuing care plan that includes the essential elements that are necessary for him/her to maintain abstinence and continue recovery.

RP: _____

_____

24. Discuss with family members the connection between relapse proneness and addictive behavior.

RP: _____

_____

25. In a family session, review what each member can do to assist the client in recovery.

RP: _____

_____

26. Provide the family members with information about the client's proneness for relapse and the steps that he/she must take to recover successfully.

RP: _____

_____

—. _____

    _____

RP: _____

    _____

—. _____

    _____

RP: _____

    _____

—. _____

    _____

RP: _____

    _____

DIAGNOSTIC SUGGESTIONS

Axis I: 312.8   Conduct Disorder
         296.xx   Bipolar I Disorder
         296.89   Bipolar II Disorder
         301.13   Cyclothymic Disorder
         314   Attention-Deficit/Hyperactivity Disorder
         313.81   Oppositional Defiant Disorder

         _____   _____

Axis II: 301.0   Paranoid Personality Disorder
          301.20   Schizoid Personality Disorder
          301.22   Schizotypal Personality Disorder
          301.7   Antisocial Personality Disorder
          301.83   Borderline Personality Disorder
          301.81   Narcissistic Personality Disorder
          301.82   Avoidant Personality Disorder

          _____   _____

          _____   _____

SEXUAL PROMISCUITY

BEHAVIORAL DESCRIPTIONS

1. Repeated sexual encounters with a variety of partners without regard for the potential for negative consequences.
2. Repeated acts of sexual intimacy with partners with whom there is no meaningful emotional or lasting social connections.
3. A history of sexually acting out in areas that are potentially self-damaging (e.g., unprotected sex, hiring prostitutes, cruising the streets for sex, many different sexual partners).
4. Preoccupied with sexual thoughts.
5. A pattern of sexual behavior that seeks instant gratification.
6. The use of sexual behavior to cope with stress or reduce tension.
7. Overarousal to mild sexually oriented stimulation.
8. A sense of tension or affective arousal before engaging in the sexual behavior and a reduction of tension after completing the sexual act.
9. Engaging sexual behavior that is unlawful.
10. Inability to cut down or stop harmful sexual behavior.
11. Concomitant substance abuse accompanies the impulsive, emotionally detached sexual encounters.
12. Chemical dependence leads to an exchange of sex for mood-altering drugs.

__. _____
   _____
__. _____
   _____
__. _____
   _____

LONG-TERM GOALS

1. Reduce the frequency of sexual promiscuity, and increase the frequency of responsible and meaningful sexual behavior.
2. Reduce thoughts and behavior that trigger sexual promiscuity, and increase self-talk that controls behavior.
3. Maintain a program of recovery that is free from sexual promiscuity and addiction.
4. Learn the techniques that are necessary to decrease sexually promiscuous thoughts, feelings, and behaviors.
5. Learn to stop, look, listen, think, and plan before acting.
6. Learn stress reduction techniques to manage stress without the use of sexually promiscuous behavior.
7. Terminate substance abuse that accompanies sexual promiscuity.

—. _____
   _____
—. _____
   _____
—. _____
   _____

SHORT-TERM OBJECTIVES

1. Verbalize an understanding of the powerlessness and unmanageability that result from sexual promiscuity and addiction. (1)

2. Verbalize how sexual promiscuity and addiction meet the 12-step program criteria for insanity. (2)

3. Identify the negative consequences that are caused by sexual promiscuity and addiction. (3, 4, 5, 6)

THERAPEUTIC INTERVENTIONS

1. Using a step-one exercise from a 12-step program of recovery, help the client to understand how sexual promiscuity and addiction lead to powerlessness and unmanageability.

   *RP: _____

   _____

2. Using a step-two exercise from a 12-step program, help the client to see that doing the same things over

---

*RP = responsible professional.

4. Verbally identify several times when impulsivity led to sexual promiscuity addiction and subsequent negative consequences. (4, 6)

5. Increase the frequency of reviewing behavioral decisions with a trusted friend or family member for feedback regarding the consequences before the decision is enacted. (7)

6. Verbalize the biopsychosocial elements that have contributed to sexual promiscuity. (8)

7. Comply with a physician's evaluation regarding the necessity for psychopharmacological intervention, and take all medications as prescribed. (9, 10)

8. Identify the thoughts that trigger impulsive sexual behavior; then, replace each thought with a thought that is accurate, positive, self-enhancing, and adaptive. (11, 12)

9. Develop a list of accurate, positive, self-enhancing statements to read each day, particularly when feeling upset. (12)

10. List the inappropriate behaviors that are displayed when feeling anxious or uncomfortable, and replace each behavior with an action that is positive and adaptive. (13, 14)

and over again and expecting different results meets the definition of *insanity*.
RP: _____
_____

3. Assist the client in making connections between his/her sexual promiscuity and the negative consequences that he/she experienced.
RP: _____
_____

4. Assign the client to write a list of negative consequences that occurred because of his/her sexual promiscuity and addiction.
RP: _____
_____

5. Help the client to see how dangerous it is to act impulsively (i.e., you don't have time to think, you can't plan effectively, you don't consider all the consequences, etc.).
RP: _____
_____

6. Explore times when the client acted too quickly on impulses, resulting in sexually promiscuous behavior and negative consequences.
RP: _____
_____

7. Conduct a session with the spouse, significant other, sponsor, or family member and the client to develop a contract for the client re-

11. Practice a relaxation exercise twice a day for 10 to 20 minutes. Then, practice relaxing when feeling upset or uncomfortable. (14)

12. Practice the assertive formula, "I feel . . . When you. . . . I would prefer it if. . . ." (15)

13. Identify situations where assertiveness has been implemented and the resulting consequences. (16)

14. Practice stopping, looking, listening, thinking, and planning before acting. (17, 18)

15. List instances when "stop, look, listen, think, and plan before acting" has been implemented, citing the positive consequences. (18)

16. Verbalize an understanding of a 12-step program's step three, regarding the role of a higher power and how this step can be used in recovery from sexual promiscuity and addiction. (19, 20)

17. Write an autobiography detailing the exact nature of wrongs that were committed, and relate each of these wrongs to sexual promiscuity. (21)

18. Disclose any history of sexual abuse in childhood, and relate that experience to current patterns of sexual behavior. (22, 23)

ceiving feedback prior to engaging in sexually promiscuous acts.
RP: _____

_____

8. Probe the client's biopsychosocial history and help him/her to see the precipitants of his/her sexual promiscuity (e.g., family patterns of promiscuity, low self-esteem, sexual abuse, etc.).
RP: _____

_____

9. Physician examine the client, order medications as indicated, titrate medications, and monitor for side effects.
RP: _____

_____

10. Monitor for side effects and effectiveness when the client takes medications ordered by the physician.
RP: _____

_____

11. Help the client to uncover dysfunctional thoughts that lead to sexual promiscuity, and then replace each one with an accurate, positive, self-enhancing, and adaptive thought.
RP: _____

_____

12. Help the client to develop a list of positive, accurate, self-enhancing thoughts to

19. Verbalize why a meaningful relationship is necessary for true sexual intimacy. (24)

20. Identify those factors that contribute to difficulty with establishing intimate, trusting relationships. (25)

21. Identify triggers to sexual promiscuity and coping behaviors for each trigger. (26, 27)

22. List personal advantages of monogamous sexual intimacy. (28)

23. Develop and write out a continuing care program that includes the recovery group meetings and any further therapy that is necessary for recovery. (29)

__. _____
    _____
__. _____
    _____
__. _____
    _____

read to himself/herself each day, particularly when feeling tense or disparaged.
RP: _____
    _____

13. Probe the client's behaviors used to cope with anxiety, and then use modeling, role playing, and behavior rehearsal to teach him/her new behaviors that are positive and adaptive (e.g., talking to someone about the problem, taking a time-out, calling the sponsor, going to a meeting, engaging in exercise, practicing relaxation, etc.).
RP: _____
    _____

14. Using relaxation techniques (e.g., progressive relaxation, self-hypnosis, or biofeedback), teach the client how to relax completely. Assign the client to relax whenever he/she feels tense or anxious.
RP: _____
    _____

15. Using modeling, role playing, and behavior rehearsal, teach the client how to use the assertive formula, "I feel . . . When you. . . . I would prefer it if . . ." in difficult situations that the client is facing.
RP: _____
    _____

16. Review implementation of assertiveness and feelings about it, as well as the consequences of it; redirect as necessary.

    RP: _____

    _____

17. Using modeling, role playing, and behavior rehearsal, teach the client how to use "stop, look, listen, think, and plan before acting" in several current situations.

    RP: _____

    _____

18. Review the use of "stop, look, listen, think, and plan before acting" in day to day living and identify the positive consequences; redirect as necessary.

    RP: _____

    _____

19. Using a step-three exercise from a 12-step program, teach the client how to turn his/her will and life over to the care of the higher power; discuss how this step can be beneficial in recovery from sexual promiscuity and addiction.

    RP: _____

    _____

20. Teach the client about the 12-step program concept of a higher power, and discuss how the client can use a

higher power effectively in
recovery.
RP: _____

_____

21. Using a step-four exercise
from a 12-step program, assign the client to write an
autobiography of the exact
nature of his/her wrongs
and to relate these wrongs
to sexual promiscuity and
addiction.
RP: _____

_____

22. Explore the client's history
of sexual abuse.
RP: _____

_____

23. Relate the client's childhood
sexual abuse to his/her
current pattern of sexual
promiscuity; refer the client
for ongoing counseling that
is focused on overcoming
the effects of the sexual
abuse.
RP: _____

_____

24. Teach the importance of a
meaningful relationship to
allow for true intimacy in a
sexual encounter.
RP: _____

_____

25. Explore the client's history
of rejection or neglect that
may have led to an inability
to form and/or maintain

trusting, close, intimate relationships.
RP: _____

_____

26. Assist the client in identifying thoughts and situations
that trigger urges to act out
sexually.
RP: _____

_____

27. Develop with the client
adaptive behaviors to cope
with trigger situations.
RP: _____

_____

28. Assist the client in identifying a list of personal advantages for him/her
becoming monogamous in
sexually intimate behavior
(e.g., increased self-esteem,
development of trust and
respect from others, living
within a spiritual value
system, reduced health
risk, etc.).
RP: _____

_____

29. Help the client to develop
an aftercare plan that includes attending recovery
groups regularly, getting a
sponsor, and any further
therapy that is necessary to
recover from sexual promiscuity and any other addictive behavior.
RP: _____

_____

__. _____

_____

RP: _____

_____

__. _____

_____

RP: _____

_____

__. _____

_____

RP: _____

_____

DIAGNOSTIC SUGGESTIONS

Axis I:	296.xx	Bipolar I Disorder
	302.4	Exhibitionism
	302.2	Pedophilia
	302.82	Voyeurism
	302.9	Paraphilia NOS
	312.80	Conduct Disorder
	309.3	Adjustment Disorder with Disturbance of Conduct
	312.9	Disruptive Behavior Disorder NOS
	312.30	Impulse-Control Disorder NOS
	V71.01	Adult Antisocial Behavior
	V71.02	Child or Adolescent Antisocial Behavior
	_____	_____
	_____	
Axis II:	301.70	Antisocial Personality Disorder
	301.83	Borderline Personality Disorder
	301.81	Narcissistic Personality Disorder
	_____	_____
	_____	_____

SOCIAL ANXIETY

BEHAVIORAL DEFINITIONS

1. Excessive fear and worry about social circumstances that have no factual or logical basis.
2. Constant worry about social interactions that prevent the client from feeling comfortable in group meetings.
3. Tendency to believe that others are blaming self for the slightest imperfection or mistake.
4. Fear of saying or doing something foolish in a social situation due to lack of confidence in social skills.
5. Symptoms of autonomic hyperactivity in social situations such as cardiac palpitations, shortness of breath, sweaty palms, dry mouth, trouble swallowing, nausea, or diarrhea.
6. Symptoms of motor tension such as restlessness, tiredness, shakiness, or muscle tension.
7. Use of addictive behavior in an attempt to control anxiety symptoms.
8. Symptoms of hypervigilance in social settings such as feeling constantly on edge, difficulty concentrating, sleep problems, irritability.

—. _____

_____

—. _____

_____

—. _____

_____

LONG-TERM GOALS

1. Interact socially without excessive anxiety.
2. Develop the social skills that are necessary to reduce excessive anxiety in social situations, and terminate reliance on addiction as a coping mechanism.
3. Maintain a program of recovery that is free from addiction and excessive social anxiety.
4. Decrease thoughts that trigger anxiety, and increase positive, self-enhancing self-talk.
5. Learn the relationship between anxiety and addiction.
6. Form relationships that will enhance a recovery support system.

—. _____
   _____
—. _____
   _____
—. _____
   _____

SHORT-TERM OBJECTIVES

1. Keep a daily journal of social anxiety rating, including the situations that cause anxious feelings and the negative thoughts that fueled social anxiety. (1, 6)

2. Acknowledge the powerlessness and unmanageability that are caused by excessive social anxiety and addiction. (2, 3, 4)

3. List reasons why social anxiety led to more addiction and addiction led to more social anxiety. (2, 3)

THERAPEUTIC INTERVENTIONS

1. Assign the client to keep a daily record of social anxiety, including a description of each situation that caused anxious feelings, the rating of anxiety using Subjective Units of Distress (SUDs), and thoughts that triggered the anxiety. Process the journal material, helping the client to uncover the dysfunctional, distorted thoughts that fueled the social anxiety.

   *RP: _____

   _____

_____

*RP = responsible professional.

4. Verbalize the irrationality (12-step program's concept of *insanity*) of excessive social anxiety and addiction. (3, 4, 5)

5. Verbalize an understanding of the principle of how irrational thoughts form the basis for social anxiety. (1, 5, 6)

6. List five specific worries, and use logic and reasoning to replace irrational thoughts with reasonable thoughts. (5, 6)

7. Implement positive self-talk to reduce or eliminate the social anxiety. (6, 7, 8, 9)

8. List 10 positive self-enhancing statements to be read several times a day, particularly when feeling anxious. (9, 10)

9. Comply with a physician's evaluation to determine if psychopharmacological intervention is warranted. Take any medications as directed. (11, 12)

10. List five ways in which a higher power can assist in a program of recovery from social anxiety and addiction. (13, 14)

11. Report on three instances when worries and anxieties were turned over to the higher power. (13, 14, 15)

12. Identify the fears that were learned in the family of origin. Relate these fears to

2. Help the client to see how social anxiety and powerlessness over addiction have made his/her life unmanageable.
   RP: _____
   _____

3. Teach the client about the relationship between social anxiety and addiction (i.e., how the substance was used to treat the anxious symptoms and why more substance use became necessary).
   RP: _____
   _____

4. Teach the client about the 12-step program concept of *insanity,* and help him/her to see how social anxiety and addiction are insane.
   RP: _____
   _____

5. Assist the client in understanding the irrational nature of his/her thoughts that underlie the social fears.
   RP: _____
   _____

6. Help the client to identify five specific worries, and then facilitate the client's use of logic and reasoning to challenge the irrational thoughts that are associated with the fear.
   RP: _____
   _____

current social anxiety levels. (16, 17, 18)

13. Write a specific plan to follow when anxious and tempted to engage in addictive behaviors to reduce stress. (7, 14, 19, 20, 21)

14. Develop a leisure program that will increase pleasurable activities and affirm self. (20)

15. Practice relaxation techniques twice a day for 10 to 20 minutes. (21)

16. Exercise at least three times a week at a training heart rate for at least 20 minutes. (22)

17. Write an autobiography, detailing those behaviors in the past that are related to current social anxiety or guilt and the use of addiction as a means of escape. (3, 16, 17, 23)

18. Increase the frequency of speaking up with confidence in social situations. (24, 25, 26)

19. Develop a program of recovery that includes helping others at regular recovery group meetings. (27)

__. _____
  _____

__. _____
  _____

__. _____
  _____

7. Help the client to develop reality-based cognitive messages that can replace distorted thoughts and will increase self-confidence in coping with social fears and anxieties.
RP: _____
  _____

8. Reinforce the client's use of more realistic, positive messages to himself/herself in interpreting life events.
RP: _____
  _____

9. Assign the client to read *What to Say When You Talk to Yourself* (Helmstetter) and to process key ideas with the therapist.
RP: _____
  _____

10. Assist the client in developing a list of 10 self-affirming statements to read to himself/herself several times a day, particularly when feeling anxious.
RP: _____
  _____

11. Physician determine if psychopharmacological intervention is warranted, order medication, titrate medication, and monitor for side effects.
RP: _____
  _____

12. Monitor the client for psychotropic medication

prescription compliance,
for side effects, and for
effectiveness.

RP: _____

_____

13. Teach the client the benefits
of turning his/her will and
life over to the care of a
higher power of his/her own
understanding.

RP: _____

_____

14. Using a step-three exercise
from a 12-step recovery
program, teach the client
how to turn problems, worries, and anxieties over to a
higher power and trust that
the higher power is going to
help him/her resolve the
situation.

RP: _____

_____

15. Review the client's implementation of turning social
anxiety over to a higher
power.

RP: _____

_____

16. Probe the client's family-of-
origin history for experiences in which social
anxiety was learned, and
help him/her relate these
past events to current
thoughts, feelings, and
behaviors.

RP: _____

_____

17. Encourage and support the client in verbally expressing and clarifying his/her feelings that are associated with past rejection experiences, harsh criticism, abandonment, or trauma.
   RP: _____

   _____

18. Assign the client to read the books *Healing the Shame That Binds You* (Bradshaw) and *Facing Shame* (Fossum and Mason); process key concepts with the therapist.
   RP: _____

   _____

19. Help the client to develop an alternative constructive plan of action (e.g., implement relaxation exercises, engage in physical exercise, call a sponsor, go to a meeting, call the counselor, talk to someone, etc.) when feeling anxious and craving substance use.
   RP: _____

   _____

20. Help the client to develop a plan of engaging in pleasurable leisure activities (e.g., clubs, hobbies, church, sporting activities, social activities, games, etc.) that will increase his/her enjoyment of life, affirm himself/herself, and reduce stress.
   RP: _____

   _____

21. Use relaxation techniques (e.g., progressive relaxation, guided imagery, and biofeedback) to teach the client how to relax completely. Then, assign him/her to relax twice a day for 10 to 20 minutes.

    RP: _____

    _____

22. Using current physical fitness levels, increase the client's exercise by 10 percent a week until he/she is exercising three times a week at a training heart rate for at least 20 minutes.

    RP: _____

    _____

23. Ask the client to write an autobiography, detailing the exact nature of his/her painful experiences, as well as wrongs toward others; then, teach him/her how to begin to forgive others and himself/herself.

    RP: _____

    _____

24. Use role playing and behavior rehearsal to teach assertiveness skills to help the client to communicate thoughts, feelings, and needs more openly and directly.

    RP: _____

    _____

25. Recommend that the client read books on overcoming social anxiety (e.g., *Intimate*

Connections, by Burns, or *Shyness,* by Zimbardo).

RP: _____

_____

26. Teach the client the basics of good communication (e.g., eye contact, attentive active listening, asking questions to draw out the speaker, using "I" messages, etc.); refer him/her to a social skills training class, if indicated.

RP: _____

_____

27. Help the client to develop a structured program of recovery that includes helping others at regular 12-step recovery groups.

RP: _____

_____

__. _____

_____

RP: _____

_____

__. _____

_____

RP: _____

_____

__. _____

_____

RP: _____

_____

DIAGNOSTIC SUGGESTIONS

Axis I:

300.23	Social Phobia
300.4	Dysthymic Disorder
309.21	Separation Anxiety Disorder
291.89	Alcohol-Induced Anxiety Disorder
292.89	Substance-Induced Anxiety Disorder
296.90	Mood Disorder NOS
300.01	Panic Disorder Without Agoraphobia
300.21	Panic Disorder With Agoraphobia
300.02	Generalized Anxiety Disorder
309.24	Adjustment Disorder With Anxiety
309.28	Adjustment Disorder With Mixed Anxiety and Depressed Mood
____	_____

Axis II:

301.0	Paranoid Personality Disorder
301.83	Borderline Personality Disorder
301.82	Avoidant Personality Disorder
301.6	Dependent Personality Disorder
____	_____
____	_____

SPIRITUAL CONFUSION

BEHAVIORAL DEFINITIONS

1. Need for a higher power is not understood or accepted.
2. Fear that God is angry results in withdrawal from a higher power.
3. Anger at God leads to a rejection of any religious system or personal spiritual development.
4. Confusion about spiritual matters leading to a negative attitude about recovery.
5. Anger at God has the client refusing to seek conscious contact with God.
6. Religious convictions are condemning of addictive behavior and a 12-step program of recovery.
7. Active involvement in a religious system that does not support a 12-step recovery program.
8. Spiritual beliefs are negative toward the existence of a higher power.

__. _____
   _____
__. _____
   _____
__. _____
   _____

LONG-TERM GOALS

1. Accept that a higher power can assist in relieving addiction.
2. Learn the difference between religion and spirituality.
3. Learn and accept the 12-step concept of a higher power, or "God as we understood Him."

4. Develop a concept of a higher power that is loving and supportive to recovery.

—. _____

_____

—. _____

_____

—. _____

_____

SHORT-TERM OBJECTIVES

1. Verbalize the powerlessness and unmanageability that result from spiritual confusion and addictive behavior. (1, 2, 3, 4, 5)

2. Verbalize an understanding of how spiritual confusion leads to addictive behavior. (2)

3. Verbalize how spiritual confusion leads to a negative attitude toward working a 12-step program of recovery. (3)

4. List five times when spiritual confusion led to addiction. (4)

5. Verbalize how addiction and spiritual confusion left self spiritually bankrupt. (4, 5)

6. Verbalize an understanding of the 12-step concept of

THERAPEUTIC INTERVENTIONS

1. Using a 12-step recovery program's step-one exercise, help the client to accept that he/she is powerless over spiritual confusion and addictive behavior and that his/her life is unmanageable.

   *RP: _____

   _____

2. Probe the client's history of spiritual confusion, and show him/her how this confusion contributed to addiction and a negative attitude toward recovery.

   RP: _____

   _____

3. Show the client how negative attitudes toward spiritual matters make recovery difficult.

   RP: _____

   _____

_____

*RP = responsible professional.

"God as we understood Him." (6)

7. Verbalize how many different religions and cultures can work a 12-step program of recovery. (7)

8. Verbalize an understanding of a higher power's grace and willingness to forgive. (8, 9, 10)

9. List 10 ways in which a higher power can assist in recovery from spiritual confusion and addiction. (11)

10. Read and verbalize an understanding of page 449 in the *Big Book* [Alcoholics Anonymous (AA)]. (12)

11. Meet with a clergyperson who is familiar with 12-step recovery; discuss the higher power and how it can assist in recovery. (13)

12. Meet with a temporary sponsor, or a 12-step recovery program contact person; discuss plans for resolving spiritual confusion and addiction. (14)

13. Verbalize the need to begin a spiritual journey, as outlined in the 12 steps. (13, 14, 15)

14. Make a written plan to continue a spiritual journey as outlined in the 12 steps. (15, 16)

15. Write a letter to the higher power, sharing feelings and asking for specific needs in recovery. (17)

4. Help the client to identify how addiction led to spiritual confusion.
RP: _____

_____

5. Using a 12-step recovery program's step-two exercise, help the client to see the insanity of his/her spiritual confusion and addictive behavior, and help him/her to see that a higher power can assist in relieving the addiction.
RP: _____

_____

6. Teach the client about the 12-step recovery program's concept of "God as we understood Him" and how this relates to his/her spiritual confusion.
RP: _____

_____

7. Teach the client how many different religions and cultures can implement a similar 12-step program of recovery.
RP: _____

_____

8. Teach the client that the higher power will forgive him/her for the wrongs that he/she has committed.
RP: _____

_____

9. Assign the client to read books on the process of for-

16. Make a decision to turn own will and life over to the higher power, as it is understood. (18)

17. Practice prayer and meditation at least once a day. (18, 19, 20)

18. Keep a prayer journal, writing down all of the things that have been prayed for and what new spiritual insights have been gained. (20)

19. Begin each day by asking the higher power for direction and support; then, ask, "What is the next step in my relationship with you?" Write down each insight that is gained from the higher power; share with the primary therapist. (20, 21)

20. Develop a written personal recovery plan that includes attending recovery groups regularly, getting a sponsor, helping others in recovery, and any other treatment that is necessary to recover from spiritual confusion and addiction. (22)

21. Family members verbalize a connection between spiritual confusion and addictive behavior. (23, 24)

22. Family members verbalize what each can do to assist the client in recovery. (25)

giveness (e.g., *Forgive and Forget* by Smedes).
RP: _____
_____

10. Assign the client to read *Addiction and Grace* (May) and process key ideas.
RP: _____
_____

11. Teach the client about the importance of a higher power in a 12-step program, and list many ways that a higher power can assist him/her in recovery.
RP: _____
_____

12. Assign the client to read page 449 in the *Big Book* (AA); then, teach him/her how everything that happens in the world is a part of God's good plan.
RP: _____
_____

13. Arrange for the client to meet a clergyperson who is familiar with 12-step recovery programs, and encourage the client to share his/her thoughts and feelings about the higher power.
RP: _____
_____

14. Arrange for the client to meet with a contact person, or temporary sponsor, and discuss the 12-step recovery

__. _____

_____

__. _____

_____

__. _____

_____

program, spiritual confu-
sion, and addiction.

RP: _____

_____

15. Assign the client to read
"How It Works" in the *Big
Book* (AA) and to discuss
the three pertinent ideas
that are outlined at the end
of the chapter: (1) "We were
alcoholic and could not
manage our own lives"; (2)
"Probably no human power
could have relieved our alcoholism"; and (3) "God
could and would if He were
sought").

RP: _____

_____

16. Using the 12 steps as a
guide, help the client to
make a written plan to
continue his/her spiritual
journey.

RP: _____

_____

17. Assign the client to write a
letter to the higher power,
sharing how he/she thinks
and feels and asking for
what he/she wants to aid
him/her in recovery.

RP: _____

_____

18. Using a 12-step recovery
program's step-three exercise, teach the client how to
turn problems over to a
higher power.

RP: _____

_____

19. Assign the client to read Chapter 11 in AA's *Twelve Steps and Twelve Traditions*. Teach the client how to pray (talk to God) and meditate (listen for God); then, assign the client to pray and meditate at least once each day.

    RP: _____

    _____

20. Assign the client to keep a prayer journal, writing down his/her prayers and new insights gained about the higher power's will for his/her life.

    RP: _____

    _____

21. Assign the client to ask God to come into his/her life each day, and then ask, "God what is the next step in my relationship with you?" Have the client write down each insight that he/she has gained from God and share these with the primary therapist.

    RP: _____

    _____

22. Help the client to develop a personal recovery plan that includes attending recovery groups regularly, getting a sponsor, helping others in recovery, and any other treatment that is necessary

to recover from spiritual
confusion and addiction.

RP: _____

_____

23. Discuss with family members the connection between
spiritual confusion and addictive behavior.

RP: _____

_____

24. In a family session, review
what each member can do to
assist the client in recovery.

RP: _____

_____

25. Provide the family members
with information about
spiritual confusion and the
steps that the client must
take to recover successfully.

RP: _____

_____

__. _____

_____

RP: _____

_____

__. _____

_____

RP: _____

_____

__. _____

_____

RP: _____

_____

DIAGNOSTIC SUGGESTIONS

Axis I: V62.89   Religious or Spiritual Problem
                V62.4   Acculturation Problem
                _____   _____
                _____   _____

SUBSTANCE ABUSE/DEPENDENCE

BEHAVIORAL DEFINITIONS

1. A maladaptive pattern of substance use manifested by increased tolerance and withdrawal.
2. Inability to stop or cut down use of the mood-altering drug once started, despite the verbalized desire to do so and the negative consequences that continued use brings.
3. Blood work (e.g., elevated liver enzymes, electrolyte imbalance, etc.) and physical indicators (e.g., stomach pain, high blood pressure, malnutrition, etc.) reflect the results of a pattern of heavy substance use.
4. Denial that chemical dependence is a problem despite feedback from significant others that the use of the substance is negatively affecting him/her and others.
5. Frequent blackouts when using.
6. Continued substance use despite knowledge of experiencing persistent physical, legal, financial, vocational, social, or relationship problems that are directly caused by the use of the substance.
7. Increased tolerance for the drug demonstrated by the need to use more to become intoxicated or to recall the desired effect.
8. Physical withdrawal symptoms (e.g., shaking, seizures, nausea, headaches, sweating, anxiety, insomnia, and/or depression) when going without the substance for any length of time.
9. Arrests for addiction-related offenses (e.g., driving under the influence, minor in possession, assault, possession/delivery of a controlled substance, shoplifting, breaking and entering, etc.).
10. Suspension of important social, recreational, or occupational activities because they interfere with using.
11. Large time investment in activities to obtain the substance, to use it, or to recover from its effects.
12. Continued use of a mood-altering chemical despite a physician's warning that using it is causing health problems.

—. _____
_____
—. _____
_____
—. _____
_____

LONG-TERM GOALS

1. Accept the powerlessness and unmanageability over mood-altering substances, and participate in a recovery-based program.
2. Withdraw from mood-altering substance, stabilize physically and emotionally, and then establish a supportive recovery plan.
3. Accept own chemical dependence and begin to actively participate in a recovery program.
4. Establish a sustained recovery, free from the use of all mood-altering substances.
5. Establish and maintain total abstinence while increasing knowledge of the addiction and the process of recovery.

—. _____
_____
—. _____
_____
—. _____
_____

SHORT-TERM OBJECTIVES

1. Cooperate with a medical assessment and an evaluation of the necessity for pharmacological intervention. (1, 2)

THERAPEUTIC INTERVENTIONS

1. Physician perform a physical exam and write treatment orders, including, if necessary, prescription of medications.

    *RP: _____

    _____

_____

*RP = responsible professional.

2. Take prescribed medications as directed by the physician, and report as to compliance, side effects, and effectiveness. (3, 4)

3. Report acute withdrawal symptoms. (5)

4. Provide honest and complete information for a chemical dependence biopsychosocial history. (6)

5. Attend didactic sessions and read assigned material in order to increase knowledge of addiction and the process of recovery. (7, 8, 9, 10)

6. Attend group therapy sessions to share thoughts and feelings that are associated with reasons for, consequences of, feelings about, and alternatives to addiction. (11, 12)

7. List 10 negative consequences resulting from or exacerbated by substance dependence. (13, 14)

8. Verbally admit to powerlessness over the mood-altering substances. (13, 14)

9. Verbalize an understanding of the problems that are caused by the use of mood-altering substances and, therefore, the need to stay in treatment. (13, 14, 15)

10. Verbalize a recognition that mood-altering chemicals were used as the primary coping mechanism to escape from stress or pain and that

2. Physician monitor the side effects and effectiveness of medication, titrating as necessary.
   RP: _____
   _____

3. Staff administer the client's prescribed medications.
   RP: _____
   _____

4. Monitor the client's prescribed psychotropic medications for compliance, side effects, and effectiveness.
   RP: _____
   _____

5. Assess and monitor the client's condition during withdrawal using a standardized procedure (e.g., Clinical Institute of Withdrawal Scale) as needed.
   RP: _____
   _____

6. Complete thorough family and personal biopsychosocial histories that focus on addiction.
   RP: _____
   _____

7. Assign the client to attend a chemical dependence didactic series to increase his/her knowledge of the patterns and effects of chemical dependence.
   RP: _____
   _____

8. Require the client to attend all chemical dependence di-

they resulted in negative consequences. (16)

11. List the negative emotions that were caused by or exacerbated by substance dependence. (17)

12. Develop a list of the social, emotional, and family factors that contributed to substance dependence. (6, 18)

13. List 10 reasons to work on a plan for recovery from addiction. (15, 19)

14. List 10 lies that were used to hide substance dependence. (20)

15. Verbalize five ways in which a higher power can assist in recovery. (21, 22)

16. Practice turning problems over to a higher power each day. Record each event and share these with the primary therapist. (21, 22)

17. Practice healthy communication skills to reduce stress and increase positive social interaction. (23)

18. Practice problem-solving skills. (24)

19. List the reasons for substance use and the ways in which the same things can be attained in an adaptive manner. (25)

20. Verbalize options to substance use in dealing with stress and in finding pleasure or excitement in life. (22, 24, 25, 26)

dactics; ask him/her to identify several key points attained from each didactic and to process these points with the therapist.
RP: _____
_____

9. Ask the client to read substance abuse literature (e.g., *Cannabis and Cognitive Functioning* by Solowij, *Cocaine Addiction* by Washton, or *Alcohol Abuse* by Sales) and to process with the therapist five key points that were gained from the reading.
RP: _____
_____

10. Require the client to read pages 1 to 52 in the *Big Book* [Alcoholics Anonymous (AA)] and to gather five key points from it to process with the therapist.
RP: _____
_____

11. Assign the client to attend group therapy that is focused on addiction issues.
RP: _____
_____

12. Direct group therapy that facilitates the sharing of causes for, consequences of, feelings about, and alternatives to addiction.
RP: _____
_____

21. Develop a written leisure skills program to decrease stress and improve health. (26, 27)

22. Practice stress management skills to reduce overall stress levels and attain a feeling of relaxation and comfort. (28)

23. Exercise at a training heart rate for at least 20 minutes at least three times per week. (29)

24. Complete a fourth-step inventory and share with a clergyperson or someone else in the program. (30)

25. List the triggers (persons, places, and things) that may precipitate a relapse. (16, 18, 25, 31)

26. Make a written plan to cope with each high-risk or trigger situation. (31, 32)

27. Practice saying no to alcohol and drugs. (33)

28. Write a personal recovery plan that includes attending recovery group meetings regularly, aftercare, getting a sponsor, and helping others in recovery. (34, 35)

29. Take a personal inventory at the end of each day, listing the problems in recovery, the plans to address these problems, and five things to be grateful for that day. (35, 36)

30. Enter the continuing care treatment setting necessary

13. Assign the client to complete an AA first-step paper, admitting to powerlessness over mood-altering chemicals, and present it in group therapy or to a therapist for feedback.
    RP: _____
    _____

14. Ask the client to make a list of the ways in which chemical use has negatively impacted his/her life, and process this list with the therapist or group.
    RP: _____
    _____

15. Assist the client in listing reasons why he/she should stay in chemical dependence treatment.
    RP: _____
    _____

16. Explore how addiction was used to escape from stress, physical and emotional pain, and boredom. Confront the negative consequences of this pattern.
    RP: _____
    _____

17. Probe the sense of shame, guilt, and low self-worth that have resulted from addictive behavior and its consequences.
    RP: _____
    _____

18. Using the biopsychosocial history, assist the client in

to maintain abstinence and maximize chances for recovery. (37)

31. Family members verbalize an understanding of their role in the disease and the process of recovery. (38, 39, 40, 41)

32. Family members decrease the frequency of enabling the chemically dependent child after verbally identifying their enabling behaviors. (41, 42, 43, 44)

33. Meet with family members to help each one develop a program of recovery from the family disease aspects of chemical dependence. (44, 45)

34. In a family session, discuss the tools of recovery: honesty, recovery group meetings, and seeking a higher power. (46)

35. List three things that each family member can do to assist the client in recovery. (47, 48)

__. _____

_____

__. _____

_____

__. _____

_____

understanding the familial, emotional, and social factors that contributed to the development of chemical dependence.

RP: _____

_____

19. Assign the client to write a list of 10 reasons to be abstinent from addiction.

RP: _____

_____

20. Help the client to see the dishonesty that goes along with addiction. Have them list 10 lies that they told to hide substance use. Then, teach them why honesty is essential to recovery.

RP: _____

_____

21. Teach the client about the 12-step recovery program's concept of a higher power and how this can assist in recovery.

RP: _____

_____

22. Using a 12-step recovery program's step-three exercise, teach the client about the 12-step recovery program's concept of *turning it over*. Then, assign him/her to turn over problems to the higher power each day. Have the client record the event and discuss the results.

RP: _____

_____

23. Teach the client healthy communication skills (e.g., using "I" messages, reflecting, active listening, empathy, being reinforcing, sharing, etc.)
    RP: _____
    _____

24. Using modeling, role playing, and behavior rehearsal, teach the client how to solve problems in an organized fashion (e.g., write the problem, think accurately, list the options of action, evaluate alternatives, act, monitor results.)
    RP: _____
    _____

25. Assist the client in clarifying why he/she was using substances; help him/her to identify other ways to get the same things.
    RP: _____
    _____

26. Show the client how to get good things out of life without mood-altering substances.
    RP: _____
    _____

27. Assign the client to list the pleasurable activities that he/she plans to use in recovery.
    RP: _____
    _____

28. Using progressive relaxation or biofeedback, teach

the client how to relax, and
then assign him/her to
relax twice a day for
10 to 20 minutes.
RP: _____

_____

29. Using current physical fitness levels, help the client
to exercise three times a
week. Then, increase the
exercise by 10 percent a
week, until he/she is exercising at a training heart
rate for at least 20 minutes
at least three times a week.
RP: _____

_____

30. Assign the client to complete
a fourth-step inventory;
then, make arrangements
for him/her to share this
with a clergyperson or someone else in recovery.
RP: _____

_____

31. Using a 12-step recovery
program's relapse preven-
tion exercise, help the client
to uncover his/her triggers
for relapse.
RP: _____

_____

32. Teach the client about high-
risk situations (e.g., negative emotions, social
pressure, interpersonal conflict, positive emotions, and
test of personal control); assist him/her in making a

written plan to cope with each high-risk situation.

RP: _____

_____

33. Using modeling, role playing, and behavior rehearsal, teach the client how to say no to alcohol/drugs; then, practice saying no in high-risk situations.

RP: _____

_____

34. Help the client to develop a personal recovery plan that includes attending recovery group meetings regularly, aftercare, getting a sponsor, and helping others in recovery.

RP: _____

_____

35. Help the client to understand the necessity for working on a personalized recovery program every day to maintain abstinence.

RP: _____

_____

36. Encourage the client to take a personal inventory each night, listing the problems that he/she had that day, making a plan to deal with any problems, and then listing five things for which he/she was grateful that day.

RP: _____

_____

37. Discuss continuing care options with the client (e.g.,

regular meetings, therapy, halfway house, group home, therapeutic community, etc.).

RP: _____

_____

38. Teach the family members the family aspects of the addiction process and the recovery process.

RP: _____

_____

39. Direct the client's family to attend Al-Anon, Nar-Anon, or Tough Love meetings.

RP: _____

_____

40. Ask the client's family to attend the family education component of the treatment program.

RP: _____

_____

41. Assign appropriate reading that will increase the family members' knowledge of the disease and recovery process: *Bradshaw on the Family* (Bradshaw), *Adult Children of Alcoholics* (Woititz), or *It Will Never Happen to Me* (Black).

RP: _____

_____

42. Educate the client's family in the dynamics of enabling and tough love.

RP: _____

_____

43. Monitor the client's family for enabling behaviors, and redirect them in the family session as appropriate.
RP: _____

_____

44. Assist the client's family members in implementing and sticking with tough-love techniques.
RP: _____

_____

45. Help the family members to develop their own individual relapse prevention plans for the client; facilitate a session where plans are shared with the chemically dependent member.
RP: _____

_____

46. In a family session, help the client to discuss substance abuse and the tools of recovery: honesty, recovery group meetings, and a higher power.
RP: _____

_____

47. Help the client to list three things that each family member can do to assist him/her in recovery.
RP: _____

_____

48. In a family session, have the client sign a contract to attend all aftercare activities.
RP: _____

_____

—. _____

_____

RP: _____

_____

—. _____

_____

RP: _____

_____

—. _____

_____

RP: _____

_____

_____

DIAGNOSTIC SUGGESTIONS

Axis I:

305.00	Alcohol Abuse
305.70	Amphetamine Abuse
305.20	Cannabis Abuse
305.60	Cocaine Abuse
305.30	Hallucinogen Abuse
305.90	Inhalant Abuse
305.50	Opioid Abuse
305.90	Phencyclidine Abuse
305.40	Sedative, Hypnotic, or Anxiolytic Abuse
305.90	Other (or Unknown) Substance Abuse
303.90	Alcohol Dependence
304.40	Amphetamine Dependence
304.30	Cannabis Dependence
304.20	Cocaine Dependence
304.50	Hallucinogen Dependence
304.60	Inhalant Dependence
304.00	Opioid Dependence
304.90	Phencyclidine Dependence
304.10	Sedative, Hypnotic, or Anxiolytic Dependence
304.90	Other (or Unknown) Substance Dependence
304.80	Polysubstance Dependence
_____	_____
_____	_____

SUBSTANCE-INDUCED DISORDERS

BEHAVIORAL DEFINITIONS

1. Memory impairment (amnestic disorder) that persists beyond the duration of substance intoxication or withdrawal effects.
2. Memory impairment and cognitive disturbance (dementia) that persist beyond the time of substance intoxication or withdrawal effects.
3. Lack of clear awareness of the environment, deficit in the ability to focus attention, memory dysfunction, language and/or perceptual disturbance (delirium) that developed during or shortly after substance intoxication or withdrawal.
4. Hallucinations or delusions that persist beyond the duration of substance intoxication or withdrawal effects.
5. Depressed mood that developed during or shortly after substance intoxication or withdrawal.
6. Markedly expansive mood that developed during or shortly after substance intoxication or withdrawal.
7. Prominent anxiety, panic attacks, or obsessions that developed during or shortly after substance intoxication or withdrawal.
8. Sleep disturbance that developed during or shortly after substance intoxication or withdrawal.
9. Sexual dysfunction that developed during or shortly after substance intoxication or withdrawal.

—. _____

_____

—. _____

_____

—. _____

_____

LONG-TERM GOALS

1. Recover from substance-induced disorder and maintain a program of recovery that is free from addiction.
2. Improve long- and short-term memory and maintain abstinence from substance abuse.
3. Recover clear memory and an awareness of the environment, realistic perceptions, coherent communication, and focused attention, and maintain abstinence from substance abuse.
4. Terminate hallucinations and/or delusions and maintain abstinence from substance abuse.
5. Elevate depressed mood to normal functioning and maintain abstinence from substance abuse.
6. Moderate expansive mood to a normal level and abstain from substance abuse.
7. Reduce anxiety symptoms significantly and abstain from substance abuse.
8. Restore normal sleep patterns and maintain abstinence from substance abuse.
9. Participate in medical management of substance-induced disorder and addictive behavior.
10. Accept the need to work a 12-step program to recover from substance-induced disorder and addiction.

—. _____
_____
_____

—. _____
_____
_____

—. _____
_____

SHORT-TERM OBJECTIVES

THERAPEUTIC INTERVENTIONS

1. Verbalize an acceptance of the need for a safe place in which to receive treatment for the substance-induced disorder and chemical dependence. (1, 2, 3)

1. Welcome the client to treatment and explain that he/she is in a safe place. Encourage him/her to stay in

2. Verbalize an understanding that the signs and symptoms of the substance-induced disorder are caused by chemical dependence. (2)

3. Verbalize an understanding that the substance-induced disorder is not permanent and will improve if abstinence is maintained. (2, 3)

4. Report any thoughts of causing harm to self or others. (4, 5)

5. Verbalize feelings that surround the substance-induced disorder and addiction. (4, 5, 6)

6. Cooperate with periodic assessments of the substance-induced disorder, intoxication, and withdrawal. (5, 6, 7)

7. Submit to a physical examination to assess bodily functions and the need for psychotropic medication. (7)

8. Take prescribed medications as directed by the physician, and report as to symptoms, medication compliance, effectiveness, and side effects. (8, 9)

9. Cooperate with a complete psychological assessment, and comply with all recommended treatment plans. (10)

treatment long enough to enter recovery.
*RP: _____

_____

2. Teach the client about his/her substance-induced disorder, and directly relate his/her signs and symptoms to his/her chemical abuse.
RP: _____

_____

3. Teach the client that his/her symptoms will improve if he/she remains abstinent from substance abuse.
RP: _____

_____

4. Assess the client's potential for harm to himself/herself or others, and take precautionary steps if needed; encourage reporting any thoughts of causing harm to himself/herself or others.
RP: _____

_____

5. Encourage the client to share his/her feelings that surround the substance-induced disorder and addictive behavior.
RP: _____

_____

6. As often as necessary assess the client with standard instruments (e.g., the Beck Depression Inventory, Beck Anxiety Inventory, Clinical

---

*RP = responsible professional.

10. Take in fluids and nourishment as indicated by the medical staff. (11)

11. Stay with a staff member during severe symptoms of substance-induced disorder, intoxication, or withdrawal. (12)

12. Reduce environmental stimulation to decrease excessive anxiety, perceptual disturbances, and irritability. (13)

13. Talk with a treatment peer that is further along in the program, and discuss plans for recovery. (14)

14. Verbalize the need for further treatment, and develop a written plan to address substance-induced disorder and addiction. (15, 16)

15. Family members verbalize an understanding of the connection between substance-induced disorder and addiction. (17)

16. List three things that each family member can do to assist the client in recovery. (18)

__. _____

_____

__. _____

_____

__. _____

_____

Institute of Withdrawal Scale, Narcotics Withdrawal Scale, Mental Status Examination, Cognitive Screening Capacity Examination, etc.).

RP: _____

_____

7. Physician examine the client, write treatment orders as indicated, titrate medications, and monitor for side effects and effectiveness.

RP: _____

_____

8. Medical staff carry out orders as directed by the physician and administer medications.

RP: _____

_____

9. Monitor the client's medication compliance, symptoms, side effects, and effectiveness of the prescribed medication.

RP: _____

_____

10. Psychologist complete a psychological assessment of the client, and make recommendations for treatment.

RP: _____

_____

11. Encourage the client to take the fluids and nourishment as ordered by the physician.

RP: _____

_____

12. Assign a staff member to stay with the client during severe substance-induced disorder, intoxication, or withdrawal.

RP: _____

_____

13. Adjust the client's environment until there is minimal stimulation that might exacerbate excessive anxiety, perceptual disturbances, and irritability.

RP: _____

_____

14. Ask treatment peers to encourage the client during recovery.

RP: _____

_____

15. Teach the client about 12-step recovery, and encourage him/her to stay in treatment.

RP: _____

_____

16. Help the client to develop a written plan to treat his/her substance-induced disorder and addictive behavior.

RP: _____

_____

17. In a family session, explain the connection between substance-induced disorder and addictive behavior.

RP: _____

_____

18. Help the client to list three
     things that each family
     member can do to assist
     him/her in recovery.

     RP: _____

          _____

___.   _____

          _____

     RP: _____

          _____

___.   _____

          _____

     RP: _____

          _____

___.   _____

          _____

     RP: _____

          _____

DIAGNOSTIC SUGGESTIONS

Axis I: 291.0   Alcohol Intoxication Delirium
             291.0   Alcohol Withdrawal Delirium
             291.2   Alcohol-Induced Persisting Dementia
             291.1   Alcohol-Induced Persisting Amnestic Disorder
             291.5   Alcohol-Induced Psychotic Disorder, With
                        Delusions
             291.3   Alcohol-Induced Psychotic Disorder, With
                        Hallucinations
             291.89   Alcohol-Induced Mood Disorder
             291.89   Alcohol-Induced Anxiety Disorder
             291.89   Alcohol-Induced Sexual Dysfunction
             291.89   Alcohol-Induced Sleep Disorder
             291.9   Alcohol-Related Disorder NOS
             292.81   Other (or Unknown) Substance–Induced
                        Delirium
             292.11   Other (or Unknown) Substance–Induced
                        Psychotic Disorder, With Delusions

292.12	Other (or Unknown) Substance–Induced Psychotic Disorder, With Hallucinations
292.84	Other (or Unknown) Substance–Induced Mood Disorder
292.89	Other (or Unknown) Substance–Induced Anxiety Disorder
292.89	Other (or Unknown) Substance–Induced Sexual Dysfunction
292.89	Other (or Unknown) Substance–Induced Sleep Disorder
_____	_____
_____	_____

SUBSTANCE INTOXICATION/ WITHDRAWAL

BEHAVIORAL DEFINITIONS

1. Cognitive, behavioral, or emotional changes (alcohol on breath, belligerence, mood lability, cognitive impairment, impaired judgment, slurred speech, ataxia) developed shortly after ingesting, inhaling, injecting, or snorting a mood-altering substance.
2. Abnormal autonomic reactivity (e.g., elevated or decreased vital signs, tachycardia, dilated or constricted pupils, diaphoresis, flushed face, etc.) subsequent to the introduction of a mood-altering substance into the body.
3. Admits to recently abusing a mood-altering chemical.
4. Urine test, blood screen, or Breathalyzer™ indicates recent substance use.
5. Psychological symptoms caused by substance withdrawal (e.g., irritability, anxiety, anger, emotional lability, depression, hallucinations, delusions, etc.)
6. Intoxication or withdrawal symptoms causing significant impairment in cognitive, psychomotor, or emotional functioning.
7. Preoccupation with strong cravings, leaving treatment, and using mood-altering chemicals.

—. _____

_____

—. _____

_____

—. _____

_____

LONG-TERM GOALS

1. Stabilize condition medically, behaviorally, emotionally, and cognitively, and return to functioning within normal parameters.
2. Recover from substance intoxication/withdrawal and participate in a chemical dependence assessment.
3. Accept the severity of the substance use problem and enter a program of recovery.
4. Understand the extent of the danger to self and others when intoxicated.
5. Understand the reasons for substance intoxication/withdrawal and make plans to resolve the issues that led to use.

—. _____
_____
—. _____
_____
—. _____
_____

SHORT-TERM OBJECTIVES

1. Verbalize an acceptance of the need to be in a safe place to recover from substance intoxication/withdrawal. (1, 2)

2. Verbalize an agreement to cooperate with the medical management of substance intoxication/withdrawal. (2, 3)

3. Sign a release of information to allow significant others to be informed about admission and condition. (4)

THERAPEUTIC INTERVENTIONS

1. Welcome the client to the treatment setting; explain substance intoxication and the procedures that will be used to arrest symptoms.
   *RP: _____
   _____

2. Teach the client the importance of staying in treatment to recover from substance intoxication and possible withdrawal.
   RP: _____
   _____

_____

*RP = responsible professional.

4. Meet with the physician, and take all medications as prescribed. (5, 6)

5. Report as to medication compliance, effectiveness, and side effects. (6, 7)

6. Cooperate with assessments of substance intoxication and possible withdrawal complications. (5, 8)

7. Participate in taking a biopsychosocial assessment that will measure the extent of addiction/dependency. (9)

8. Agree to stay with a staff member or treatment buddy during severe intoxication/withdrawal. (10)

9. Report any change in symptoms of intoxication/withdrawal to the medical staff. (8, 11)

10. Blood work shows no presence of mood-altering substances. (12)

11. Vital signs stabilized within normal parameters. (8, 13)

12. Cognitive, behavioral, and emotional functioning returned to preintoxication status. (10, 14)

13. Share the feelings that surround admission for substance intoxication/withdrawal. (9, 15)

14. Verbalize thoughts of causing harm to self or others. (15, 16)

3. Inform the client of what he/she can expect during intoxication and withdrawal, and encourage him/her to cooperate with medical management; ask him/her to sign a consent-to-treat form.
RP: _____

_____

4. Encourage the client to sign a release of information; then, contact the significant others to gain support for the client's admission to treatment.
RP: _____

_____

5. Physician examine the client, educate the client about substance intoxication and withdrawal, order medications as appropriate, titrate medications, and monitor for side effects and effectiveness.
RP: _____

_____

6. Medical staff will carry out the orders of the physician and administer medications as directed.
RP: _____

_____

7. Monitor the client's medications for compliance, side effects, and effectiveness.
RP: _____

_____

15. Cooperate in reducing environmental stimulation to prevent exacerbation of symptoms. (17)

16. Learn and cooperate with the rules of the treatment program. (18)

17. Agree to follow through with a personal recovery plan that addresses addiction issues as determined by the biopsychosocial assessment. (9, 19, 20)

18. In a family session, discuss the connection between withdrawal symptoms and addiction. (21)

19. Read letters of support from family members. (22)

__. _____
   _____

__. _____
   _____

__. _____
   _____

8. Medical staff monitor the client's vital signs and administer the Clinical Institute of Withdrawal Scale, the Narcotic Withdrawal Scale, or equivalent measures of the client's functioning during withdrawal.
   RP: _____
   _____

9. Complete a biopsychosocial assessment to determine the extent of the client's addiction and the need for treatment.
   RP: _____
   _____

10. Assign a staff member to remain with the client until he/she is through intoxication and withdrawal.
    RP: _____
    _____

11. Teach the client what signs and symptoms he/she might experience during substance intoxication and/or withdrawal; then, encourage him/her to report any significant change in symptoms to the medical staff.
    RP: _____
    _____

12. Monitor the client's status via blood tests and report findings in the clinical chart.
    RP: _____
    _____

13. Monitor the client's vital signs, and document the findings in his/her chart.
RP: _____

_____

14. Evaluate the client's cognitive, behavioral, and emotional status as detoxification progresses, reporting the results on his/her chart.
RP: _____

_____

15. Probe the client's feelings that surround his/her substance intoxication and admission for treatment.
RP: _____

_____

16. Assess danger to the client or others; encourage him/her to report any thoughts of causing harm to himself/herself or others.
RP: _____

_____

17. Help the client to reduce environment stimulation to a level that will not exacerbate symptoms.
RP: _____

_____

18. Teach the client the rules of the treatment program, and encourage him/her to follow the rules while in treatment.
RP: _____

_____

19. Teach the client that sub-
    stance withdrawal means
    substance dependence; then,
    help him/her to make plans
    for treatment and recovery.
    RP: _____

    _____

20. Share the results of the
    chemical dependence as-
    sessment, and discuss the
    options for the treatment of
    addiction/dependence.
    RP: _____

    _____

21. In a family session, discuss
    withdrawal symptoms
    and the connection with
    addiction.
    RP: _____

    _____

22. Encourage family members
    to write letters of support to
    the client; then, have
    him/her read the letters.
    RP: _____

    _____

__. _____

    _____

    RP: _____

    _____

__. _____

    _____

    RP: _____

    _____

__. _____

    _____

    RP: _____

    _____

DIAGNOSTIC SUGGESTIONS

Axis I:	303.00	Alcohol Intoxication
	292.89	Amphetamine Intoxication
	305.90	Caffeine Intoxication
	292.89	Cannabis Intoxication
	292.89	Cocaine Intoxication
	292.89	Hallucinogen Intoxication
	292.89	Opioid Intoxication
	292.89	Phencyclidine Intoxication
	292.89	Sedative, Hypnotic, or Anxiolytic Intoxication
	291.81	Alcohol Withdrawal
	292.0	Amphetamine Withdrawal
	292.0	Cocaine Withdrawal
	292.0	Opioid Withdrawal
	292.0	Sedative, Hypnotic, or Anxiolytic Withdrawal
	292.89	Other (or Unknown) Substance Intoxication
	292.0	Other (or Unknown) Substance Withdrawal
	_____	_____
	_____	_____

SUICIDAL IDEATION

BEHAVIORAL DEFINITIONS

1. Recurrent or ongoing suicidal ideation without any plans.
2. Ongoing suicidal ideation with a specific plan.
3. Recurrent thoughts of and wish for death.
4. Profound feelings of helplessness, hopelessness, and worthlessness.
5. History of suicide attempts.
6. Experienced recent significant losses (e.g., divorce, death of spouse, illness, loss of job, etc.), which have led to suicidal thoughts.
7. Chemical dependence or other addictive behavior that exacerbates depression, hopelessness, and suicidal ideation.
8. Losses due to addictive behavior (e.g., financial, familial, vocational, etc.) trigger suicidal feelings.
9. Belief that others would be better off if he/she were dead.

—. _____

_____

—. _____

_____

—. _____

_____

LONG-TERM GOALS

1. Resolve the wish for death, find new hope, and enter a program of recovery that is free of addiction and suicidal ideation.
2. Terminate all suicidal urges, express hope for the future, and remain abstinent from all mood-altering substances.

3. Enter at the level of care that is necessary to protect self from suicidal impulses.

4. Understand the relationship between suicidal ideation and addictive behavior.

5. Develop a sense of self-worth to other addicts and family members.

—. _____
   _____

—. _____
   _____

—. _____
   _____

SHORT-TERM OBJECTIVES

1. Verbalize specific suicidal thoughts, feelings, plans, and actions. (1, 6, 7)

2. Sign a no-self-harm contract that states that nothing will be done to harm self while in treatment and will contact a staff member if feeling suicidal. (2)

3. Agree to the level of care that is necessary to protect self from suicidal impulses. (1, 2, 3, 4)

4. Agree to stay with a staff member until suicidal threat resolves. (1, 2, 3, 4)

5. Verbalize an understanding of how suicide risk is magnified by addiction. (5, 6)

THERAPEUTIC INTERVENTIONS

1. Assess the dangerousness of the suicidal ideation by asking the client to share suicidal feelings, thoughts, plans, and behaviors.
   *RP: _____
   _____

2. Have the client sign a no-self-harm contract that states that he/she will do nothing to harm himself/herself while in treatment, and that he/she will contact a staff member if feeling suicidal.
   RP: _____
   _____

3. Discuss the levels of care that are available (e.g., locked room, staying close by a staff member, transfer

---

*RP = responsible professional.

6. Verbalize the reasons for feeling helpless, hopeless, and worthless. (1, 6, 7)

7. Identify the losses sustained because of addiction. (6, 7)

8. Verbalize feeling a sense of importance to family members and other addicts in recovery. (8)

9. Meet the physician for an assessment for the need for psychotropic medication. (9)

10. Take all medications as directed. (10, 11)

11. Keep a record of self-defeating thoughts, and replace each dysfunctional thought with positive, self-enhancing self-talk. (12, 13)

12. List the reasons for new hope for the future. (13, 14, 15, 16)

13. List 10 reasons for wanting to live. (14, 17, 18)

14. Verbalize new hope for resolving interpersonal conflicts because of being in addiction treatment. (19, 20)

15. Verbalize an understanding of the 12-step *attitude of gratitude;* then, list five things to be grateful for each day. Share this with therapist. (21)

16. Verbalize coping strategies that will elevate depressed mood. (22)

17. Encourage someone else in recovery at least once a day.

to a more intensive level of care, etc.); then, decide upon the level of care that will be necessary to protect the client from suicidal impulses.
RP: _____
_____

4. Assign a staff member to stay with the client until his/her suicidal threat is resolved.
RP: _____
_____

5. Assist the client in understanding how the feelings of shame, loss, and hopelessness are exacerbated by addictive behavior.
RP: _____
_____

6. Review the losses (e.g., marital, familial, social, legal, financial, health, occupational, etc.) that have resulted from addictive behavior and led to suicidal hopelessness.
RP: _____
_____

7. Explore the client's reasons for suicidal ideation: feelings of helplessness, hopelessness, and worthlessness.
RP: _____
_____

8. Help the client to see the meaning behind the 12-step recovery program's saying,

Record these events and share with therapist. (16, 23)

18. Verbalize an understanding of the 12-step concept of a higher power and how this can be used to recover from suicidal ideation and addictive behavior. (24)

19. Practice prayer and meditation at least once each day. (24, 25)

20. In a family session, discuss the connection between suicidal ideation and addiction. (26)

21. List three things that each family member can do to assist the client in recovery. (27)

—. _____
   _____

—. _____
   _____

—. _____
   _____

"What we cannot do alone, we can do together." Help him/her to see that other addicts need his/her support in recovery.
RP: _____
    _____

9. Physician examine the client, discuss suicidal ideation and addiction, order medications as indicated, titrate medications, and monitor for side effects.
RP: _____
    _____

10. Staff administer the client's prescribed medications.
RP: _____
    _____

11. Monitor the client's medication for compliance, side effects, and effectiveness.
RP: _____
    _____

12. Assist the client in developing an awareness of his/her cognitive messages that reinforce hopelessness and helplessness.
RP: _____
    _____

13. Assign the client to keep a daily record of self-defeating thoughts (e.g., thoughts of hopelessness, helplessness, worthlessness, catastrophizing, negatively predicting the future, etc.). Challenge each thought for accuracy; then, replace each dysfunc-

tional thought with a thought that is positive and self-enhancing.

RP: _____

_____

14. Provide the client with reasons for new hope in recovery (e.g., being in treatment offers hope, working with trained professionals who can act as an advocate, other addicts can encourage them, staff members are supportive, etc.).

RP: _____

_____

15. Encourage the client regarding the excellent chances for recovery from addiction and depression if he/she works the 12-step program.

RP: _____

_____

16. Assign the client to read "the promises" on pages 83 and 84 of the Alcoholics Anonymous (AA) *Big Book,* and encourage the client to verbalize hope for the future.

RP: _____

_____

17. Help the client to list 10 reasons to live (e.g., positive people, places, or things that are a part of his/her life).

RP: _____

_____

18. Assign the client to write a list of the positive people, places, and things in his/her life.
RP: _____

_____

19. Help the client to see the new hope that addiction treatment brings to the resolution of interpersonal conflicts.
RP: _____

_____

20. Meet with the client and a significant other with whom there is conflict to begin a process of conflict resolution.
RP: _____

_____

21. Teach the client about the 12-step recovery program's concept of the *attitude of gratitude;* then, assign him/her to list five things for which he/she is grateful each day.
RP: _____

_____

22. Assist the client in developing coping strategies for suicidal ideation (e.g., more physical exercise, less internal focus, increased social involvement, and more expression of feelings).
RP: _____

_____

23. Assign the client to encourage someone in treatment

each day; record each event and discuss with the therapist.

RP: _____

_____

24. Teach the client about the 12-step recovery program's concept of a higher power; encourage the client to ask God for direction each day.

RP: _____

_____

25. Assign the client to read Chapter 11 in the *Twelve Steps and Twelve Traditions* (AA); then, encourage him/her to pray and meditate at least once each day.

RP: _____

_____

26. In a family session, have the client discuss the connection between suicidal ideation and addiction.

RP: _____

_____

27. Help the client to list three things that each family member can do to assist in recovery; assign the client to share these with the family members and report back to the therapist.

RP: _____

_____

__. _____

_____

RP: _____

_____

___.   _____

_____

RP: _____

_____

___.   _____

_____

RP: _____

_____

DIAGNOSTIC SUGGESTIONS

Axis I:	291.89	Alcohol-Induced Mood Disorder
	292.84	Amphetamine-Induced Mood Disorder
	292.84	Cocaine-Induced Mood Disorder
	292.84	Inhalant-Induced Mood Disorder
	292.84	Opioid-Induced Mood Disorder
	292.84	Phencyclidine-Induced Mood Disorder
	292.84	Sedative-, Hypnotic-, or Anxiolytic-Induced Mood Disorder
	292.84	Other (or Unknown) Substance–Induced Mood Disorder
	296.xx	Major Depressive Disorder
	300.4	Dysthymic Disorder
	296.xx	Bipolar I Disorder
	296.89	Bipolar II Disorder
	309.xx	Adjustment Disorder
	_____	_____
	_____	_____
Axis II:	301.83	Borderline Personality Disorder
	_____	_____
	_____	_____

TREATMENT RESISTANCE

BEHAVIORAL DEFINITIONS

1. Severe denial of addiction in spite of strong evidence of increase tolerance, loss of control, and many negative consequences of addictive behavior.
2. Substitutes a secondary problem as the focus of concern rather than admit that addiction is the primary problem.
3. Angry at family members, court, or employer for giving an ultimatum for treatment.
4. Refuses to cooperate with the treatment plan and is a constant risk for terminating treatment.
5. Verbally abusive to treatment providers and other clients, is irritable, restless, and angry.
6. Dishonesty to self and others has led to believing own lies rather than the facts regarding addictive behavior.
7. Constantly phones friends or family members, demanding that they take him/her out of treatment.
8. Refusing to talk to or bond with treatment peers.

—. _____

_____

—. _____

_____

—. _____

_____

LONG-TERM GOALS

1. Accept the truth about the problems in which addiction has resulted, and enter a program of recovery.
2. Accept the powerlessness and unmanageability that addictive behavior has brought to his/her life, and actively engage in the treatment process.
3. Learn the facts about addictive behavior, and make a logical decision about the treatment that is necessary to arrest addiction.
4. Resolve anger at others, and accept the responsibility for the problems that are caused by addictive behavior and the need for treatment.

—. _____
   _____
   _____
—. _____
   _____
   _____
—. _____
   _____

SHORT-TERM OBJECTIVES

1. Verbalize the reasons for resisting treatment. (1, 2)
2. Share the feelings that surround admission to treatment. (2)
3. Cooperate with a bio-psychosocial assessment and accept the treatment recommendations. (3)
4. Cooperate with a physician's examination. (4)
5. Listen to the results of the assessments, and make a rational, informed choice about the treatment that is

THERAPEUTIC INTERVENTIONS

1. Probe the reasons why the client is resisting treatment; check for the accuracy of his/her beliefs about addiction.
   *RP: _____
   _____

2. Encourage the client to share the fear, sadness, shame, and anger that he/she feels about coming to treatment.
   RP: _____
   _____

---

*RP = responsible professional.

needed to arrest addiction.
(3, 4, 5)

6. List 10 times when addictive behavior led to negative consequences. (6)

7. Sign a release of information to key family members, friends, employer, and coworkers so they can be contacted to support treatment. (7, 8)

8. Concerned family members, friends, employer, or coworkers express their concerns about the client's addiction. (7, 8)

9. Sign a release of information to the probation, parole, or court services worker so information can be shared about treatment. (9)

10. Discuss the reasons for treatment resistance with treatment peers, and listen to their feedback. (10, 11)

11. Verbalize an understanding of the treatment process. (12)

12. Stay with a staff member or treatment buddy until the threat of leaving treatment resolves. (13)

13. Discuss the options for treatment, and make informed plans to enter treatment in the least restrictive environment that is necessary to control addiction. (14)

14. List five lies that were told to hide addiction. (15)

3. Conduct a biopsychosocial assessment, and collect laboratory results and collateral information from friends and relatives. Share these results with the client.
RP: _____

_____

4. Physician examine the client, and share the results of the history and physical, pointing out signs and symptoms of prolonged and excessive addiction.
RP: _____

_____

5. Using the biopsychosocial assessments, help the client to make an informed choice about treatment.
RP: _____

_____

6. Help the client to see the extent of his/her addiction by showing him/her a number of negative consequences that resulted from addictive behavior.
RP: _____

_____

7. Ask the client to sign releases of information, and meet with the client's employer, family, friends, and/or coworkers to enlist their support for him/her to remain in treatment.
RP: _____

_____

15. Develop a written personal recovery plan that includes the treatment that is necessary to maintain abstinence. (16)

16. In a family session, discuss the connection between treatment resistance and addiction. (17)

17. Make a list of three things that each family member can do to assist the client in recovery. (18)

__. _____

_____

__. _____

_____

__. _____

_____

8. Assign concerned family, friends, employer, and coworkers to write letters, stating specific instances when the client's addiction hurt them, and to share what they are going to do if the client refuses treatment. Have each person read the letters to the client in a group setting.

RP: _____

_____

9. Ask the client to sign a release of information, and contact his/her probation, parole, or court services worker to elicit support for treatment.

RP: _____

_____

10. In a group setting, encourage the client to share why he/she does not want to remain in treatment. Facilitate other clients' confrontation of denial and support for the need for treatment.

RP: _____

_____

11. Encourage the client to discuss with peers and staff his/her plans to leave treatment.

RP: _____

_____

12. Teach the client about the treatment process, and encourage him/her to stay in

treatment as long as necessary to bring the addiction under control.

RP: _____

_____

13. Assign a staff member or treatment peer to stay with the client until the risk of leaving treatment is resolved.

RP: _____

_____

14. Discuss the levels of care that are available (e.g., recovery group meetings, counseling, outclient treatment, day treatment, residential treatment, partial hospitalization, and hospitalization), and help the client to make an informed decision about entering treatment.

RP: _____

_____

15. Help the client to admit to the lies that he/she told to hide his/her addiction.

RP: _____

_____

16. Help the client to develop a written personal recovery plan detailing the treatment that is necessary to maintain abstinence.

RP: _____

_____

17. In a family session, help the client to discuss the connec-

tion between treatment resistance and addiction.

RP: _____

_____

18. Help the client to list three things that each family member can do to assist in recovery.

RP: _____

_____

—. _____

_____

RP: _____

_____

—. _____

_____

RP: _____

_____

—. _____

_____

RP: _____

_____

DIAGNOSTIC SUGGESTIONS

Axis I:	305.00	Alcohol Abuse
	305.70	Amphetamine Abuse
	305.20	Cannabis Abuse
	305.60	Cocaine Abuse
	305.30	Hallucinogen Abuse
	305.90	Inhalant Abuse
	305.50	Opioid Abuse
	305.90	Phencyclidine Abuse
	305.40	Sedative, Hypnotic, or Anxiolytic Abuse
	305.90	Other (or Unknown) Substance Abuse
	303.90	Alcohol Dependence
	304.40	Amphetamine Dependence

304.30	Cannabis Dependence
304.20	Cocaine Dependence
304.50	Hallucinogen Dependence
304.60	Inhalant Dependence
304.00	Opioid Dependence
304.90	Phencyclidine Dependence
304.10	Sedative, Hypnotic, or Anxiolytic Dependence
304.90	Other (or Unknown) Substance Dependence
304.80	Polysubstance Dependence
_____	_____
_____	_____

Appendix A

BIBLIOTHERAPY SUGGESTIONS

Adult-Child-of-an-Alcoholic Traits

Al-Anon Family Group (1994). *From Survival to Recovery: Growing Up in an Alcoholic Family.* Virginia Beach, VA: Al-Anon Family Group.

Alcoholics Anonymous (1974). *Big Book.* New York: Alcoholics Anonymous General Services Office.

Bowden, J., H. Gravitz, C. Wegscheider, and J. Bowden (1987). *Recovery: A Guide for Adult Children of Alcoholics.* New York: Fireside.

Kritsberg, W. (1998). *The Adult Children of Alcoholics Syndrome: From Discovery to Recovery.* New York: Bantam Books.

Woititz, J. G. (1990). *Adult Children of Alcoholics.* Palm Coast, FL: Health Communications.

Anger

Alberti, R., and M. Emmons (1990). *Your Perfect Right.* San Luis Obispo, CA: Impact.

Bilodeau, L. (1992). *The Anger Workbook.* Minneapolis, MN: Compcare Publications.

Gottlieb, M. (1999). *The Angry Self: A Comprehensive Approach to Anger Management.* Redding, CT: Zeig, Tucker and Theisen, Inc.

Harbin, T. (2000). *Beyond Anger: A Guide for Men: How to Free Yourself from the Grip of Anger and Get More Out of Life.* New York: Marlowe and Co.

Lee, J., and B. Stott (1995). *Facing the Fire: Experiencing and Expressing Anger Appropriately.* New York: Bantam Doubleday Dell.

Lerner, H. (1997). *The Dance of Anger: A Woman's Guide to Changing the Patterns of Intimate Relationships.* New York: Harper-Collins.

McKay, M., P. Rogers, and J. McKay (1989). *When Anger Hurts: Quieting the Storm Within.* Oakland, CA: New Harbinger Publications.

Smedes, L. (1991). *Forgive and Forget: Healing the Hurts We Don't Deserve.* San Francisco: Harper.

Williams, R., and V. Williams (1998). *Anger Kills: Seventeen Strategies for Controlling the Hostility That Can Harm Your Health.* New York: Harper Mass Market Paperbacks.

Antisocial Behavior

Patterson, G., J. Reid, and T. Dishion (1997). *Antisocial Boys*. Eugene, OR: Castalia Publishing Company.

Samenow, S. (1984). *Inside the Criminal Mind*. New York: Times Books.

Sells, S., N. Schiff, and J. Haley (1998). *Treating the Tough Adolescent: A Family-Based, Step-by-Step Guide*. New York: Guilford Press.

Anxiety

Antony, M., and R. Swinson (2000). *The Shyness and Social Anxiety Workbook: Proven Techniques for Overcoming Your Fears*. Oakland, CA: New Harbinger Publishers.

Bradshaw, J. (1988). *Healing the Shame That Binds You*. Deer Field Beach, FL: Health Communications.

Burns, D. (1986). *Intimate Connections*. New York: New American Library.

Dayhoff, S. (2000). *Diagonally Parked in a Parallel Universe: Working Through Social Anxiety*. Placitas, NM: Effectiveness-Plus Publications.

Fossum, M., and M. Mason (1989). *Facing Shame*. New York: W. W. Norton & Co.

Goldman, C., and S. Babior (1996). *Overcoming Panic, Anxiety, and Phobias: New Strategies to Free Yourself from Worry and Fear*. Duluth, MN: Whole Person Associates.

Helmstetter, S. (1997). *What to Say When You Talk to Yourself*. Fine Communications.

Peurifoy, R. (1995). *Anxiety, Phobias, and Panic: A Step-by-Step Program for Regaining Control of Your Life*. New York: Warner Books.

Rapee, R. (1999). *Overcoming Shyness and Social Phobia: A Step-by-Step Guide*. Northvale, NJ: Jason Aronson.

Zimbardo, P. (1987). *Shyness: What It Is and What to Do about It*. New York: Addison-Wesley.

Attention-Deficit/Hyperactivity Disorder (ADHD)

Barkley, R. (2000). *Taking Charge of ADHD: The Complete, Authoritative Guide for Parents*. New York: Guilford Press.

Hollowell, E., and J. Ratey (1995). *Driven to Distraction: Recognizing and Coping With Attention Deficit Disorder from Childhood Through Adulthood*. New York: Simon & Schuster.

Ingersoll, B. (1995). *Distant Drums, Different Drummers: A Guide for Young People with ADHD*. Buffalo, NY: Cape Publishing.

Kelly, K., and P. Ramundo (1996). *You Mean I'm Not Lazy, Stupid or Crazy?!: A Self-Help Book for Adults with Attention Deficit Disorder*. New York: Fireside.

Murphy, K., and S. Levert (1995). *Out of the Fog: Treatment Options and Coping Strategies for Adult Attention Deficit Disorder.* New York: Hyperion.

Quinn, P., and J. Stern (1992). *Putting on the Brakes: Young People's Guide to Understanding Attention Deficit Hyperactive Disorder.* Washington, DC: Magination.

Attention-Deficit/Inattentive Disorder

Barkley, R. (2000). *Taking Charge of ADHD: The Complete, Authoritative Guide for Parents.* New York: Guilford Press.

Hollowell, E., and J. Ratey (1995). *Driven to Distraction: Recognizing and Coping with Attention Deficit Disorder from Childhood Through Adulthood.* New York: Simon & Schuster.

Ingersoll, B. (1995). *Distant Drums, Different Drummers: A Guide for Young People with ADHD.* Buffalo, NY: Cape Publishing.

Kelly, K., and P. Ramundo (1996). *You Mean I'm Not Lazy, Stupid or Crazy?!: A Self-Help Book for Adults with Attention Deficit Disorder.* New York: Fireside.

Murphy, K., and S. Levert (1995). *Out of the Fog: Treatment Options and Coping Strategies for Adult Attention Deficit Disorder.* New York: Hyperion.

Quinn, P., and J. Stern (1992). *Putting on the Brakes: Young People's Guide to Understanding Attention Deficit Hyperactive Disorder.* Washington, DC: Magination.

Borderline Traits

Kreisman, J., and H. Straus (1991). *I Hate You—Don't Leave Me: Understanding Borderline Personality Disorder.* New York: Avon.

Mason, P., R. Kreger, and L. Siever (1998). *Stop Walking on Eggshells: Coping When Someone You Care About Has Borderline Personality Disorder.* Oakland, CA: New Harbinger Publications.

Moskovitz, R. (1996). *Lost in the Mirror: An Inside Look at Borderline Personality Disorder.* Dallas, TX: Taylor Publishers.

Santoro, J., and R. Cohen (1997). *The Angry Heart: Overcoming Borderline and Addictive Disorders: An Interactive Self-Help Guide.* Oakland, CA: New Harbinger Publications.

Childhood Trauma

Barnhill, J., R. Rosen, and R. Granet (1999). *Why Am I Still So Afraid: Understanding Post Traumatic Stress Disorder.* New York: Dell Publication Co.

Bradshaw, J. (1988). *Healing the Shame That Binds You.* Deer Field Beach, FL: Health Communications.

Draper, P. (1996). *Haunted Memories: Healing the Pain of Childhood Abuse.* Old Tappan, NJ: Fleming H. Revell Co.

Flannery, R., Jr. (1995). *Post-Traumatic Stress Disorder: The Victims Guide to Healing and Recovery.* New York: Crossroad/Herder & Herder.

Gil, E. (1984). *Outgrowing the Pain.* New York: Dell Publishing.

Matsakis, A. (1996). *I Can't Get Over It: A Handbook for Trauma Survivors.* Oakland, CA: New Harbinger Publications.

Matsakis, A. (1998). *Trust After Trauma: A Guide to Relationships for Survivors and Those Who Love Them.* Oakland, CA: New Harbinger Publications.

Schiraldi, G. (1999). *The Post-Traumatic Stress Disorder Sourcebook: A Guide to Healing, Recovery and Growth.* Lincolnwood, IL: Lowell House.

Dependent Traits

Alberti, R., and M. Emmons (1990). *Your Perfect Right.* San Luis Obispo, CA: Impact.

Alcoholics Anonymous (1974). *Big Book.* Alcoholics Anonymous General Services Office.

Beattie, M. (1987). *Codependent No More: How to Stop Controlling Others and Start Caring for Yourself.* San Francisco: Harper.

Drews, T. R. (1980). *Getting Them Sober: A Guide for Those Living with Alcoholism.* South Plainfield, NJ: Bridge Publishing.

Evans, P. (1992). *The Verbally Abusive Relationship.* Holbrook, MA: Bob Adams Inc.

Helmfelt, R., F. Minirth, and P. Meier (1985). *Love Is a Choice.* Nashville, TN: Nelson.

Norwood, R. (1985). *Women Who Love Too Much.* Los Angeles: Tarcher.

Pittman, F. (1998). *Grow Up!* New York: Golden Books.

Walker, L. (1979). *The Battered Woman.* New York: Harper & Row.

Whitfield, C. (1990). *A Gift to Myself: A Personal Guide to Healing My Child Within.* Deerfield Beach, FL: Health Communications, Inc.

Whitfield, C. (1993). *Boundaries and Relationships: Knowing, Protecting and Enjoying the Self.* Deerfield Beach, FL: Health Communications, Inc.

Depression

Burns, D. (1990). *The Feeling Good Handbook.* New York: Plume.

Cronkite, K. (1995). *On the Edge of Darkness: Conversations About Conquering Depression.* New York: Delta.

O'Connor, R. (1999). *Undoing Depression: What Therapy Doesn't Teach You and Medication Can't Give You.* New York: Berkley Publishing Group.

Thorn, J., and L. Rothstein (1993). *You Are Not Alone: Words of Experience and Hope for the Journey Through Depression.* New York: Harperperennial.

Yapko, M. (1998). *Breaking the Patterns of Depression.* New York: Main Street Books.

Eating Disorders

Claude-Pierre, P. (1999). *The Secret Language of Eating Disorders: The Revolutionary New Approach.* (1999). New York: Vintage Books.

Costin, C. (1997). *The Eating Disorder Source Book: A Comprehensive Guide to the Causes, Treatments, and Prevention of Eating Disorders.* Los Angeles: Lowell House.

Jantz, G. (1995). *Hope, Help, and Healing for Eating Disorders: A New Approach to Treating Anorexia, Bulimia, and Overeating.* Wheaton, IL: Harold Shaw Publishers.

Leith, L. (1998). *Exercising Your Way to Better Mental Health.* Morgantown, WV: Fitness Info Technology.

Sacker, I., and M. Zimmer (1995). *Dying to Be Thin: Understanding and Defeating Anorexia and Bulimia.* New York: Warner Books.

Siegel, M., J. Brisman, and M. Weinshell. (1997). *Surviving an Eating Disorder: Strategies for Family and Friends.* New York: Harper-Collins.

Family Conflicts

Beattie, M. (1987). *Codependent No More.* Center City, MN: Hazelden.

Covey, S. R., and Covey, S. M. (1998). *The 7 Habits of Highly Effective Families: Building a Beautiful Family Culture in a Turbulent World.* New York: Golden Books Publishing Company.

Page, S., and S. Page (1998). *How One of You Can Bring the Two of You Together: Breakthrough Strategies to Resolve Conflicts and Reignite Your Love.* New York: Bantam Doubleday Dell.

Robinson, J. (1997). *Communication Miracles for Couples: Easy and Effective Tools to Create More Love and Less Conflict.* New York: Conari Publishing.

Sherven, J., and J. Sniechowski (1997). *The New Intimacy: Discovering the Magic at the Heart of Your Differences.* Palm Coast, FL: Health Communications.

Weinhold, B., and J. Weinhold (1989). *Breaking Free of the Co-Dependency Trap.* Walpole, NH: Stillpoint Publishing.

Gambling

Berman, L., and M. Siegel (1998). *Behind the 8-Ball: A Guide for Families of Gamblers.* Center City, MN: Hazelden Publishing.

Eadington, W., and J. Cornelius (2000). *The Downside: Problem and Pathological Gambling.* Las Vegas, NV: University of Nevada Press.

Federman, E., C. Drebing, and C. Krebs (2000). *Don't Leave It to Chance: A Guide for Families of Problem Gamblers.* Oakland, CA: New Harbinger Publications.

Gamblers Anonymous (1989). *Combo Book.* Los Angeles: Gamblers Anonymous International Service Office.

Herscovitch, A. (1999). *Alcoholism and Pathological Gambling: Similarities and Differences.* Holmes Beach, FL: Learning Publications.

May, G. (1991). *Addiction and Grace.* San Francisco: Harper San Francisco.

Grief/Loss Unresolved

Caplan, S., and G. Lang (1995). *Grief's Courageous Journey: A Workbook.* New Oakland, CA: Harbinger Publications.

Childs-Gowell, E. (1992). *Good Grief Rituals: Tools for Healing: A Healing Companion.* Barrytown, NY: Station Hill Press.

Harris-Lord, J., and E. Wheeler (1991). *No Time for Goodbyes: Coping With Sorrow, Anger, and Injustice After a Tragic Death.* New York: Pathfinder Publications.

James, J., and R. Friedman (1998). *The Grief Recovery Handbook: The Action Program for Moving Beyond Death, Divorce, and Other Losses.* New York: Harper-Collins.

Obershaw, R. (1998). *Cry Until You Laugh: Comforting Guidance for Coping With Grief.* Minneapolis, MN: Fairview Publications.

Westberg, G. (1986). *Good Grief: A Constructive Approach to the Problem of Loss.* Minneapolis, MN: Fortress Press.

Impulsivity

Garber, S., R. Freedman-Spizman, and M. Garber (1995). *Is Your Child Hyperactive? Inattentive? Impulsive? Distractable?: Helping the ADD/Hyperactive Child.* New York: Villard Books.

Hollowell, E., and J. Ratey (1994). *Driven to Distraction.* New York: Simon & Schuster.

Melody, P., and A. Miller (1992). *Facing Love Addiction: Giving Yourself the Power to Change the Way You Love—The Love Connection to Codependence.* San Francisco: Harper San Francisco.

Quinn, D., and J. Stern (1992). *Putting on the Brakes.* Washington, DC: Magination Press.

Legal Problems

Kheel, T. *The Keys to Conflict Resolution: Proven Methods of Settling Disputes Voluntarily.* (1999). New York: Four Walls Eight Windows.

Mnookin, R., S. Peppet, and A. Tulumello (2000). *Beyond Winning: Negotiating to Create Value in Deals and Disputes.* Cambridge, MA: Harvard University Press.

Seidenberg, R., and W. Dawes (1997). *The Father's Emergency Guide to Divorce-Custody Battle.* New York: J. E. S. Books, Inc.

Smith, G., and S. Abrahms (1998). *What Every Woman Should Know About Divorce and Custody: Judges, Lawyers, and Therapists Share Winning Strategies on How to Keep the Kids, the Cash and the Family.* New York: Perigee.

Stewart, J. (2000). *The Child Custody Book: How to Protect Your Children and Win Your Case.* Atascadero, CA: Impact Publishers, Inc.

Strohm, R., ed. (1997). *Solving Your Financial Problems: Getting Out of Debt, Repairing Your Credit and Dealing With Bankruptcy* (Layman's Law Guide). Broomall, PA: Chelsea House Publishing.

Living Environment Deficiency

Alberti, R., and M. Emmons (1990). *Your Perfect Right.* San Luis Obispo, CA: Impact.

Forward, S., and D. Frazier (1998). *Emotional Blackmail.* New York: HarperCollins.

Gordon, S. (1981). *The Teenage Survival Book.* New York: Times Books.

Kaplan, L. (1997). *Coping with Peer Pressure.* Center City, MN: Hazelden.

Kritsberg, W. (1998). *The Adult Children of Alcoholics Syndrome: From Discovery to Recovery.* New York: Bantam Books.

Sachs, S. (1997). *Street Gang Awareness: A Resource Guide for Parents and Professionals.* Minneapolis, MN: Fairview Press.

Mania/Hypomania

Bradley, L. (2000). *Manic Depression: How to Live While Loving a Manic Depressive.* Houston, TX: Emerald Ink Publications.

Granet, R., and E. Ferber (1999). *Why Am I Up, Why Am I Down?: Understanding Bipolar Disorder.* New York: Dell.

Mondimore, F. (1999). *Bipolar Disorder: A Guide for Patients and Families.* Baltimore, MD: Johns Hopkins University Press.

Olson, B., and M. Olson (1999). *Win the Battle: The 3-Step Lifesaving Formula to Conquer Depression and Bipolar Disorder.* Worchester, MA: Chandler House Press.

Papolos, D., and J. Papolos (1999). *The Bipolar Child: The Definitive and Reassuring Guide to Childhood's Most Misunderstood Disorder.* New York: Broadway Books.

Waltz, M. (2000). *Bipolar Disorders: A Guide to Helping Children and Adolescents.* Sebastopol, CA: O'Reilly & Associates.

Medical Issues

Cousins, N. (1991). *Anatomy of an Illness as Perceived by the Patient.* New York: Bantam Doubleday.

Dollemore, D., and A. Feinstein, eds. (1996). *Symptoms: Their Causes and Cures: How to Understand and Treat 265 Health Concerns.* New York: Bantam Books.

Griffith, W., and M. Pederson (1992). *Complete Guide to Symptoms, Illnesses and Surgery for People Over 50.* New York: Perigee.

Winter, H., and M. Griffith (2000). *The Complete Guide to Symptoms, Illnesses, and Surgery.* New York: Perigee.

Narcissistic Traits

Brown, N. (1998). *The Destructive Narcissistic Pattern.* Westport, CT: Praeger Publications.

Donaldson-Pressman, S., and R. Pressman (1997). *The Narcissistic Family: Diagnosis and Treatment.* San Francisco: Jossey-Bass.

Forrest, G. (1995). *Alcoholism, Narcissism and Psychopathology.* Leonia, NJ: Jason Aronson.

Lowen, A. (1997). *Narcissism: Denial of the True Self.* Greenwich, CT: Touchstone.

Schwartz-Salant, N. (1982). *Narcissism and Character Transformation: The Psychology of Narcissistic Character Disorders.* Toronto, ON: Inner City Books.

Solomon, M. (1992). *Narcissism and Intimacy: Love and Marriage in an Age of Confusion.* New York: W. W. Norton & Company.

Nicotine Dependence

Ashelman, M. (2000). *Stop Smoking Naturally.* New York: NTC/Contemporary Publishing.

Baer, A. (1998). *Quit Smoking for Good: A Supportive Program for Permanent Smoking Cessation.* Freedom, CA: Crossing Press.

Burton, D. (1986). *American Cancer Society's Freshstart: 21 Days to Stop Smoking.* New York: Pocket Books.

Fisher, E., and C. Koop (1998). *American Lung Association 7 Steps to a Smoke Free Life.* New York: John Wiley and Sons.

Lynch, B., and R. Bonnie, eds. (1994). *Growing Up Tobacco Free: Preventing Nicotine Addiction in Children and Youths.* Washington, DC: National Academy Press.

Rogers, J., and J. Rubinstein (1995). *You Can Stop Smoking.* New York: Pocket Books.

Occupational Problems

Gill, L. (1999). *How to Work With Just About Anyone: A 3-Step Solution for Getting Difficult People to Change.* New York: Fireside.

Hirsh, S., and J. Kise (1996). *Work it Out: Clues for Solving People Problems at Work.* Palo Alto, CA: Davies-Black Publishing.

Johnson, S. (1998). *Who Moved My Cheese?: An Amazing Way to Deal With Change in Your Work and in Your Life.* New York: Putnam Publishing Group.

Lloyd, K. (1999). *Jerks at Work: How to Deal With People Problems and Problem People.* Franklin Lakes, NJ: Career Press.

Scanlon, W. (1991). *Alcoholism and Drug Abuse in the Workplace.* Westport, CT: Praeger Publications.

Oppositional Defiant Behavior

Bodenhamer, G. (1884). *Back in Control: How to Get Your Children to Behave.* New York: Simon and Schuster Trade.

Greene, R. (1998). *The Explosive Child: A New Approach for Understanding and Parenting Easily Frustrated, "Chronically Inflexible" Children.* New York: Harper-Collins.

Hepp, E., M. Fleishman, and P. Espeland (1996). *Fighting Invisible Tigers: A Stress Management Guide for Teens.* Minneapolis, MN: Free Spirit Publishing.

Kindlon, D., M. Thompson, D. Kindlon, and T. Barker (1999). *Raising Cain: Protecting the Emotional Life of Boys.* New York: Ballantine Publishing Group.

McCoy, K., and C. Wibbelsman (1995). *A Teenagers Guide to Friends, Failure, Sexuality, Love, Rejection, Addiction, Peer Pressure, Families, Loss, Depression, Change, and Other Challenges of Living.* New York: Berkley Publishing Group.

Riley, D. (1997). *The Defiant Child: A Parents Guide to Oppositional Defiant Disorder.* Dallas, TX: Taylor Publishing Company.

Smedes, L. (1991). *Forgive and Forget: Healing the Hurts We Don't Deserve.* San Francisco: Harper.

Parent-Child Relational Problems

Bodenhamer, G. (1884). *Back in Control: How to Get Your Children to Behave.* New York: Simon and Schuster Trade.

Dreikurs, R., and V. Soltz (1964). *Children the Challenge.* New York: Hawthorne Books.

Hepp, E., M. Fleishman, and P. Espeland (1996). *Fighting Invisible Tigers: A Stress Management Guide for Teens.* Minneapolis, MN: Free Spirit Publishing.

McCoy, K., and C. Wibbelsman (1995). *A Teenagers Guide to Friends, Failure, Sexuality, Love, Rejection, Addiction, Peer Pressure, Families, Loss, Depression, Change, and Other Challenges of Living.* New York: Berkley Publishing Group.

Seixas, J., and G. Youcha (1985). *Children of Alcoholics: A Survivor's Manual.* New York: Crown Publishers.

Sells, S. (1998). *Treating the Tough Adolescent: A Family Based, Step-by-Step Guide.* New York: Guilford Press.

Steinberg, L., and A. Levine (1997). *You and Your Adolescent: A Parent's Guide for Ages 10 to 20.* New York: Harper-Collins.

Partner Relational Conflicts

Asker, S. (1999). *Plan B: How to Get Unstuck from Work, Family, and Relationship Problems.* New York: Perigee.

Beck, A. (1989). *Love is Never Enough: How Couples Can Overcome Misunderstanding, Resolve Conflicts, and Solve Relationship Problems Through Cognitive Therapy.* New York: Harper-Collins.

Crenshaw, R. (1981). *Expressing Your Feelings: The Key to an Intimate Relationship.* New York: Irvington Publications.

Page, S. (1998). *How One of You Can Bring the Two of You Together: Breakthrough Strategies to Resolve your Conflicts and Reignite Your Love.* New York: Bantam Doubleday.

Robinson, J. (1997). *Communication Miracles for Couples: Easy and Effective Tools to Create More Love and Less Conflict.* Berkeley, CA: Conari Press.

Stern, S. (1999). *He Just Doesn't Get It: Simple Solutions to the Most Common Relationship Problems.* New York: Pocket Books.

Peer Group Negativity

Gordon, S. (1981). *The Teenage Survival Book.* New York: Times Books.

Kaplan, L. (1997). *Coping with Peer Pressure.* Center City, MN: Hazelden.

Kritsberg, W. (1998). *The Adult Children of Alcoholics Syndrome: From Discovery to Recovery.* New York: Bantam Books.

Sachs, S. (1997). *Street Gang Awareness: A Resource Guide for Parents and Professionals.* Minneapolis, MN: Fairview Press.

Posttraumatic Stress Disorder (PTSD)

Coffey, R. (1998). *Unspeakable Truths and Happy Endings: Human Cruelty and the New Trauma Therapy.* Towson, MD: Sidran Press.

Flannery, R. B., Jr. (1995). *Post-Traumatic Stress Disorder: The Victim's Guide to Healing and Recovery.* New York: Crossroad/Herder & Herder.

Freyd, J. (1998). *Betrayal Trauma: The Logic of Forgetting Childhood Abuse.* Cambridge, MA: Harvard University Press.

Matsakis, A. (1996). *I Can't Get Over It: A Handbook for Trauma Survivors.* New Oakland, CA: Harbinger Publications.

Matsakis, A. (1998). *Trust After Trauma: A Guide to Relationships for Survivors and Those Who Love Them*. Oakland, CA: New Harbinger Publications.

Rosenbloom, D., M. Williams, and B. E. Watkins (1999). *Life After Trauma: A Workbook for Healing*. New York: Guildford Publications.

Schiraldi, G. (1999). *The Post-Traumatic Stress Disorder Sourcebook: A Guide to Healing, Recovery, and Growth*. Lincolnwood, IL: Lowell House.

Psychosis

Adamec, C., and D. Jaffe (1996). *How to Live With a Mentally Ill Person: A Handbook of Day-to-Day Strategies*. New York: John Wiley and Sons.

Granet, R., and E. Ferber (1999). *Why Am I Up, Why Am I Down?: Understanding Bipolar Disorder*. New York: Dell.

Mondimore, F. (1999). *Bipolar Disorder: A Guide for Patients and Families*. Baltimore, MD: Johns Hopkins University Press.

Mueser, K. (1994). *Coping with Schizophrenia: A Guide for Families*. Oakland, CA: New Harbinger Publications.

Olson, B., and M. Olson (1999). *Win the Battle: The 3-Step Lifesaving Formula to Conquer Depression and Bipolar Disorder*. Worchester, MA: Chandler House Press.

Papolos, D., and J. Papolos (1999). *The Bipolar Child: The Definitive and Reassuring Guide to Childhood's Most Misunderstood Disorder*. New York: Broadway Books.

Torrey, F. (1995). *Surviving Schizophrenia: A Manual for Families Consumers and Providers*. New York: Harperperennial Library.

Waltz, M. (2000). *Bipolar Disorders: A Guide to Helping Children and Adolescents*. Sebastopol, CA: O'Reilly & Associates.

Relapse Proneness

Dorsman, J. (1998). *How to Quit Drugs for Good: A Complete Self-Help Guide*. Roseville, CA: Prima Publishing.

Duwors, G. (2000). *White Knuckles and Wishful Thinking: Learning from the Moment of Relapse in Alcoholism and Other Addictions*. Kirkland, WA: Hogrefe and Huber Publishers.

Gorski, T. (1987). *Passages Through Recovery: An Action Plan for Preventing Relapse*. Center City, MN: Hazelden.

Gorski, T., and M. Miller (1986). *Staying Sober: A Guide for Relapse Prevention*. Scottdale, PA: Herald Publishing House.

Washton, A. (1991). *Cocaine Addiction: Treatment, Recovery, and Relapse Prevention*. New York: W. W. Norton & Company.

Washton, A., and D. Boundy (1990). *Willpower's Not Enough: Understanding and Recovering from Addictions of Every Kind*. New York: Harper-Collins.

Sexual Promiscuity

Carnes, P. (1991). *Don't Call It Love: Recovery from Sexual Addiction*. New York: Bantam Books.

Carnes, P. (1992). *Out of the Shadows: Understanding Sexual Addiction*. Center City, MN: Hazelden Information Education.

Means, M. (1999). *Living With Your Husband's Secret Wars*. Grand Rapids, MI: Fleming H. Revell Co.

Melody, P., and A. Miller (1992). *Facing Love Addiction: Giving Yourself the Power to Change the Way You Love—The Love Connection to Codependence*. San Francisco: Harper San Francisco.

Social Anxiety

Antony, M., and R. Swinson (2000). *The Shyness and Social Anxiety Workbook: Proven Techniques for Overcoming Your Fears*. Oakland, CA: New Harbinger Publishers.

Bradshaw, J. (1988). *Healing the Shame That Binds You*. Deer Field Beach, FL: Health Communication.

Burns, D. (1986). *Intimate Connections*. New York: New American Library.

Dayhoff, S. (2000). *Diagonally Parked in a Parallel Universe: Working Through Social Anxiety*. Placitas, NM: Effectiveness-Plus Publications.

Fossum, M., and M. Mason (1989). *Facing Shame*. New York: W. W. Norton & Co.

Helmstetter, S. (1997). *What to Say When You Talk to Yourself*. Fine Communications

Rapee, R. (1999). *Overcoming Shyness and Social Phobia: A Step-by-Step Guide*. Northvale, NJ: Jason Aronson.

Zimbardo, P. (1987). *Shyness: What It Is and What to Do about It*. New York: Addison-Wesley.

Spiritual Confusion

Alcoholics Anonymous (1974). *Big Book*. Alcoholics Anonymous General Services Office.

Alcoholics Anonymous World Services, Inc. (1981). *Twelve Steps and Twelve Traditions*. New York: Alcoholics Anonymous World Services, Inc.

Carter, L. (1997). *The Choosing to Forgive Workbook*. Nashville, TN: Thomas Nelson.

Foster, R. (1988). *Celebration of Discipline: The Path to Spiritual Growth*. San Francisco: Harper and Row.

Graham, B. (1984). *Peace With God*. Dallas, TX: Word.

May, G. (1991). *Addiction and Grace*. San Francisco: Harper San Francisco.

Parachin, J. (1999). *Engaged Spirituality: Ten Lives of Contemplation and Action*. St. Louis, MO: Chalice Press.

Perkinson, R. (2000). *God Talks to You.* Bloomington, IN: 1st Books.

Smedes, L. (1991). *Forgive and Forget: Healing the Hurts We Don't Deserve.* San Francisco: Harper.

Willard, D. (1988). *The Spirit of the Disciplines.* New York: Harper and Row.

Substance Abuse/Dependence

Alcoholics Anonymous (1974). *Big Book.* Alcoholics Anonymous General Services Office.

Black, C. (1991). *It Will Never Happen to Me.* New York: Ballantine Books.

Bradshaw, J. (1996). *Bradshaw on the Family.* Deer Field Beach, FL: Health Communications.

Fanning, P. (1996). *The Addiction Workbook: A Step-by-Step Guide to Quitting Alcohol and Drugs.* Oakland, CA: New Harbinger Publications.

May, G. (1991). *Addiction and Grace.* San Francisco: Harper San Francisco.

Sales, P. (1999). *Alcohol Abuse: Straight Talk Straight Answers.* Honolulu, HI: Ixia Publications.

Solowij, N. (1998). *Cannabis and Cognitive Functioning.* New York: Cambridge University Press.

Washton, A. (1991). *Cocaine Addiction: Treatment, Recovery, and Relapse Prevention.* New York: W. W. Norton & Company.

West, J., and B. Ford (1997). *The Betty Ford Center Book of Answers: Help for Those Struggling With Substance Abuse and for the People Who Love Them.* New York: Pocket Books.

Woititz, J. G. (1990). *Adult Children of Alcoholics.* Palm Coast, FL: Health Communications.

Substance-Induced Disorders

Antony, M., and R. P. Swinson (2000). *The Shyness and Social Anxiety Workbook: Proven Techniques for Overcoming Your Fears.* Oakland, CA: New Harbinger Publishers.

Burns, D. (1990). *The Feeling Good Handbook.* New York: Plume.

Cronkite, K. (1995). *On the Edge of Darkness: Conversations About Conquering Depression.* New York: Delta.

Dayhoff, S. A. (2000). *Diagonally Parked in a Parallel Universe: Working Through Social Anxiety.* Placitas, NM: Effectiveness-Plus Publications.

Goldman, C., and S. Babior. (1996). *Overcoming Panic, Anxiety, and Phobias: New Strategies to Free Yourself from Worry and Fear.* Duluth, MN: Whole Person Associates.

O'Connor, R. (1999). *Undoing Depression: What Therapy Doesn't Teach You and Medication Can't Give You.* New York: Berkley Publishing Group.

Peurifoy, R. Z. (1995). *Anxiety, Phobias, and Panic: A Step-by-Step Program for Regaining Control of Your Life.* New York: Warner Books.

Rapee, R. M. (1999). *Overcoming Shyness and Social Phobia: A Step-by-Step Guide.* Northvale, NJ: Jason Aronson.

Thorn, J., and L. Rothstein (1993). *You Are Not Alone: Words of Experience and Hope for the Journey Through Depression.* New York: Harperperennial.

Yapko, M. (1998). *Breaking the Patterns of Depression.* New York: Main Street Books.

Substance Intoxication/Withdrawal

Alcoholics Anonymous World Services, Inc. (1976). *Alcoholics Anonymous.* New York: Alcoholics Anonymous World Services, Inc.

Alcoholics Anonymous World Services, Inc. (1981). *Twelve Steps and Twelve Traditions.* New York: Alcoholics Anonymous World Services, Inc.

Denning, P., and A. Marlatt (2000). *Practicing Harm Reduction Psychotherapy: An Alternative Approach to Addictions.* New York: Guilford Press.

Fanning, P. (1996). *The Addiction Workbook: A Step-by-Step Guide to Quitting Alcohol and Drugs.* Oakland, CA: New Harbinger Publications.

May, G. (1991). *Addiction and Grace.* San Francisco: Harper San Francisco.

Perkinson, R. (1997). *Chemical Dependency Counseling: A Practical Guide.* Thousand Oaks, CA: Sage Publications.

West, J., and B. Ford (1997). *The Betty Ford Center Book of Answers: Help for Those Struggling With Substance Abuse and for the People Who Love Them.* New York: Pocket Books.

World Service Office, Inc. (1988). *Narcotics Anonymous.* Van Nuys, CA: World Service Office, Inc.

Suicidal Ideation

Alcoholics Anonymous World Services, Inc. (1981). *Twelve Steps and Twelve Traditions.* New York: Alcoholics Anonymous World Services, Inc.

Burns, D. (1990). *The Feeling Good Handbook.* New York: Plume.

Cronkite, K. (1995). *On the Edge of Darkness: Conversations About Conquering Depression.* New York: Delta.

Ellis, T. E., and C. F. Newman (1996). *Choosing to Live: How to Defeat Suicide Through Cognitive Therapy.* Oakland, CA: New Harbinger.

Jamison, K. R. (2000). *Night Falls Fast: Understanding Suicide.* New York: Vintage Books.

O'Connor, R. (1999). *Undoing Depression: What Therapy Doesn't Teach You and Medication Can't Give You.* New York: Berkley Publishing Group.

Thorn, J., and L. Rothstein (1993). *You Are Not Alone: Words of Experience and Hope for the Journey Through Depression.* New York: Harperperennial.

Yapko, M. (1998). *Breaking the Patterns of Depression.* New York: Main Street Books.

Treatment Resistance

Alcoholics Anonymous World Services, Inc. (1976). *Alcoholics Anonymous.* New York: Alcoholics Anonymous World Services, Inc.

Alcoholics Anonymous World Services, Inc. (1981). *Twelve Steps and Twelve Traditions.* New York: Alcoholics Anonymous World Services, Inc.

Fanning, P. (1996). *The Addiction Workbook: A Step-by-Step Guide to Quitting Alcohol and Drugs.* Oakland, CA: New Harbinger Publications.

May, G. G. (1991). *Addiction and Grace.* San Francisco: Harper San Francisco.

West, J. W., and B. Ford. (1997). *The Betty Ford Center Book of Answers: Help for Those Struggling With Substance Abuse and for the People Who Love Them.* New York: Pocket Books.

World Service Office, Inc. (1988). *Narcotics Anonymous.* Van Nuys, CA: World Service Office, Inc.

Appendix B

INDEX OF DSM-IV™ CODES ASSOCIATED WITH PRESENTING PROBLEMS

Acculturation Problem   V62.4
  Living Environment Deficiency
  Spiritual Confusion

Acute Stress Disorder   308.3
  Anxiety
  Grief/Loss Unresolved
  Posttraumatic Stress Disorder

Adjustment Disorder   309.xx
  Posttraumatic Stress Disorder
  Suicidal Ideation

**Adjustment Disorder
With Anxiety**   309.24
  Anxiety
  Grief/Loss Unresolved
  Social Anxiety

**Adjustment Disorder
With Depressed Mood**   309.0
  Depression
  Grief/Loss Unresolved

**Adjustment Disorder With
Disturbance of Conduct**   309.3
  Grief/Loss Unresolved
  Impulsivity
  Legal Problems
  Peer Group Negativity
  Sexual Promiscuity

**Adjustment Disorder With Mixed
Anxiety and Depressed Mood**   309.28
  Anxiety
  Depression
  Grief/Loss Unresolved
  Social Anxiety

**Adjustment Disorder With Mixed
Disturbance of Emotions and
Conduct**   309.4
  Anger
  Antisocial Behavior
  Attention-Deficit/Hyperactivity
    Disorder
  Attention-Deficit/Inattentive Disorder
  Grief/Loss Unresolved
  Oppositional Defiant Behavior
  Peer Group Negativity

Adult Antisocial Behavior   V71.01
  Anger
  Antisocial Behavior
  Family Conflicts
  Impulsivity
  Legal Problems
  Peer Group Negativity
  Sexual Promiscuity

Alcohol Abuse   305.00
  Substance Abuse/Dependence
  Treatment Resistance

Bulimia Nervosa   **307.51**
  Eating Disorders

Caffeine Intoxication   **305.90**
  Substance Intoxication/Withdrawal

Cannabis Abuse   **305.20**
  Substance Abuse/Dependence
  Treatment Resistance

Cannabis Dependence   **304.30**
  Substance Abuse/Dependence
  Treatment Resistance

Cannabis Intoxication   **292.89**
  Substance Intoxication/Withdrawal

**Child or Adolescent Antisocial
Behavior**   **V71.02**
  Anger
  Antisocial Behavior
  Family Conflicts
  Impulsivity
  Legal Problems
  Oppositional Defiant Behavior
  Peer Group Negativity
  Sexual Promiscuity

Cocaine Abuse   **305.60**
  Substance Abuse/Dependence
  Treatment Resistance

Cocaine Dependence   **304.20**
  Substance Abuse/Dependence
  Treatment Resistance

**Cocaine-Induced Mood
Disorder**   **292.84**
  Suicidal Ideation

Cocaine Intoxication   **292.89**
  Substance Intoxication/Withdrawal

Cocaine Withdrawal   **292.0**
  Substance Intoxication/Withdrawal

Conduct Disorder   **312.8**
  Anger
  Antisocial Behavior
  Attention-Deficit/Hyperactivity
    Disorder
  Attention-Deficit/Inattentive Disorder
  Family Conflicts

Impulsivity
Legal Problems
Oppositional Defiant Behavior
Relapse Proneness
Sexual Promiscuity

**Conduct Disorder/Adolescent-Onset
Type**   **312.82**
  Peer Group Negativity

Cyclothymic Disorder   **301.13**
  Depression
  Mania/Hypomania
  Narcissistic Traits
  Relapse Proneness

**Delirium Due to . . . [*Indicate the
General Medical Condition*]**   **293.0**
  Medical Issues

Delusional Disorder   **297.1**
  Psychosis

**Dependent Personality
Disorder**   **301.6**
  Adult-Child-of-an-Alcoholic Traits
  Anxiety
  Borderline Traits
  Childhood Trauma
  Dependent Traits
  Eating Disorders
  Family Conflicts
  Social Anxiety

Depersonalization Disorder   **300.6**
  Posttraumatic Stress Disorder

Depressive Disorder NOS   **311**
  Adult-Child-of-an-Alcoholic Traits
  Dependent Traits
  Depression
  Grief/Loss Unresolved
  Occupational Problems

**Disruptive Behavior Disorder
NOS**   **312.9**
  Attention-Deficit/Hyperactivity
    Disorder
  Attention-Deficit/Inattentive Disorder
  Impulsivity
  Sexual Promiscuity